Gospel Revelation

in Three Treatises

1. The Nature of God
2. The Excellencies of Christ
3. The Excellency of Man's Immortal Soul

by JEREMIAH BURROUGHS

The Late Preacher of the Gospel
at Stepney, and St. Giles Cripplegate, London

Edited by Dr. Don Kistler

"Let them praise the Name of the Lord, for His Name alone is excellent."

PSALM 148:13

"My Beloved is white and ruddy, the chiefest of ten thousand."

SONG OF SOLOMON 5:10

"Fear not them which kill the body, but are not able to kill the soul."

MATTHEW 10:28

SOLI DEO GLORIA PUBLICATIONS
. . . for instruction in righteousness . . .

Soli Deo Gloria Publications

A division of Ligonier Ministries, Inc.

P.O. Box 547500, Orlando, FL 32854

(407) 333-4244/FAX 333-4233

www.ligonier.org

Gospel Revelation was first published in 1660.

This Soli Deo Gloria reprint, in which spelling, formatting, and grammatical changes have been made, is ©2006 by Soli Deo Gloria Publications.

ISBN 1-56769-069-6

Library of Congress Cataloging-in-Publication Data

Burroughs, Jeremiah, 1599-1646.
  Gospel revelation / by Jeremiah Burroughs ; edited by Don Kistler.
– 1st modern ed.
      p. cm.
  Originally published: 1660.
  ISBN 1-56769-069-6 (alk. paper)
  1. God–Biblical teaching. 2. Jesus Christ–Person and offices
–Biblical teaching. 3. Salvation–Biblical teaching. 4. Sermons,
English–17th century. 5. Congregational churches–Sermons.
I. Kistler, Don. II. Title.
BS544.B87 2006
230'.59–dc22

                                                        2005036218

Contents

THE NATURE OF GOD

THE EXCELLENCY OF CHRIST

THE EXCELLENCY OF THE SOUL

THE NATURE OF GOD

Ten Points on the Nature of God

"For His name alone is excellent."

PSALM 148:13

*M*en who live without God in the world are in a dreadful condition. It is evil to be without bread, without friends, or without outward comforts; how great an evil is it then to be without God in the world? They who live without God in the world are those who did not know Him, who had no interest in Him. Therefore, seeing that there are so many poor, wretched creatures, so many families who live without God in the world, who know nothing of Him, who live as if they expected nothing from Him, and fear no evil to come from Him at all, I promised to labor to set forth before you something of God that might help you to know Him, to show you what He is. And to that end we turn to

Psalm 148:13: "For His name alone is excellent."

This psalm is a psalm of praise, praising God for all the glorious manifestations of Himself in His great works, and calling upon all creatures to praise Him because He is glorious in every creature. But the psalmist does not rest in praising God for the glory of Him that appears in the creatures, but he takes rise from there to praise and bless God for what there is in Himself, above that which appears in any creature. For it is clear that to this the psalmist arises in my text: "Let them praise the name of the Lord, for His name alone is excellent. His glory is above the earth and heaven." The earth and heaven, and all creatures therein, are called to praise God's name; and David praises the name of God for what appeared there, but he says, "Praise the Lord, for His name alone is excellent, and His glory is above the earth and heaven." The phrase "His name," the name of God, is either taken for God Himself, or for the manifestation of God. Often in Scripture it is taken for God Himself. "The name of the Lord is a strong tower; the righteous run unto it, and are safe" (Proverbs 18:10); that is, God Himself is the strength and tower. He is the object of the trust of His people; and so it is with other Scriptures.

It may also stand for that whereby God may be known. "His name is great in Israel" (Psalm 76:1). And here we are to understand both; for "His name alone is excellent," that is, God Himself alone is excellent; the name of Him, and of Him alone, is high, is lifted up, is excellent. We are to understand that by "the name of God" here. God Himself, as well as His manifestations, appears in the words at the end of the verse: "His glory is above the earth and heaven." Now God's manifestation is either in heaven or on earth. But there is a further glory of God that is in Himself, that is beyond all that is or can be manifested in or to any creature.

So, from the words thus opened, there are these two doctrinal points: one (and I will only touch on it) is raised from the connection of the words with the former; and the other is the substance of the text, and that we shall abide a while upon.

DOCTRINE 1. A gracious heart is not satisfied with praising God only for His works, but rises higher to praise Him, and especially to praise Him for Himself, for what He is in Himself.

A gracious heart does not stop with the works of God; nor is it only enlarged to praise God for what it sees in God's works, but it will rise higher than all the works of God and praise Him especially for what He is in Himself. "Thyself, O Lord, is excellent; the glory that is in Thyself is above the earth, and above the heaven." While we praise God for what we see in His works, our thoughts and hearts are limited; for God's manifestations of Himself are infinite, and so there is not that spaciousness that a gracious heart desires to let out itself in; but when it can rise up to God Himself, and look at the infinite excellency that there is in Him above all that appears in His works, then the heart that is enlarged with grace can expatiate itself to the uttermost; and that is what delights him. Then is a gracious heart indeed in its own element, when it is expatiating itself even in God Himself.

Further, God, in setting Himself before the soul in way of covenant, not only tells those whom He takes into covenant that He will do such and such things for them, but He would have them to close with Himself. "I will be your God" (Jeremiah 24:7; 31:33; 32:38; Ezekiel 11:20). The Lord told Abraham that He would be his "exceeding great reward" (Genesis 15:1). But that would not satisfy Abraham. "What wilt Thou give me?" (verse 2), having an eye to Christ and the enjoyment of God

in Him. So let God say that He will do never such things for a
gracious heart, that is not enough unless God Himself is the
portion of the soul; the soul cannot be satisfied with anything
that God does. If God should say to one whose heart He has
enlarged with grace, "I will give you all the world to possess;
you shall have all the glory, all the pomp, all the sweetness, all
the comforts in the world; nay, more than that, I will make ten
thousand worlds more, and give you them all, and they shall
all have more excellency than this present world has"—why, all
this would not satisfy a heart enlarged with grace for its portion.
Though such a one sees himself unworthy of the least crumb
of bread, yet it cannot be satisfied with all the world. What then
will satisfy him? Only God Himself, for so God propounds Himself unto His people in way of covenant: "I will be thy God. I
will be your portion" (see Psalm 16:5). And upon this, those
who are in covenant with Him, though they rejoice to see God
manifesting Himself in all His names, bless God for beholding
as much as they do of Him in His works. But the thing that their
hearts are most upon is God Himself, the excellency that there
is in God above all His works.

And as it is in praising God, so also it is in other workings of
the heart towards God. For example, grace does not love God
so much for what God gives to it as for what God is Himself;
that is the difference between true sanctifying grace and common grace; common grace may make me love God for what I
receive from Him, or for what I hope to receive from Him; but
sanctifying grace makes me love God for what He is in Himself
more than for what I receive from Him or expect to receive.

And so there may be the fear of God for some works of God.
When God manifests His power and dreadfulness in His works
in thundering or lightning, then the heart of a sinner may fear
God though there is no grace. But where there is grace, such a

one fears God more because of that excellency he sees in God Himself than from any dreadful works of God. And this would be a good rule to try yourselves by. You say, "Fear God." Why? If you fear God, if it is the right fear of God, you will fear God more for what you see in God Himself than for any works of God, than for any works of His judgments, threatenings, and the like.

And so it is in the desires of the heart after God. Where the heart is gracious, it works after God for Himself and not for His gifts. It is an argument of a false love, a whorish love, for the wife to love her husband for what she shall have by him, and not to love his person more. It is a sign of a base, slavish spirit for a child to love his father because he gives him meat and drink and clothes, and will leave him an inheritance, and not rather to love the very person of his father. Just so the heart is but false with God that loves God, and that desires after God, for anything that God does more than for what God is. And as these workings of heart, love, fear, and desire are more in respect of God Himself than of His works, so praises of God and delighting in God, where they are from true grace, are more from what the soul sees in God than from the manifestation of all the glory of God in all His works. As the text says, "Praise the name of the Lord, for His name is excellent. His glory is above the earth and heaven." But I shall let this pass.

The main point in the text that we are to pitch on is this:

DOCTRINE 2. God is a most excellent Being above all things.

The work that I now have to do is to endeavor to present God in the excellency of His being to you. Only you must know by way of caution, before we begin, that God dwells in that light that is unapproachable (1 Timothy 6:16). That is, it is but little that we do or can know of God. And before we begin to set forth the excellency of God's being to you, you must know that there is infinitely more than either the tongue of man or angel can express. When we have done all we can, there is more in God that is beyond what we can say or that angels can preach unto you. I say, there is more than the glorious light of the sun is beyond a little glittering of a glow-worm in the night, more than all the sea is beyond and above a spoonful, a drop of water.

And further, by way of caution, you must know that it is impossible to set before you the excellency of God's being, and yet to speak so as that everything should be plain to every-one. Many things in the opening of God's nature to you must have some difficulty in them, because the subject that we are speaking of is so high above us. Especially must it be difficult to unclean spirits, to spirits that have always been groveling below in the dirt, to drowsy spirits that think nothing to be excellent but to eat and drink and satisfy their flesh. When they hear the excellency of God's being set out unto them, it must be an argument above their reach; it cannot be expected that it is profitable to speak so that their hearts should close with what is said, to apprehend it.

But we do not know what God may do in going along with His Word, how He may come by His Spirit even to those who are of the weakest capacity. Therefore I shall endeavor to do that which is my work, that is, to show you something of God, what an excellent Being He is, and so leave the work of the Spirit of God to Himself, to make known those things that shall be propounded, and to settle them upon your hearts. Where-fore, then, "God is an excellent Being above all things."

1. "He is, and there is none else besides Him." The truth is, we can scarcely say that anything is except God. In Exodus 3:14,

when God came to Moses to send him to Pharaoh, and Moses would know the name of God, He bid him say, "I am that I am. I am hath sent me." And God only describes Himself thus unto Moses: "I am," that is, "I am a being." And so the name Jehovah is a name proper to God that signifies God's being. Now Moses might say, "Lord, is this a name that will distinguish Thee from anything else, to say 'I am'? Cannot any man say, 'I am'?" Yet God gives this name of His as His proper name, meaning, "I am a being," and "I am that being that I am." And that is all the name God would tell Moses when Moses desired to know so much of Him and how he might express Him who sent him, "I am that I am."

It is God's being that is proper, and all other creatures in comparison of this God have but a shadow of being. Therefore, in Proverbs 8:21, wisdom (that is, godliness) says there, "I cause to inherit substance." The words are translated by the learned, "that which is, grace carries to God." And so by grace being carried to God, we come to inherit that which is, as if all the while we inherited anything in the world, we did not inherit that which is.

God Himself properly is. So we read in Isaiah 45:5–6: "I am Jehovah, and there is none else besides Me." In other words, "There is nothing that has a being besides Me," that is, not such a being, as we shall further open, yea, and in comparison no being. Therefore, in Isaiah 40:15, 17 we have a most excellent expression of the excellency of God's being in comparison to all other things: "All the nations of the world are as the drop of the bucket, and as the small dust of the balance." In comparison to God, "Yea, they are all as nothing, and less than nothing."

What an expression is here! Take all the nations of the world, put them all together, and they are all but as the drop of the bucket that you shall see hang a little at the bottom, but as a little dust of the balance. How soon may you take your finger and wipe off the drop of the bucket? Why, so even all nations of the world may as soon perish in respect of God. Yea, it is as if the Holy Ghost had said too much when He compared the nations of the world to God, as if He should say, "What, did I say they were as the drop of the bucket, and as the small dust in the balance? Nay, they are nothing at all! Nay, and I must go lower, they are less than nothing!"

And thus you see that the name of God alone is excellent because indeed He is such a being that in comparison to Him there is nothing that is worthy of the name of a being. The fortieth chapter of the prophecy of Isaiah will be a good chapter to read in your families to set out the greatness of God, for that is the work I am about, which is to show you what a God you have to deal with in all your ways, and that the name of God is excellent. Read that chapter, and you will find God's name set out there as excellent indeed.

2. God is a present Being. "I am," He says, that is, God enjoins Himself, that infinite being of Himself, together; there is no succession at all in the being of God as there is in other creatures. The creature enjoys but little of its own being. I beseech you to consider the difference between God and the creature in this. When I say that He is a present being, that is set forth in the words, "I am." I say, the creature enjoys but very little of its own being. Why? Because whatsoever is past it cannot enjoy, and whatsoever is to come it does not yet enjoy. Now all that it enjoys of itself, it is only what it has at this present instant. But with God there is nothing past and there is nothing to come. There is nothing past, I say, and in respect of God's being there is nothing to come, for His being is always present. He always says, "I am." Therefore Christ, speaking of His divine nature in

John 8:58, says, "Before Abraham was, I am." Christ did not say, "I was before Abraham was," no, but "Before Abraham was, I am." Certainly this would not have been good English for any creature to so speak. If any man should say thus, "Before such a thing was, I am"; if any angel should say so, this would not be proper speech. But Christ says, "Before Abraham was, I am," because Christ, in regard of His divine nature, has no succession of being at all.

We cannot say that God has so many years added to Him since the world began. God was as eternal before the world was as He is now, or ever shall be. It cannot be said that He was nor will be, but always it may be said "I am," that is, "I am, I was, and I will be." The difference of time is in respect of the creature, not in respect of God. And that is the reason for that phrase in Scripture that "a thousand years with God are as one day, and one day as a thousand years" (2 Peter 3:8). There is no difference of time with God at all, and therefore He alone is excellent.

Third, this being of God is in all places. His excellency is everywhere throughout the world, and that, first, is not virtually only. God is not in every place only virtually by His power; that is, He works in every place, but He is in every place. But He is in every place essentially. Second, God is not in every place by motion, from one place to another, and so gradually is in all places, but God is every moment in every place.

3. God is not in every place to fill heaven and earth, that is, one part in one place and another in another, as a great thing that fills such a room, one part is in one place, and another is in another. But God fills heaven and earth, that is, all of God is everywhere; all that God is, is in every place. Yea, further, God is as much beyond every place as He is in every place. He is as

much beyond the circumference of the heavens and the earth as He is in them; yea, if God should make ten thousand worlds more, He would fill all those as well as He does this one, without any motion at all. He would not move from one place to another to fill up ten thousand worlds (if there were so many new ones made), but in the same instant in which they were all made, that immense being of His would fill up all. Surely God is a most excellent being than above all other things whatsoever.

4. I intend but merely to present the chief things of the excellency of God before you, and not to stand handling these at large, for every one of them might require a large tract. Now I wish only to present before you what a God it is with whom you have to deal: God is a Being who is all-sufficient in Himself. He stands in no need of any creature. In Acts 17:25, He has need of nothing, of none of us. He has enough within Himself. Before the world was, God was as blessed in Himself as now He is; nothing can be added to Him. There is such an excellency even in God's being itself that nothing can be added to Him. We are poor creatures who stand in need of a thousand things continually: the air to breathe in, the earth to bear us, fire to warm us, clothes to cover us, meat and drink, and a thousand such things. We stand in need of the meanest creature, and if God should take away the use of some mean contemptible creature, our lives would be made miserable to us. But it is the excellency of God's being that He has need of nothing. He has all within Himself, and all the creatures in heaven and earth cannot add to Him. No, if there were ten thousand worlds more, although God possessed them all, yet they would not add one whit unto what is in God Himself. God has an essential and an attributed glory. His attributed glory is augmented or diminished by man's obedience or disobedience—therefore

sinners are said to rob God of His glory, and saints to give Him glory—but His essential glory cannot be increased or diminished. Therefore, though the Lord has made the heaven and earth, and all therein, yet we must not think that God is ever a whit the better for these things, or has the more glory. He had as much glory and blessedness in Himself as He now has or can have. When all the angels and saints shall be eternally blessing God in heaven, yet they can add nothing to God's glory. We say that the sun is a glorious creature, but does that add any light to the sun? So for saints and angels to be praising and blessing God, what does that add to God? And in this the name of God is excellent.

5. His name alone is excellent in that His excellency is universal, that is, all excellencies that are in all creatures in heaven and earth are all in Him virtually and eminently. He has them all in His own being. Psalm 94:9: "Shall not He that made the ear hear? He that formed the eye, shall not He see?" The argument there will confirm to us that whatsoever is in the creature that has any excellency in it, that excellency is in God in an eminent way. With regard to the creature, one has one drop of excellency, another has another drop of excellency in it, and so a third a third; every creature has its particular excellency in it. But God is a universal good. All excellencies in all creatures are in God: all beauty, all comfort, all goodness. Whatsoever has any loveliness or desirableness in it, I say, it is all in God; and I do not know any one consideration that will help us more to understand God while we are here in the flesh than this; for in regard of our weakness, we can know little or nothing of God but by looking into the creature, and so rising from them to God.

Now, then, when we come to look upon the creatures, and we see an excellency in one creature and another in another, if we can conceive, as it were, the quintessence of all these excellencies drawn out, and conceive a Being that has all these together in Him, this Being is an excellent Being indeed. This would make us to look upon God above the creature, when we look upon everything that is good in the creature to be in God Himself. Why, then, whatever the creature has to draw the heart, why that, the soul says, is in God. And, indeed, this one consideration of God, and presenting God to the soul in this manner, is a special work of God's converting a soul to Himself. When the Lord intends to draw a soul to Himself, to have the heart that was let out after creature comforts now to close with Himself and choose Himself for his Portion, the Lord shows this to the soul: "Soul, what would you have? You would have this and the other comfort to delight and content you? Know that there can be nothing in any creature that you see, but what you may have it in Me." Now this indeed we cannot see by sense; the comforts of the creature are sensibly before us, and we see them by our senses. But God is above our senses. God He is above our reason, and there must be faith to close with Him. But when God would convert a soul to Himself, He shows Himself in such a way to the soul that the soul sees that there is all the good in Him that there is in the creature, and that it is in God in a more satisfying and eminent manner.

Certainly, whatsoever there is in the effect must be in the causes. Now as all effects are to be resolved into the causes, so all causes are to be resolved into this excellent Being that is the First Cause of all things; for these causes that are effects have other causes of them, yet those causes are effects of some higher causes. At length we must come to the First Cause, and all must be resolved into that. Nay, all excellencies in the creature are more in God than the excellency of the effect is in its causes; for when an effect is resolved into the causes, if they are not united to produce such an effect, they cannot do immediately the thing that the effect could do. But all excellency is so in God. Look at what power any creature has, or what thing it can do by any excellency it has, and that God can do; look at what comfort it can bring by any good it has in it, and the same comfort God can bring.

So all is to be resolved into God. Not that God has all formally in Him, such as fire, air, meat, or drink; but what good there is here, what excellency there is here, is eminently in God—that is, God is able to do of Himself by His own being whatsoever any creature is able to do, though all the creatures in the world should be annihilated (taken away) and you only left live. God, by His immediate power, is able to let out all that variety of comforts that all the creatures in the world before could do. Now we can find all made up in God. We say sometimes that in some good dish, all dishes are made up; but that is just a similitude. But here it is really so that whatsoever any child of God loses in the creature, such a one can find it to be made up in God. Indeed, this is the art and skill of religion. Godliness teaches this art and skill, to make up whatsoever is wanting in a creature in God Himself. And that is the chief ground of the satisfaction and contentment of a gracious heart in the want of creature comforts; and because the men of the world have no skill in this mystery, they think it is a mere notion, a conceit of men, and therefore they are not able to apprehend any reality in it. That is why they vex and fret so much when they want creature comforts, for they do not know where to go to make them up in any other being. But the saints know that all is in God, that all excellency in all creatures is in God. Therefore, when you look thus upon God as having all good that all creatures have, and that in Himself; and when you come thus to God, as such a Being so much above all creatures—then you have in same measure a right apprehension of God.

6. The name of God is excellent above all; for not only all excellencies in the creature are in Him, but all those varieties of excellencies that are scattered up and down severally in creatures are united into one excellency in Him. Water may have the quintessence of many herbs in it; there are many things in the water at that time. Though it is but one drop of water, yet there are many in it. So there is such a union of all excellencies in things in God that it is but one in God; there is an indivisible union of all variety. Things that are various in the creature are all united in one in God; and that must be a glorious excellency indeed. If one man had all the beauty, strength, and all the wisdom that all the men in the world ever had or have united into one, what beauty, what strength, what wisdom would that one man have! Now it is so in God that all beauty, wisdom, and strength are united into one excellency, so that God is one otherwise than any other creature can be one. Other creatures may be made one by composition, but God is not one by the union of many things together; for there is but one thing in God. God is but one. There is a variety, as we conceive, such as when the sun shines upon different glasses, red, blue, or yellow, it has a variety. Aye, but all this is but one sun. So all the attributes of God that we speak of at divers times are the several manifestations of that one excellency that there is in God all united into one. Therefore by this the saints come to be more happy, for they may not only enjoy all good that there is in the creature, but enjoy it all in one. And we say that the stronger a thing is, the more it is united. Now in God all good whatsoever is united in one: all good in the creature, yea, and all good in Himself, that is, all His attributes. This is how you must conceive of God.

Only the manifestation is diverse; and therefore you must not conceive that there is any one thing in Him more than another. You may not conceive of God as if there were more mercy than justice, more justice than mercy, or more of either of these than there is of truth, wisdom, or holiness. Indeed, God may manifest Himself unto the creature more in one thing than in another, but as they are in His own being they are not only one as much as the other, but they are all but one thing, only several manifestations, as but one sun that has divers reflections by divers glasses. So all God's attributes are but one excellency that is in Him; therefore His name is excellent above all things because He is but one God in this manner.

7. Not only all good and excellency is in God, but all possible good. Whatever can possibly be imagined (as we know that the power of God that made the world could make thousands of worlds) all this is in Him, and it is infinitely in Him. When we speak of anything being in God, we must be sure that we do not limit our thoughts. When we speak of God as being a great God, we must not limit it; for He is great, but infinitely so. Speaking of His wisdom, He is wise, but infinitely wise; and the same is true of His holiness, justice, truth, and knowledge. All must be looked upon without any bounds whatsoever. In the creature there are such and such things, but they are all limited by their causes; but God, having no causes at all to limit Him, is therefore infinite. Whatsoever is in Him is infinitely in Him. Whatsoever is in Him is not only infinite in the kind, as there is all the wisdom and holiness that can be, but it is absolutely infinite. Since it is in Him, it is so infinite that there is no kind of being but is included within it. Speak but any one thing of God, I say, and it is not only infinite in the kind, but so as it includes whatsoever has being, in the infinite ocean of being that is in Himself.

We are very ready when we look upon God to have limited thoughts, and therein we bring Him down to the same level as the creature. This is the very reason God hates images as much as He does, because that image makes a kind of a representation of Him, as though He were finite. Papists tell us that they do not think that such an image is God, aye, but being put in mind of God by such an image in a way limits the infiniteness that is in God—and therefore God hates it, and will not have that infinite excellency of His to be represented by any image whatsoever. Whenever you think or speak of God, do not only compare Him with that which is in the creature; but when you have made your comparison, let your thoughts be infinitely above that. There is no one attribute of God that helps us more to understand what God is than when we conceive Him to be infinite in all that He is or has.

8. Further, all the good and excellency that there is in God is eternally in Him. It may be that such and such a creature has an excellency, but how long has it had it? It was not long ago that it was nothing. But God has been what He has been (if we may speak so) eternally. Now that is a mighty voracious consideration, the consideration of eternity. A man who is an accountant, if he writes a figure of one, add but six zeroes to it, and it is a million. Now if he should be adding and adding all his lifetime, yea, if he should have lived from the beginning of the world to have added to the figure of one, what an infinite sum would this be! But it is nothing to eternity. If you look back to eternity, it is nothing; or if you look forward to eternity, it is nothing. The saints indeed shall live eternally in respect of that which is to come: the souls and bodies of the saints shall be eternally for time to come with God, and the souls and bodies of the ungodly shall be eternally in hell. Now all the

excellency that there is in God is eternally in God, whichever way you look.

9. Not only eternally are these things in Him, but they are immediately in Him—and therefore His name alone is excellent; it is immutable, that is, God has such an infinite excellency that it is impossible that He could be better, or other than He is. If God should be otherwise than He is, He would instantly cease to be a God. The being of God has that excellency in it so that there can be no addition nor subtraction. Add anything to Him and you destroy Him; take anything from Him and you destroy His being; alter anything in Him and He ceases to be God. So James 1:17 says, "With Him there is no shadow of change." Indeed, there is a change in the creature, but nothing at all in God. If you bring a piece of wax to the sun, it melts it; but do the same with clay and it hardens it. Here are different effects of the sun, but the sun is the same. Bring the creature in one disposition to God, and the love and delight of God are on it; bring the creature in another disposition to God, and the wrath of God is upon it. God is the same, the only variety is in the creature. And therefore His name alone is excellent. The creature, whatsoever excellence it has changes up and down. As there is no shadow of change with God, so there is no shadow of constancy in the creature.

10. In the next place, all these things are essentially in God. Whatever is in God is His being; it is God Himself. This one thing would greatly help you to understand the nature of God, that whatsoever can be truly said of God is God Himself. For example, God's wisdom is God Himself. God's mercy is God Himself. God's power is God Himself. It is not so in the creature: a man's wisdom is not a man's being; they are separable,

and one may be separated from the other. But God's wisdom is God's being. A man's power and strength are not his being, but God's are. So a man's mercy and goodness are not his being, but God's are; and therefore (as before) these things that are variously conceived by us are not only one in God, but His very being. This mightily adds to the glory of God, that whatsoever is in God is the very essence and being of God Himself. These things that we speak of God (as I told you), because God is infinitely above us, it is very hard to make them plain to every understanding. And no marvel, because we have fallen so far from Him. And as I have gone along, I fear that a great many are ready to think, "Lord, what are these things? We cannot apprehend them." Why, then, go your way home and be humbled for that great fall of mankind. Oh, how far man has fallen by his sin? We see now why God dwells in the thick cloud and darkness. Oh, how far I am fallen from God! For God made man at first able to know Him. Certainly Adam knew all these things perfectly: it was the happiness of Adam in his first creation to be able to look upon the face of God and know what such things as these meant. But since our fall, we are said not only to be in the dark, but to be darkness itself (Ephesians 5:8). And therefore it is but very little that we can know of God.

We have such a sight of God as a poor man who lives all his days in a dungeon. If he should one day have a little crevice opened, where a little beam of the sun should shine, certainly he would stand and admire it if he never saw it before; but how little would that man know of the nature of the sun who had but a little crevice opened for a beam to shine in a little time? Truly all that the ministers of God can ever tell you, or if God should send His angels to preach to open the nature of God to you, it could be nothing other than a little glimmering. But I hope if you bend your minds you may know so much as to make you desire the knowledge of Him; for if there is no other effect than this, yet it will be worth the while to make you to see that you do not know God. And therefore, your thoughts not being thus of God as I have spoken, the truth is that you have made God unto yourselves but as an idol (for if we conceive otherwise of God than He is, we do but make Him an idol to ourselves). Now, oh, that it might have but this effect at least (this that I have said, with some few other things that are to be spoken), to cause men and women to humble themselves before God for want of the knowledge of God, and to be crying to God, that He would be pleased to make Himself known unto them in another way than they have known Him, so that when they come to worship God, they may be able to look upon Him in another way than they have done.

Therefore, I beseech you, do not be so discouraged as to think, "I shall never know these things. If God is thus, I shall never know what He is." Do not be discouraged, for this God is able to communicate Himself beyond the way that any creature is able to communicate itself. God can let Himself out to any creature as much as He pleases. And it does not matter whether the creature is capable or not; the Lord can make it capable. Therefore, do not discouraged because of your weakness. But if, in the uprightness of your heart, you seek God, and desire to know Him above all things, "If thou searchest after the knowledge of God as after silver" (Proverbs 2:3-4), you shall come to know God more than ever you did. And certainly to have but a few glimpses of this infinite First Being of all things is a kind of infinite satisfaction unto the souls of the servants of God; and though at first they find it hard to know God, yet by seeking long after the knowledge of Him, they find the knowledge of God that they would not be without for ten thousand, thousand worlds. It's only the rational creature who is able to know anything of God at all; and this is a great part of that worship and homage you owe to God, that you should know Him, and so that you might honor Him as God, that you might glorify Him as God.

O my brethren, how would people live if they had but the real sight of such a God, with whom they have to deal in all their ways? When we put you upon searching to know what God is, we do not put you upon searching to get notions to discuss. I confess that in the right knowledge of the infinite First Being of all things, there are most excellent notions to be learned. But what I endeavor to put you on to is that you might search to know this God to the end that you might fear Him, and choose Him to be your Portion, that you might have Him and serve Him; and blessed is the soul that shall thus know Him.

Eight Additional Points on the Nature of God

"For His name alone is excellent."

PSALM 148:13

11. All excellencies are in God purely and are unmixed; that is, God has all excellencies in Him, and nothing but excellency. The creature may have some excellency, but it has a mixture of imperfections. It may have some power, but there is a mixture of weakness; it may have some goodness, but there is a mixture of some kind of evil in creatures as they are in themselves. The very angels themselves, though they are upheld by God, yet have that in them that might make them sin against God if He left them to themselves. So there is a mixture of weakness in all creatures, but God alone is excellent; for He has nothing in Him but that which is excellent. 1 John 1:5: "The Lord is light, and in Him there is no darkness." This cannot be said of any creature, that the creature has excellency in

21

him, and there is no darkness at all in him; for there is darkness in every creature. But the Lord is light, and in Him there is no darkness. What is said concerning light here may be said concerning anything else about God. The Lord has such and such excellencies, and in Him there is no defect; all is in Him purely.

12. Next, all is in God originally; that is, all is from Himself. Now there is no excellency in God that is by participation. He has it from Himself and in Himself. Whatever the creature has, it has derivatively, not originally; it receives it from another. But all that is in God is in Him originally: it is in Himself, by Himself, and from Himself. All is in Him as the spring of all kinds of excellency.

13. But as all is in Him originally, that is, He has all from Himself, so God is the Fountain of all excellency to all creatures whatsoever. If there is any good in any creature, it is but a beam from this sun, and a drop from this infinite ocean. It all flows from that infinite sea of all good that lets itself out to this creature or the other creature, in this or the other manner. So God is the Fountain of all good to all creatures whatsoever; they are to look upon Him as having all coming from Him. And therefore He alone is excellent, and His glory is above the heavens and earth.

14. Further, as all things are from Him, so they depend upon Him. As all excellencies that are in the creature come from God, so they have their absolute dependence upon God. God needs do nothing to destroy a creature; if He but withdraws Himself from it, it falls to nothing immediately. Take the most glorious angels, and the highest heavens, sun, moon, stars,

sea, and earth, and if God should but withdraw His hand from these creatures they would presently fall down to nothing. They depend upon God as the light depends upon the sun; there is no more light if the beams of the sun are withdrawn, and if God withdraws His influence from the creature, it can do nothing and it is nothing immediately. So that the influence there is from God to the creature is to maintain the creature in his being; every moment the Lord must put forth as infinite a power to maintain you and me and every creature, as He did at first to make the world (Hebrews 1:3).

It is God's excellence to uphold all things, since they so depend upon Him. If a workman makes a house and he goes away, the house can stand without him. But when God built the world, the world could not stand one moment without Him. And not only must God have an influence into the creature to preserve its being, but likewise to enable the creature to act. The creature cannot act one moment without God; no creature can stir in the least degree unless the Lord concurs with it. Therefore, the name of God alone is excellent. "In [or by] Him we live, we move, we have our being" (Acts 17:28); not only we are upheld in our being and lives, but we move. We cannot stir one moment but God must concur with His creature for its motion and actions.

15. God alone is excellent in His operation, in His power, in the manner of His working. Though God gives a power to other creatures to work, yet God works in a different way from all other creatures.

First, God does whatsoever He pleases either in heaven or earth. The will of God, as I showed you before, cannot be beyond God's power. God cannot will to do more than He has power to do. Therefore the Lord does whatsoever He pleases in heaven and earth (Psalms 115:3; 135:6; Ecclesiastes 8:3). The power of every creature can but work within the sphere so far as the causes give a virtue and efficacy; so far it is able to work, and no farther.

Second, the power of God appears in that the Lord does the greatest and most difficult things as easily as He does the least and the easiest. For example, God makes the whole world as easily as He can make a crumb of dirt. God can make the heavens, sun, moon and stars, and all the seas and earth, with as much ease as He can make a fly. God can make ten thousand angels as soon as He can make one worm. And therefore God can as soon speak the word to the soul of a man who is dead to live (John 5:25). He can as soon raise all the dead out of their graves as He can give them a piece of bread to eat while they are alive. Such is the infiniteness of God's operation.

Third, God is excellent in all that He does. There is nothing that God does at any time but was decreed to be done from eternity. That is the excellency of God's working; the creature works something, but perhaps a man did not think of what he does until a few days ago. But God does nothing, nor ever will do anything, but what was decreed from all eternity that He would do; and God will never do anything to all eternity but what He had decreed from all eternity before. Yet it is for us creatures to observe according to His revealed will. This is the excellency of God above all creatures whatever.

Fourth, God is so far from needing any matter to work upon, or instrument to work by, when He does anything as there is no more required for any creature to be or work at any time when God would have it, but the alone act of God's will thus was from eternity. For example, the world was not made six thousand years ago. God willed from all eternity that there should be a world in time, and there was nothing required to make this world but that act of God's will that was from all eternity that it should be at that time. Man wills and decrees to do such a thing and then, when the time comes, he stirs himself up and takes this tool or instrument, and puts forth a power that he did not put forth before. But the act of God's will from all eternity was sufficient to make all creatures that have been made ever since, and to provide for all creatures that ever since have been provided for. One act of God's will has done all this; and that act of the will of God that has been from all eternity has done it. There are not several acts of God's will, but God's act is Himself.

Fifth, where God has done any work, all His works add nothing to Him. The creature has something added to him by his works. For example, a workman can make a house, and so he has the benefit of dwelling in it to keep off the weather; and so he makes cloth, and has the benefit of that. But all the works of God add nothing to Him. A man can do something by the work that he has made that he could not do without his work: but God can do nothing by any work that He has made but He can do the same without that work. When He has made all His works, they are not helpful to Him (but this was a branch of the all sufficiency of God).

16. God alone is excellent in the manner of His communication of Himself. God so communicates Himself to His creatures as one creature cannot to another.

First, God can let out as much of Himself as He will to any creature. One creature cannot let out as much of himself as he pleases to another. For instance, a man who has learning cannot make another as learned as he will; a man who has holiness and goodness cannot make another as holy and as good as he will—but God can. This is God's propriety. He can let out as much of Himself as He pleases. As much holiness, as much goodness, as much power as He pleases, He is able to let out.

Second, when the creature communicates any excellency, the more it lets out, the less it has. But God never has a whit less by what He lets out to His creatures. For example, the sea is full of water, yet if you take out but a little water the sea has that much less. Therefore, some of the church fathers would set out eternity by this, that if a sparrow should but once in a thousand years fetch one drop of water from the sea in its bill, the sparrow would sooner empty all the sea than the torments of the damned should be at an end. So if a drop of water is taken out of the sea, the sea has one drop less water. But God is such an infinite ocean of being, of excellencies, of happiness that, let Him let out and communicate never so much of Himself, yet He has as much still as He ever had. God has let out excellency and good to all His creatures ever since the world began. All the good, the comfort, the happiness, the sweetness, the beauty and excellency of all creatures have been from God, that infinite Fountain. But this Fountain is as full as it ever was, and will be as full to all eternity as it ever was. And here lies the excellency of God beyond all creatures whatsoever.

17. God alone is excellent; there is no comparison to be made between Him and anything else. For example, take the creature in whatever way we think it comes nearest to God, and, the truth is, to speak properly, it comes no nearer to God than those things that we think come less. When we say that God is a great God and fills all places, if you should suppose a body that should fill all this world, it is no nearer to God's immensity than a moat that flies in the sun. Or think of it in this way: if an accountant should write down numbers all his lifetime and add them together, they would come, we think, to an infinite sum.

Yet if all those numbers were years, all those infinite millions of years come no nearer to God's eternity than one minute does. And the reason that I give is unanswerable is because there must always be an infinite distance between what is finite and what is infinite—and there cannot be anything greater than an infinite distance. Now take such a body as should fill the space between heaven and earth, there remains still an infinite distance between the immensity of God and this body; and take so many numbers of years as possibly can be imagined by men or angels, yet there will remain an infinite distance between God's eternity and those numbers of years. Now there cannot be anything greater than an infinite distance; therefore all those years do not come nearer to eternity than a minute, and all the greatness does not come nearer to immensity than a moat in the sun. God is beyond all comparison whatsoever, and the understanding that God is an infinite Being will help us to understand all the rest that I have named.

18. There is one more thing about the nature of God, and that is this: He is the last end of all things. He is the highest end, for which all creatures have their being; and the more any creature is subservient unto God, the more excellency a creature has. "For of Him, and through Him, and to Him are all things, to whom be glory forever" (Romans 11:36). All things must tend to God as the highest end; and cursed is the creature that shall challenge to be the highest end of any good thing whatsoever. This makes it to be a cursed thing for any man to make himself to be his last end, to make his name, honor, or credit to be the end that he aims at. And indeed, this is the very thing that makes pride to be so great a sin. The Scripture never speaks of any other thing as it does of pride; it is said of other sins that God hates the workers of iniquity, but it is said of no other sin

that God resists it, only the sin of pride (James 4:6; 1 Peter 5:5). Why? Because a proud man crosses God in that which is indeed His excellency, and that is this: that God is the highest end of all things, for whom all things were made. A proud man crosses God in this. No, he says, I will aim at myself as the highest end. We may aim at our own good in a subordinate way, but we must be sure to lift up God as the highest end of all because He is excellent above all. Now put all these together:

First, that God He is, and there is none else. He is such a Being as, by comparison with Him, nothing else has a being. He is that Being that has no succession; that is always the same. He is an excellency in all places that fills all places without any local motion at all. He is a Being who has all sufficiency in Himself. He has all excellencies; in Him is an universality of all excellencies. He has all excellencies united in one that are scattered up and down in creatures; yea, all the attributes of God are in Him but one. He has in Him all possible good whatsoever; all things that are in God are equally in Him; they are all infinitely in Him; they are eternally, immutably, essentially, purely, without mixture, originally. He is the Fountain of all good to the creature; all excellency in the creature absolutely depends upon Him. He is excellent in His operations. He can do whatsoever He will. He can do the greatest thing as easily as the least; and one act from eternity is enough to do all that He ever has done. He can communicate as much of Himself as He will to His creature; and He has never a whit the less in Himself. There can be no comparison between Him and the creature; the highest creature comes no nearer Him than the least, and He is the highest end of all things whatsoever. And this God is our God! This is the God WHOM we profess to serve, whom we profess to worship; and these are to be the thoughts that we are to have of God when we come before Him.

Now you cannot but imagine that there must be an abundance of streams of use and application that must follow from these things. All that I have done thus far is to present what God is.

Now I think I hear many who give their minds to understand what God is saying within themselves, "Oh, that we did but acknowledge God to be thus. Surely there is a farther excellency in God than we have imagined, and might we have but further sight into these things that have been thus briefly presented to us, oh, of what excellent use might all these be!"

SERMON 3

The Application

"For His name alone is excellent."

PSALM 148:13

I shall endeavor therefore to present to you, and even as briefly as I have done the other, the several uses that may flow from all these things.

USE 1. Oh, what infinite cause we have to be ashamed of these low thoughts we have had of God! If God is thus as He has been even but a little presented to us now, and by what we see, we may gather that there is infinitely more in God, and that God is infinitely higher than ever we thought of, then, upon the very hearing of such things as these are, and especially we being conscious to ourselves how little we are able to understand of them, we may see cause to be ashamed of the poor and low thoughts that we have had of this infinite Majesty, of the unworthy thoughts that we have had of Him when we have come into the presence of God. You have come to pray to God, but have you come to prayer as unto such a God? Have you had such kind of thoughts as these are, that He is that High Majesty? Certainly you cannot sanctify God's name but you must have high thoughts of God. And though I will not say that those do not sanctify God's name who do not have every one of these thoughts of God, yet this much I will say, that those who have not apprehended every one of these things regarding God have not sanctified God's name as much as they should; for we are to apprehend what it is possible for us to apprehend here in this world, or otherwise we do not sanctify God's name so as we ought.

When we come to God in prayer, or to worship Him in any other duty of His worship, if we do not apprehend God as much as we possibly can in this world, we do not sanctify God's name as much as we ought to do—and we ought to be ashamed that we do not have such apprehensions of God as we might possibly have. If God is such a God as this, what poor thoughts of God are these that He is as an old man in heaven? Some have such poor apprehensions of God, and when they hear the Scripture speak of God's eyes, ears, and hands, they think that God has a body, when the Scripture is but speaking to our capacities, that is, saying that what a man can do with his eyes, hands, or ears, God is able to do by His infinite power.

I appeal to you, do you have apprehensions of the majesty and glory of God beyond all majesty and glory that any creature is capable of in this world? We do not sanctify God's name unless, I say, we apprehend God being higher in majesty and glory than all creatures in the world are. Suppose you were to come to a king who had all the glory and honor put upon him that any creature ever had in this world—with what fear and trembling would we come before such a majesty as this? But if you have not come with greater trembling and fear before God when you came into His presence, if you have not come with higher thoughts of that God with whom we have to deal, you have not glorified God as God. No marvel then if people are so slight and vain in the duties of God's worship; they do not know what a God He is with whom they have to do.

USE 2. This shows you the dreadful evil there is in sin. Why? Because it is against such a God as this God is. Do you know whom it is that you sin against? O you sinner! Do you know whom it is that you strike at? It is this infinite God who is thus presented to you, "whose name alone is excellent, and whose glory is above the earth and heavens." Know, sinner, and may the Lord smite this upon your heart, you who are a wicked and ungodly man all the days of your life, you have done nothing else but fight against this God, this infinite and glorious God; you have been an enemy to Him all the days of your life, and every time you renew your sins, you do nothing else but strike at this infinite God, and provoke the wrath of this infinite Deity against your soul and body. And dare you stand out against this God? Will you put it to the trial to see whether that God whom you sin against is such a God as this? Will you put it to the trial, that God should set you apart to make you an object upon whom to exercise all the infinite power that there is in God, to bring evil, misery, and torments upon you for your sin?

This is the case of all desperate sinners who go on in a desperate way of sin. The language of their sin is this: "I hear much spoken concerning the greatness, excellency, and glory of God. I'll try and venture, I'll put it to the experiment whether God is such a God as He has manifested Himself to be in His Word or not." Oh, woe to that creature who shall come to feel what the greatness of God means! Oh, it is infinitely better for you to fall down before Him! And therefore this should be the exhortation to all sinners: consider, O sinful man or woman, what a

God it is before whom you come! Shall the potsherd strive with his Maker? Let one potsherd strive with another, but let not the creature strive with the Almighty; for He will be infinitely too hard for you, and He alone will appear to be excellent. You lift up your will above His will, as if so be that you could rise above this infinite God. But know this, that in spite of your heart He will be above you. He has you under His feet this moment, and the sword of His justice is at your very heart. He can take your heart's blood when He pleases and send you down to eternal miseries; there is no striving with such a God as this, who alone is excellent. The Word has proceeded out of His mouth in righteousness, that every knee must bow unto Him, and every tongue must confess this God (Isaiah 45:23; Romans 14:11). Certainly, one way or another He will have His glory out of you. God can as well cease to be as not to have His glory out of every creature. Do but consider this, and learn to tremble before this God. "The Lord is excellent and glorious above all things," and He is resolved that He will have His glory from every creature one way or another; and if it proves that He comes upon you to force it out of you, better ten thousand times that you had never been born. Therefore, according to the exhortation of the Holy Ghost in Scripture, oh, let us humble ourselves under the mighty hand of God (1 Peter 5:6; James 4:10). Let us all say, "Thou, O Lord, art alone excellent. Thy glory is above the heavens and earth, and the desire of our souls is to lift up Thy name as the excellent thing above all creatures." While we live here in this world, this is our excellency; and blessed is that man or woman who comes to see this to be his or her excellency, namely, that they might lift up God's name in the place where He has set them. Heretofore we have lifted up other things as excellent, such as an estate, and the like. But the Lord has made us to see that He alone is excellent; and His excellency has darkened all the excellency of the creature in our eyes. We see nothing excellent but God, and all in order unto God. It is a good sign of the work of grace in a man or woman, when they shall see so much of the excellency of God that God's excellency shall darken all the excellency in the world.

Oh, how vile is sin then, that is committed against such a God as this is! Nothing in the world can show a soul the evil of sin but the sight of God. If we should tell you never so much of the terrors of the law, and of hellfire, though you might see something of sin's desert, yet until you come to see with what a God you have to deal, you can never know what the evil of sin means. "Against Thee, Thee only have I sinned" (Psalm 51:4), said David; that was the thing that struck David's spirit. David knew that it was against God that he sinned. When God comes to the conscience of a sinner, and presents Himself before his conscience, He says, "O wretched sinner, it is I whom you have sinned against." Christ did so in Acts 9:4 unto Saul: "Saul, Saul, why persecutest thou Me?" So God shall say, "Sinner, sinner, why do you rebel against Me?" If God would but give us one sight of Himself, so that we might behold Him as He is upon His throne in this excellency of His name above all things, it would be impossible that the heart of a sinner would not break at such a sight.

Certainly one day every sinner shall have a sight of God. Happy it is for us now to have such a sight of God here in this world that may cause us to see the evil of our sins; for otherwise the sight of God hereafter will certainly sink our souls into the bottomless gulf of horror and despair. When Daniel was about to confess his sin in Daniel 9, mark how he begins. He wanted to get his heart to be affected with his sin, and the sins of the people, so mark how he begins his prayer in verse 4: "And I prayed unto the Lord my God, and made my confession, and said, 'O Lord, the great and dreadful God.' " Thus he begins: "I made confession. I prayed and made confession of sin, and said, 'O Lord, the great and dreadful God.' " First he looked upon how great and dreadful God was; and this caused him to confess his sin with humiliation.

You who say your prayers, and who confess that you are sinners, if at the beginning of your prayers, when you go to confess your sin, you would cast one eye up to heaven and behold this God upon His throne, and see Him to be the great and dreadful God, it would cause you to confess sin in another manner than ever yet you have done. It is a good thing, therefore, in our prayers, when we are about to confess sin, first to set before our souls the greatness and the dreadfulness of that God whom we have sinned against. When the prophet Daniel would humble proud Belshazzar in Daniel 5:23, mark what he said, "And the God in whose hand thy breath is, and whose are thy ways, hast thou not glorified." This speech set home upon a man's conscience would be enough to break the proudest and stoutest heart in the world, if the eyes of the proudest, stoutest sinner were opened to see God in His glory, and to hear the Lord speak thus to him, that God in whose hand is the breath of your nostrils, and all your ways, that is the God whom you have not glorified. You do not think with whom it is that you have to deal; but that is the God whom you have heard preached of thus, "whose name alone is excellent." Just such an infinite and glorious Deity is that Deity that you have neglected and despised, and preferred your lusts before.

Oh, if God would but give commission to your consciences to speak this with power to you, that God who is this glorious and excellent you have sinned against, oh, it would be a wonderful force to break the hardest hearts of men. And in Psalm 104:1–2, see there how David had his heart rising against sin and sinners upon the consideration of the excellency of God. There he speaks with the same argument that we have here in the text: "Bless the Lord, O my soul. My God, Thou art very great. Thou art clothed with honor and majesty [and so he goes on] who coverest Thyself with light as with a garment." He proceeds in this psalm to describe the greatness and excellency of God. But when he was done describing God's excellency, and found his heart warmed and enlarged, and raised with the meditation of the excellency of God, mark how he breaks forth in the last words of the psalm: "Let the sinners be consumed out of the earth, and let the wicked be no more; bless thou the Lord, O my soul" (verse 35). It is as if holy David had said, "O Lord, I see Thee to be very great, and Thou art clothed with honor and majesty, and Thy name is excellent above all things. What? And are there any wretched creatures who will dare to presume to rebel against Thee who art so great, who will dare to set their will against Thy will, and to prefer their lusts before Thee? Oh, cursed be those sinners. Let the sinners be consumed from the earth, and let the wicked be no more. There is infinite reason that wicked, wretched creatures should be forever consumed, who sin against such a God as Thou art, who art so great as Thou art."

My brethren, it is no marvel that the people of God are so afraid of sin. Many of you wonder at the niceness of the consciences of many people, that they dare not commit any known sin for all the world. You wonder why they should be so nice; you think it is foolishness. Would you know the reason? It is this: God has shown unto their consciences a sight of Himself; they have had a sight of the glory of the majesty of that great God, "whose name alone is excellent." And that makes them afraid of sin forever, and makes them look upon sin as the greatest evil, and even tremble at the least temptation unto any sin whatsoever. And that is the second use, great is the evil of sin if committed against such a God.

USE 3. Hence, then, if God is this excellent above all, from the meditation of the excellency of God and His glory, we see cause to be vile in our own eyes. The higher we see God to be, the lower we should be in our own eyes; there is nothing that will take down the spirit of a man more than God. I dare say of every proud heart in the world, such a one does not know God, and never had a sight of the glory of that God with whom he has to do. The sight of God will wonderfully humble the heart before Him. Job 42:5 is very famous for this, where Job says, "With the hearing of the ear I have heard of Thee, but now mine eyes have seen Thee." What follows then? "Wherefore I abhor myself, and repent in dust and ashes" (verse 6). Job was a holy man, yet he confessed that he had merely heard of God. He never had such a sight of God as God gave him at this time, and upon the sight that he had of God, though he was a holy and a gracious man, and could stand in his uprightness, yet said, "Mine eyes have seen Thee, and therefore I abhor myself, and repent in dust and ashes."

Oh, that God would give such a sight of Himself to all your souls, to those proud, stout, and rebellious sinners who have gone on in ways of rebellion against Him. You have heard of God by the hearing of the ear, but have your eyes ever seen Him? If God would but give you a sight of what I briefly spoke to you, you would certainly fall down before Him and abhor yourselves in dust and ashes.

So the prophet Isaiah, though a godly man, yet in Isaiah 6 he heard the cherubims and seraphims praising God and crying, "Holy, Holy, Holy is the Lord of hosts" (Isaiah 6:1–3). There was a vision of God upon His throne to the prophet. What followed?

The prophet said, "Woe unto me, for I am undone!" Why? "For I am a man of polluted lips, and I dwell among a people that are of unclean lips. Woe unto me, for I am undone, for I have seen the King, the Lord of hosts!" It is as if he had said, "I see the Lord upon His throne, and I behold how the blessed angels admire His glory. Oh, woe to me, I am undone."

If so holy a man shall thus cry out at the sight of God and say, "Woe to me, I am undone, because I am a man of polluted lips!" oh, what may you do then who are people of polluted lips, polluted hearts, and polluted lives? Oh, how your lips are polluted! The prophet Isaiah was no swearer; neither was he one who would talk filthy, unclean talk. Yet he complained that he was a man of polluted lips, and cried, "Woe to me, I am undone, because I have seen the Lord."

Oh, how should your heart then be humbled? What cause at least is there that your heart should be humbled, who are as polluted as you are? The sight of God should mightily humble us before God. Psalm 8:1: "O Lord, our Lord, how excellent is Thy Name in all the earth." So says the prophet David, and then he goes on to show the excellency of God. Then he cries out in verse 4, "What is man that Thou art mindful of him, and the son of man that Thou visitest him?" It is as if he had said, "Lord, Thou who art so excellent in Thyself above all things, it is a wonder that Thou should so much as look upon man."

It may be that you look high, because you are a little above your brethren, but if you had a sight of God, you would wonder that this God should look upon you. In Psalm 113:6 you have such an expression, that God humbles Himself to behold the things that are done in heaven. What an expression is here of God's excellency! God is so excellent that He humbles Himself to behold the things that are done in heaven. Now if He is so excellent as to humble Himself to behold the things in heaven, then how God humbles Himself to behold things done in earth, to behold such wretched, vile creatures as you are! Oh, be vile in your own eyes upon the sight of the great God, and by these three questions you may have three signs whether God has ever made known Himself to you or not.

First, are you ashamed and confounded in your thoughts for those low, poor thoughts you have had of God?

Second, has the sight of God caused you to see the dreadfulness of the evil there is in sin?

Third, has the sight of God made you to be vile in your own eyes? That is good evidence that you have had some sight of God indeed.

USE 4. If God is this excellent, and His glory is so great above the earth and heavens, hence we may learn to know the vanity of the creature. Set God and the creature together, nay, set all the creature comforts in the world together, and, oh, how the vanity of all creature comforts in the world is made known to us. There are many ways to convince us that there is a vanity in all things in the world; we may be convinced by the strength of reason and by experience. Suppose that a man has an estate, and God but touches his body and keeps him on his sickbed. Such a man may say, "Oh, what a poor thing it is to enjoy all the world! Had I all the world at my command, I could have no comfort in it." And therefore, what a vanity there is in the creature.

Someone else perhaps, by arguments and reasons, will tell you that everything is vain, and that there is neither contentment nor continuance in anything in the world. When we see men who are rich and great die, and carry nothing with them, we are ready to say, "Oh, how vain the world is!" These are some means to cause us to see the vanity of the creature. But what are all these to the sight of God? The sight of the glory of God is infinitely more powerful to reveal the vanity of all things in the world to us. The man or woman who has once had a real sight of this God in His infinite excellency will not much regard what becomes of him concerning outward things in this world. He who sees God to be great will see all other things to be small.

And, indeed, we never see God to be truly excellent unless we see Him alone to be excellent. You think that you know something of God, aye, but the excellency of the creature is still glorious in your eyes. Certainly you do not know God aright. If you know God aright in His excellency, you know that He alone is excellent; and therefore, if you know no other excellency but God, all other things would be but vanity in your eyes. In 2 Corinthians 3:10, the apostle says there, concerning the glory of the law compared with the glory of the gospel, that "that which was glorious now has no glory by reason of a greater glory that is come." So I may say in this case, the things of the world that were glorious in your eyes before yet now are not glorious, but all darkened, because there is a greater glory that now comes and shines in upon you.

If a man had lived in a dark dungeon under the ground all the days of his life and never had the glimpse of any light whatsoever, never since he was born; if all of a sudden a candle should be brought to him, he would admire its glory. But if this man should afterwards be brought into the outside world and see the glory of the sun, the glory of the candle would be nothing to him. So because the men of the world have lived as it were in darkness, they have some comforts in the creature and think them to be glorious, for they know no better. But the soul that has had a sight of God comes to see that all things in the world are but darkness to him. There is nothing that can disengage the heart of a man from the creature as a sight of

God. You have a notable Scripture for how a sight of God disengages the heart of a man from the creature in Acts 7:2. "And he said, 'Men, brethren, and fathers, hearken. The God of glory appeared unto our father Abraham when he was in Mesopotamia before he dwelt in Harran, and said unto him, "Get thee out of thy country, and from thy kindred, and come into the land which I shall show thee." ' " And so he shows how Abraham was content to forsake all his friends and country. Why? Because the God of glory appeared to him. It is said upon this that when the Holy Ghost would show what it was that brought Abraham out of his country, that took his heart off from all his friends and country to go into a strange country, the Holy Ghost said, "The God of glory appeared to our father Abraham." Let a man's heart be never so glued to any contentments that are here in the world, let but the God of glory appear to that man, and all things are vanity; then the heart quickly comes off from any thing.

And indeed, though there may be many arguments that may make men and women greatly deny themselves the use of creature comforts, yet the heart is never thoroughly taken off till the God of glory appears to the soul. A notable example of self-denial is that of Moses; he might have had all the riches and glory of Egypt, might have been next to the king himself, an heir (for so some write that Pharaoh had no son, and that Pharaoh's daughter adopted Moses to the end that he might be an heir to the crown). Moses had all riches, and the treasures of Egypt at command, yet he forsook all.

"But though he forsook all for a while," yet you will say, "did he not regret it afterward?" No, says Hebrews 11:27, "By faith he forsook Egypt, not fearing the wrath of the king, for he endured, as seeing Him that is invisible." That was what made Moses forsake all the riches of Egypt, and endure, to go on and never repent for making such a choice. What was the great thing that took Moses off from the creature? It was that sight of God, that God who was invisible.

My brethren, the sight of God puts a mighty magnanimity upon a man's heart; there is nothing great to a great spirit, nor nothing can greaten the spirit of a man or woman, so as the sight of the great God. No men and women in the world have such great spirits as those who have seen the great God. And the more often any one has the sight of the great God, I say, the greater will such men's and women's spirits be. They are raised to such a height that all the world will not satisfy such a soul for its portion. And this again may be a note of trial whether you have ever seen God alone to be excellent. Has that sight ever taken your hearts off from the creature? Has it engaged your hearts fully to God Himself, so that you can say, "There is none in heaven, nor none in earth that I desire in comparison to Thee" (Psalm 73:25).

USE 5. Is God's name alone excellent? O my brethren, study to know God then. Labor to search into this excellency so far as we may, and as God gives us leave. God has revealed much of Himself to us in the Scripture, and in the book of the creature; and God expects that what is revealed of Him in the Scripture and in the book of the creature, that the rational creatures, angels, and men should labor and search to know. There is nothing so sweet, so amiable, so lovely, or so delightful to a rational creature (if it is purged from the filthiness and corruption of sin) as the sight of the infinite First Being of all things. Why, here is concluded all excellent sights whatsoever. Some men are taken with such a sight as to behold fair buildings, and others to behold brave pictures, one with one thing and another with another. Oh, but the sight of God has all sights in

it that may delight the soul and give contentment to the heart
of man or angel—and therefore labor to know the excellency
of God.

You poor creatures who have minded little all this while but
merely to understand your trades, and how you may get a shil-
ling or two to provide for your families, oh, know that here is a
higher object for you to busy your thoughts and hearts about.
Learn to know this God who alone is excellent, and do not be
discouraged at those things that have been spoken, though they
are above your reach at first. Yet if your hearts are pure and are
cleansed from filthiness, you have the promise in Matthew 5:8:
"Blessed are the pure in heart, for they shall see God." It may be
that you who are poor people can never come to get learning to
have the knowledge of arts and sciences, and such things. Aye,
but if you have clean hearts you are blessed in this, for God says
that you shall see Him. Labor to study God, and labor to know
Him more. In Psalm 91:14, mark how acceptable it is to God
for His creature to labor to know Him: "I will set him on high,
because he hath known My Name." Thy Name, O Lord, alone
is excellent, and Thy glory above the heavens and earth. And,
"I will set him on high, because he knows My Name."

"Oh," says God, "yonder is a poor creature who above
all things in the world desires to know Me. He has had a little glimpse of My glory, and, oh, how earnest his heart is to
know Me! I will reveal more of Myself to him, and then I will
set him on high because he knows My name." The Lord has a
high account of those who know His name. As for those ignorant creatures, let them be what they will in regard of outward
things, yet if they are ignorant of God, they are vile, low, and
base in God's esteem. But take a soul who knows God's name,
the Lord will set him on high; such a one is high in the very
thoughts of God, and the Lord takes pleasure to make such a

soul to be high. Paul, in Philippians 3:8, accounted "all things dung and dross." For what? "For the excellency of the knowledge of Jesus Christ." Indeed, in the knowledge of Christ God is known; and if you would study the knowledge of God, it must be in Christ. You can never know God but in Christ. In Matthew 11:27 Christ says, "No man knows the Father but the Son, and him to whom the Son shall reveal Him." It must be Christ who must reveal the glory of God to our souls, or else we can never come to know Him savingly.

USE 6. If God is this excellent above all, and His glory is thus above the earth and heaven, hence we are taught to labor to keep the sense of the infinite distance that there is between God and His creatures always in our hearts. This is a point of marvelous consequence, the sense of the distance between God and us. If God is infinitely above the creature, then God expects that we who profess any knowledge of Him should evermore have our thoughts upon God's excellency raised in a kind of infiniteness above what we think of the excellency of any creature; and our hearts then should work after God in a kind of infiniteness more than ever they worked after any creature, since there is an infinite disproportion between the excellency of God and the excellency that is in any creature.

I beseech you to observe what I am saying, for it is of marvelous use to help us to sanctify God in all our ways. As there is an infinite distance between the excellency of God and that of all creatures, so there ought to be a kind of infinite distance between what our hearts are in working after God and working after the creature; otherwise we do not lift up God's name in His excellency and glory. And indeed, a gracious heart will make it so; and in this I conceive the very work of grace consists, in that it is such a principle in the soul of a man or woman who is converted that, though such a one is a finite creature, yet it has a kind of infiniteness in the working of it after God.

You will say, "Infinite, how can that be?" True, I confess that properly it cannot be infinite; but thus it is infinite in its kind, that is, such a creature has such a principle as it would fain, if it were possible, work infinitely after God.

Further, this principle of grace causes this in the heart, that it will never limit itself in any work after God, and therefore has a kind of infiniteness. And here is the difference between one who has true grace and the most glorious hypocrite in the world: a hypocrite will ever be bounding his working after God, and think that this is enough. "What need is there for anything more? If I do this and that, why, I do well and may go to heaven at last." And so he bounds himself.

But where there is the least dram of true grace, though there are many weaknesses in the soul, yet such a soul never bounds itself in working after God. "I indeed, heretofore, have set out my heart to the creature, but now I would fain, if I could, let my heart out infinitely after God. Why? For I see an infinite distance between the good there is in the creature and the good there is in God."

Certainly where this is, there is grace; and this one note would be enough to discern the truth of grace in the heart. If the sight of God has wrought this, that whereas heretofore your heart has been let out after such and such creature comforts, now you desire, if it were possible, to let your heart out infinitely after God, here is the work of grace—and in this you go beyond any hypocrite. Oh, keep this constantly in your soul; this is the special sanctifying of God's name in all our ways. When we see that God gives us leave to let our hearts out towards the creature in some measure, then there is a great deal of danger that we should have our heart stick on the creature, and that we should not have that disproportion in the letting out of our hearts to the creature and to God as ought to be. This is the ground of all idolatry in the world; when men have seen some excellency in the creature, they have been taken with it and there have stuck, and have not been carried from the creature in God. That is the heathen's idolatry: when they see an excellency in the sun, they think that it is a god. So a Christian's idolatry may be in this: if there is any creature comfort that your heart closes with, and there you do stick, and your heart is not carried to God, yea, is not carried to God in such a disproportion as there is between Him and the creature—I say, so far as you want what you are capable of in this kind, so far you are guilty of idolatry.

Oh, that this one note might stick upon us: "There is none like unto Thee, O Lord." Can you say this out of an uprightness of your soul, as in the presence of God, "Lord, Thou that knowest all things, knowest that though I have a vile heart that is let out after the creatures more than it ought to be, yet, Lord, Thou knowest that my heart is let out after nothing so much as after Thee?" That would be a good argument of a gracious work of God upon you. Surely, if none is like the Lord, then our hearts should seek nothing so much as the Lord. We must not content ourselves with a little love to God. Is there such a disproportion between your love for the creature and your love for God as there is between God and the creature? You say that you love God, aye, but it may be that you love the creature as well. Do you think that this will satisfy God? When you hear that God's name alone is excellent, God expects that your love for Him should be in a way infinitely above that love of yours for any other creature.

USE 7. There is one thing more, with which I will conclude:

surely if God's name alone is excellent, there is a proportion in which God's people alone are the excellent people on the earth. According as a man's God is, so is he. Men conceive their excellency to be according to the excellency of him whom they serve; according as a man's God is, I say, so is he. Now if God alone is excellent, and He is your God, then you are excellent. The people of God are therefore excellent because their God is so excellent. This is the reason for the phrase that you have in Proverbs 12:26: "The righteous is more excellent than his neighbor." Why is a righteous man more excellent than his neighbor? It may be that the righteous man is a poor man and his neighbor is a rich man; perhaps this poor good man's next neighbor is a knight or a nobleman, and yet he is more excellent than his neighbor. Why? Because his God is more excellent; because the infinite Lord of heaven and earth is the portion of a righteous man. If God alone is excellent, then the righteous alone is excellent.

I will give you a Scripture or two to show that, according to the excellency of God, in proportion appears the excellency of the children of God. Compare Deuteronomy 33:26 with verse 29. Verse 26: "There is none like unto the God of Jeshurun." Then in verse 29: "Happy art thou, O Israel; who is like unto thee?" You see that there is a reflection of the glory of God upon His saints: there is none like God, and there are none like God's people. So in 2 Samuel 7:22 you have an expression to the same purpose: "Wherefore Thou art great, O Lord God, for there is none like Thee; neither is there any God besides Thee, according to all that we have heard with our ears." Then in verse 23: "And what one nation in the earth is like Thy people?"

Oh, how the saints of God should boast of their God and rejoice in Him, and be encouraged in God alone! Though you have no other portion than God alone, you have portion enough. In Micah 5:4 there is an admirable Scripture for the encouragement of the hearts of God's people in God alone: "And he shall stand and feed in the strength of the Lord, in the majesty of the name of the Lord his God." This is a prophecy of Christ, and as it is true of Christ, so it is true of all the members of Christ. They may stand when the world falls; whatsoever becomes of the world, whatsoever troubles are about them, they are to stand and rejoice themselves in the name of the Lord, in the strength of the Lord, and in the majesty of the Lord their God. The knowledge of this reference that the saints have to God is what should put courage and boldness into their hearts before all the world. Revelation 22:4: "And they shall see His face, and His name shall be in their foreheads." They shall see the face of God. And what then? Then the name of God shall be on their foreheads; they shall have a boldness and courage in the cause of God. Whatever becomes of the world, yet we have happiness enough in God. Oh, rejoice, rejoice in this, you who are the people of God; for there is none so excellent as you are, if so be that God now invests you with this excellency.

USE 8. What cause then have you to fear this God, and to serve this God in all your ways, and to worship Him as a God whose name alone is excellent? Who would not fear Him? There is none like Him. Jeremiah 10:7: "Who would not fear Thee, O King of nations?" Let this God be feared by us; let us labor to hold forth the excellency of our God in our lives and conversations, in our whole course. Oh, that it might be written upon our lives, "The name of God alone is excellent." All you who profess to have any interest in this God, you should walk so in your conversations that it may be written upon your lives, "The name of God alone is excellent, and His glory is above the earth and heavens." Oh, take heed that this blessed name

of God that alone is excellent is not dishonored and polluted
by you. We might have enlarged upon this point if we had had
the time. James calls it "that worthy name of the Lord."

You who profess yourselves to be Christians, and who profess godliness more than others, know that you have the name
of God upon you; and this name of God is excellent and glorious. Do not let it suffer by you. Oh, woe to you that ever you
were born, if you should be instruments of polluting the name
of God. I think that anyone who makes profession of God's
name should think to himself, "It would be better that I were
dead and rotting under the clods of dirt than that ever I should
live to pollute this blessed name of God that is so excellent.
What? Was I born so that I might live to have my hand in so
great a mischief as that this glorious name of God should be
darkened by me? Oh, the Lord forbid!"

Know what the name of God is that you profess; meditate
upon how excellent it is, and let this be a strong argument
to keep you from sin. When any temptation comes, set this
thought against it: "Shall I pollute this name of God that is so
infinitely excellent?" No man or woman can die with peace, or
have peace upon their sickbeds, unless they are able to look
back into their lives and to say, "Lord, though there has been
much weakness in me, and in many things I have dishonored
Thee, yet it has been my care in my generation, and in the
place that Thou hast set me, to lift up Thy name. And I have
done something through Thy grace to lift up Thy name."

Oh, that I could leave this point upon your hearts, that
everyone of you might go home and make but this one use of
it: "I have heard that the name of God alone is excellent, and
that His glory is above all. This likewise I have heard to be my
duty. I have hear that this was the great work that I was born for,
that I should do something to make God's name great before

all those with whom I converse." Think of this, everyone of you. How long have you lived? Many of you will be ready to say, "I have lived this long in such a place." And it may be that you can say that you have done no man wrong, only good. But what can you say to this question? I appeal to your conscience. Has the name of God been made great by you? Have you done anything to lift up this glorious name of God in the place wherein God has set you? It may be that you have not thought that this was your work; but this is the work that God expects from you, that you should give yourself up to study by all the means that you possibly can to lift up God's name and deny your own name—no matter if that is cast into the dirt, so long as the name of God is lifted up. Have this resolution. Oh, that you would go away with this one note stuck upon your hearts: "I am convinced that the name of God is infinitely glorious; and therefore, for the time to come, through His grace, whatever becomes of me, yet I will do what I can to lift up His name."

Consider what has been said in the text, and may the Lord give you understanding.

THE EXCELLENCY OF CHRIST

Christ Is the Great Wonder of the World

*T*here is nothing of greater concern than to know God, and His Son whom He has sent into the world. "Even this is eternal life," says Christ (John 17:3). I have therefore endeavored to open something to you concerning God so that you may have right apprehensions of that God with whom you have to deal, out of that Scripture in Psalm 148:13, "His name alone is excellent, His glory is above the earth and heaven." I have concluded for the present what I intended to present to you about God, with the meditation of the excellency of the state of those who have this God to be their God, who is so excellent and glorious. The church makes her boast of her interest in God in Psalm 48:14: "for this God is our God." Oh, happy is he who, having heard what a glorious God God is, is able to say, "This God is my God; this is my God in whom my soul has interest!"

And if the name of God is as excellent and glorious as you have heard, there is infinite cause that we should fear Him and sanctify His name in our conversations (Job 13:11). Shall not His excellence make you afraid? Oh, where is the soul that shall

51

dare to walk before this God with boldness and presumption, considering what a God He is with whom that soul has to deal? Shall not that excellency of His that has been opened unto you make you afraid, and cause you to fear such a God?

Now then, having spoken somewhat about the excellency of God, and what apprehensions we are to have of God in all our ways, I am now to speak somewhat concerning the excellency of Christ, and to show you what apprehensions you are to have of Jesus Christ. "For this is eternal life, to know Thee, and Thy Son." To know God, and not to know Him in Christ, is to very little purpose. It is no saving knowledge of God, if we were able to discourse never so much of Him, unless we know Him in Jesus Christ His Son. And therefore, for the knowledge of Christ, which I shall endeavour to present as briefly as I did the knowledge of God, you may be pleased to read with me from Isaiah 9:6 these words: "And His name shall be called Wonderful."

If you read this verse, and that which follows, you might think that you were reading an evangelist rather than a prophet, one relating a history of what was done rather than a prophecy of what was to be done. Isaiah here prophesies clearly of Christ, as if He had come at that time; and yet it was between seven hundred and eight hundred years before the coming of Christ that this prophecy was given: "Unto us a child is born, unto us a Son is given, and the government shall be upon His shoulders. And His name shall be called Wonderful." But it is the usual way of Scripture to set before us things to be done as if they were already done, to note the certainty of what God reveals to be done; and faith will make things that are not to be as if they were really present. Indeed, faith never has a proper work so much as in making things that are not present to be as if they were present, to make them real.

It was a time of great distress and trouble to the church of God when this prophecy occurred, as will appear from the seventh chapter even unto this prophecy. And frequently we find in Scripture that in times of the greatest distress of the church, there were the clearest prophecies of Christ, of the Messiah to come. Jacob prophesied of Shiloh when he was in Egypt (Genesis 49:10); and Daniel of the Messiah when he was in captivity (Daniel 9) in Babylon. And Isaiah here prophesies when the people were in great distress, "To us a child is born, unto us a Son is given, whose name is Wonderful, Counselor, the mighty God." There are four reasons why the Lord would have the prophecy of the Messiah come especially at those times when the church was in a sad, suffering condition.

First, because the only comfort of all the saints of God then was their expectation of the Messiah to come, God, therefore, propounded Christ unto them as that which might lighten all their darkness, that might sweeten all their sorrows and troubles. And indeed, there was enough in their expectation of the Savior who was to come; this was what made their hearers rejoice in the midst of all their sorrows. "Abraham saw His day and rejoiced, and was glad" (John 8:56).

Second, therefore they had the clear manifestation of Christ in the time of their outward troubles to confirm their faith in this, that however much their enemies prevailed against them, yet it was impossible that they could root out the nation of the Jews, for the great Savior of the world was to come out of them. Therefore, under God's protection, and though they might suffer somewhat, yet they could not cease from being a nation because the Messiah was to come out from them; and this was a great encouragement to them to expect mercy from God, because they were a people whom the Lord would bring the great Savior of the world out of.

Third, by propounding so great a mercy as Jesus Christ would be to the world, they might hereby have a help to their faith, that surely God would not deny them lesser mercies. What great matter was it for them to expect from God some outward affliction when God made known unto them that love and that infinite compassion, those tender bowels of His, even to send His own Son into the world for them?

Fourth, it was to teach them that the way of deliverance from any outward affliction was to exercise their faith upon Christ, the Messiah who was to come. The Lord would teach His church when it was in afflictions to not be looking so much at the present affliction that was upon them—and so to seek for outward help and means of deliverance—but would have them exercise faith upon the Messiah who was to come, though many hundred years after; and this promise of faith was so pleasing to God since it was the only means, or the chief means of deliverance from all outward afflictions: 'Nay,' said God, "if so be that they will rely upon Me, and exercise this faith upon that great promise of Mine to send My Son into the world, as for their deliverance out of these outward troubles and afflictions, it shall be but a little matter for Me to do that for them." Ordinarily, when we are exercised with outward afflictions, we only think of some natural helps and comforts contrary to those particular afflictions that are upon us, whereas indeed the way for us to sanctify God's name, to do that which is acceptable to God when any outward affliction befalls us, is immediately to exercise our faith upon the great promise of God in Jesus Christ, upon the great covenant of grace that God has made with us in Him, upon the great mercy of God in sending His Son into the world: "My condition is very sad, and I am grievously afflicted, aye, but surely the mercy that would send Jesus Christ into the world is enough to deliver me out of any affliction, or at least to bless it to me." Therefore, do not only cry to God when you are sick or in trouble to deliver you from it, but labor to exercise faith upon the covenant of grace in Christ, upon that glorious mercy of God in His Son. That is the way in which God would have us to sanctify His name. And that is the reason why, in times of great affliction, there were such clear prophecies of Jesus Christ, such as the one here in my text: "For unto us a child is born, unto us a Son is given, and His name shall be called Wonderful, Counselor...."

Now in this latter part of this verse, we have Christ set out unto us in five of His notable and famous titles:

1. Wonderful
2. Counselor
3. The Mighty God
4. The Everlasting Father
5. Prince of Peace

I intend to only speak of the first one: "His name shall be called Wonderful," because I would have some kind of proportion between what I have presented to you about God and what I shall say about Christ. As for other things more largely about God or Christ, they may come afterwards; but for now I desire only to present Christ to you in this one title of His: "His name shall be called Wonderful." The point is this:

DOCTRINE: Jesus Christ is the great wonder of the world.

This is our point of doctrine: God Himself, more than seven hundred years before He was born, gave Him this name "Wonderful." In Isaiah 19:20, we read of a Savior, "a great one," the text says. Surely Jesus Christ is a Savior, and a great one. He is the wonder of the world. In Judges 13:17–18 we have the story of the angel appearing unto Manoah. Manoah would fain know the angel's name. "And Manoah said unto the angel of the Lord, 'What is Thy name?' " (verse 17). In verse 18 we read that the angel of the Lord said unto him. "Why askest thou after my name, seeing it is secret?" Now the word that is translated in your books as "secret" is a word that signifies "wonderful." Augustine, in his questions upon the book of Judges, is confident that this angel was Jesus Christ, and that His ascending up in the sacrifice that Manoah offered was to fore-signify Jesus Christ to be the only sacrifice that should ascend up to God for a sweet savor in the nostrils of the Father. It was Jesus Christ who appeared here to Manoah, and His name is "Wonderful."

Luther had such a speech regarding Christ. He said that the most famous and wonderful and glorious miracle of all miracles is Jesus Christ. He is the wonder of the world. God is very wonderful in all His works, such as in the works of creation. Psalm 8:1: "O Lord, our Lord, how excellent is Thy name?" And in the end of that psalm we read: "O Lord, our Lord, how excellent is Thy name in all the earth?" Yea, He is wonderful in that one work of His in making our bodies. Psalm 139:14: "I am fearfully and wonderfully made," said the psalmist. God has made our very bodies fearfully and wonderfully; it is a wonderful work of God in the framing of our bodies in the womb. It was a means of the conversion of Gallen from atheism. When he saw the anatomy of a man's body and beheld the wonderful work of such a body, it forced him to acknowledge the God of nature, that there was a being above nature.

Now God is wonderful in all His works, yet all His wonderful works in the heavens, in the earth, and in the seas must all stand by and give way to this great wonder, Jesus Christ. Though the stars are glorious creatures in themselves, yet when the sun arises all their light is eclipsed and you see nothing of them.

So though God has many wonders in the world, and has done many wonderful works, yet when the Son of Righteousness arises, when Jesus Christ comes to appear, all the other works of God are darkened with the glory of this great wonder. Other things are wonderful to us because of our ignorance, because we are not able to understand the reason of things. Things are wonderful to children that are little regarded by wise and understanding men. Ignorance makes men to wonder at many things that have nothing in them; but Christ is a wonder, so as God the Father Himself accounted Him a wonder. God Himself gave Jesus Christ this name "Wonderful." He is a wonder to the angels themselves in heaven. In 1 Peter 1:12 the angels are said to desire to look into the things of the gospel, to pry into them. They stoop down to pry into those things of the gospel. Great is the mystery of godliness in Christ Jesus. Oh, there are many glorious mysteries of godliness in Jesus Christ, such things as "eye hath not seen, ear hath not heard, neither can enter into the heart of man to conceive," as the Scripture says in 1 Corinthians 2:9. Yea, they are revealed only by the Spirit of God, who searches all things, "yea, the deep things of God." The Spirit who searches the deep things of God must reveal the things of the gospel unto the soul that ever comes to the knowledge of them. It was a work of the Spirit of God to instruct Bezaleel and Aholiah in those arts of workmanship, to work in brass and the like; and it is a work of God's Spirit to show a man the reason of the things of nature. But when God's Spirit comes to reveal Christ to the soul (for it is the Spirit of God who searches the deep things of God), this puts an emphasis upon it, showing that the things of the gospel are deep things; they are things that are revealed only by God's Spirit, and not by an ordinary work of God's Spirit of God, but by an extraordinary work of the Spirit of God. That Spirit who searches the deep

things of God must declare these things to any soul who comes
to the understanding of them.

"His Name is Wonderful." Now surely He to whom God
spoke so much of before He came into the world, He who
so many wise men and prophets longed to see, He who was
the expectation and joy of the whole church of God from the
beginning of the world before He came, He who was so typified out by all the sacrifices and types of the Old Testament, by
the temple, which was the wonder of the world at that time; He
who, when He came into the world, had His birth solemnized
by the angels, a heavenly choir singing doxologies; He who had
upon His first coming the wise men from the east coming to
worship Him—surely He must be some wonderful one, some
great one. And therefore we read of the people in Luke 1:66,
that when they saw and heard of such strange things at John
the Baptist's birth, the text says, "All they that heard them laid
them up in their hearts," saying, "What manner of child shall
this be?" So when we hear of these things that were done by way
of preparation for the coming of Christ, for some two thousand
years together, and such great things that were done upon His
coming, surely it must be some wonderful one. What manner
of child is this that is given to us? Wherefore then we read of
Moses in Exodus 3:3, that when he saw that wonderful sight in
the wilderness, the bush burning and not consumed, said, "I
will go and see what yonder great sight is." So we may well say,
when Christ is propounded as being so wonderful, and when
God Himself gives Him this name, "Let us take our thoughts
from all other things, and turn aside to see this great sight, to
see what this wonder is."

Therefore, to open this wonder that is in Christ, to show
you how Christ is wonderful, how well He may challenge this
name, and how proper this title is to Him to be called "Wonder-

ful," I shall open it in these particulars:

First, Christ is wonderful in His natures.

Second, Christ is wonderful in His Person.

Third, He is wonderful in the manner of His incarnation.

Fourth, He is wonderful in the wonderful work that He came into the world for, the wonderful things that He came to do.

Fifth, He is wonderful in His anointing, in His offices.

Sixth, He is wonderful in His admirable endowments.

Seventh, He is wonderful in the glorious miracles that He wrought.

Eighth, He is wonderful in that great glory of God the Father that appears in Him.

Ninth, He is wonderful in the work of His humiliation.

Tenth, He is wonderful in His conquest.

Eleventh, He is wonderful in His exaltation, and the degrees of it.

Twelfth, He is wonderful in His saints.

Thirteenth, and last, He is wonderful, and shall be wonderful in the highest heavens, in the church triumphant.

And in all these regards we shall see what a wonderful Savior we have, and what kind of thoughts we are to have of Jesus Christ. Certainly, because of the want of the right understanding of God, and the low thoughts and apprehensions we have of Him, the name of God is little sanctified among us, so for the want of the right understanding of Jesus Christ, how little the name of God is signified in the mysteries of the gospel. We have the Word (God); we can say that God made us. We have the Word (Christ), and we hope to be saved by Jesus Christ. But, oh, how far we are either from apprehending God, such an infinite and glorious God as He has already, though very darkly, been set out unto you! And so, before we are done, though it is but in a sermon or two, you will find that your thoughts of Jesus Christ have been too low and too mean. Oh, that I could by any means heighten your thoughts of God and Christ, so that you may know the Lord, and His Son whom He has sent into the world!

First, Christ is wonderful in His natures. These headings that I have propounded all might be largely insisted on, but I think it best at first to give you a short view of things, and to present them together as briefly as I may. Christ is wonderful in His natures for He is God and man; our Savior is God, and so He is set forth unto us afterwards as the Mighty God. And is not this a wonderful thing, that mankind, fallen from God, should have no less a Savior than the Mighty God Himself? If all the angels in heaven and men in the world had undertaken to have been the saviors of one soul, they could never have done it; they could never have accomplished what they had undertaken. Such is the state of man that if ever he is saved, he must have a Savior above the angels, above all the strength that there is in all the angels in heaven and creatures in all the world, He is that God whom you have heard of whose name is above excellent, whose glory is above the heavens and earth.

But that we should be saved only by God may seem to some to be no great wonder. They will say, "Who can save us but God?" Aye, but know that here it is not God putting forth an attribute to save us, but it is God undertaking this relationship of a Savior, God putting Himself in another condition (as it were) and taking upon Him our nature. That is, therefore, what makes the wonder of a God-man, *Theoanthropos*. 1 Timothy 3:16: "Great is the mystery of godliness, God was manifested in the flesh." This is a wonderful mystery, that there should be such a

word as *Theoanthropos*. God-man is the greatest wonder that
there ever was in the world, that there should be such a thing
as should be called "God-man," that is really and verily God
and man together in one. I say, this is the greatest wonder that
ever was in the world, that divine nature and human nature
should be joined together, that we should have a Savior who
is as verily man as He is God, and as verily God as He is man;
that those two natures—the nature of God and the nature of
man—should come together in one that were so distant before
one from another. This is a wonder beyond all sense and reason, and we need a prospector's glass from God to be able to
see anything into it; we can easily believe (we think) that Christ
was God and man, but every child can do so. When you ask
your children what Christ was, you teach them that He was both
God and man. Aye, but I appeal to you, when were your hearts
taken with this as the greatest wonder in the world, that there
should ever be such a thing as God and man in one, and that
this would be the Savior of mankind? That man, who is miserable, should look up to God to save him, should look up to the
mercy of God, this would not be so wonderful; but that miserable man must be saved by one who is God-man, man and God,
this is that which, unless the Spirit of God who searches the
deep things of God (as you heard before) reveals it to a man,
it would be impossible for man ever to have such a thought as
this is. Indeed, setting out this great mystery is one great argument that the Scriptures are divine; for it is too high a thing
to have entered into the thought of a creature. It is too high
a thing that a creature should ever have such a thought that
saving a man must be by God's being a man; it cannot be imagined how such a thought could have come into a creature. This
argues the Scriptures to be from God; it is too great a mystery
for any creature ever to have imagined or thought of. This is

that which is a stumbling block to the Jews, and foolishness to the Gentiles; but it is the power and glory of God to those who shall be saved. If God should have put this to us and said, "Well, I am inclined to do good to you, and am willing to save you; but know that your estate is such that you can never be saved unless there is such a Savior, such a Mediator for you, as must be both God and man." Why, certainly both angels and men would have stood amazed at this, and would have concluded that the state of mankind was desperate then, if so be that the state of man who has fallen from God, and has sinned against Him, is such that there is no way to deliver one soul from eternal condemnation and eternal wrath but by such a Savior as must be both God and man. I say, all angels and men would have even concluded then that man must perish forever. But it is God, the wonder-working God, who has wrought this for mankind, who has sent us such a Savior as is both God and man. Surely, then, His Name may be called "Wonderful."

Christ is wonderful in His Person. Here is a greater wonder than that: God is God and man. "God and man," you will say, "that may be." He has come in the similitude of flesh, and has taken the shape of man. There may be some kind of union between the divine and human natures. But consider this second wonder: He is not only God, but the second Person in the Trinity. Consider these two things in the Person of Christ. First, He is to be looked at not merely as God, but as God, the second Person of the Trinity; and this is a great wonder in the Christian religion, for it was little known before. We read little in the Old Testament about the Trinity; it is only in Christ that the Trinity comes to be known. When we are in straits we will cry to God who made the heavens and earth to be a Savior; but for us to know that we must be saved by God in the Second Person, who is the character and graven form of His image, the

Son of God, and yet so the Son of God as He is co-eternal with His Father, equal with His Father, as the Scripture speaks, and so God the Second person in Trinity, as yet He is of the same nature that His Father is of, the same God, and yet the Son of God—the consideration of the mystery of the Trinity that appears in Christ is a great wonder above reason. We may adore it, but to search into it we are not able.

The second thing to be considered in His Person is that He is not only God and man, but God and man hypostatically united, the union of the human and divine natures. That these natures should be united both in one Person is the great wonder of the Christian religion.

There are two principal wonders in the Christian religion. I beseech you to consider them rightly.

First, there are divers Persons in one nature. That is the wonder of the Trinity; for there you have but one nature, the divine nature, but three Persons, Father, Son, and Holy Ghost. This is a wonder that the heathens knew nothing of, and was little known till Christ came.

Second, there are divers natures in one Person, that is, in Christ. Christ is God-man, but one Person united hypostatically. Now to search into this, that the same Person who is God is man, and how the human nature subsists in the Deity and has no subsistence in all in itself is in the Deity, how this is only the Scripture reveals to be so. But how it is is too deep a sea for any creature to wade into. We must stand and admire it, and adore God in it, who has revealed this as the object of our faith. But to be able to search into how such a thing can be, that that union can be in one person, is a wonder above all admiration. Indeed, it is one of the most wonderful works that God ever did in the world, to unite two such creatures who seemed to be of such distant natures as the body and the soul of man in one person; to unite a piece of earth and a piece of flesh to such a glorious thing as a rational immortal soul is, the union of these two together in one person is the greatest work, regarding the works of nature, that God ever did in the world. David saw his body as being wonderfully and fearfully made; but certainly the union of the body and soul, the soul being of the same nature with the angels, that it should be united with the body to make one person is a great wonder in the works of nature.

But God united the second Person in the Trinity to the nature of man, not to the nature of angels, for so the Scripture says, "Christ did not take upon Him the nature of angels, but the seed of Abraham" (Hebrews 2:16); for if Christ would have been united to another nature, one would have thought it would have been to an angelic nature. But to refuse that, and take man's nature, and unite it in one Person, so that it could be said that that Person who is God, the same Person is man— here is the great wonder in the Christian religion, the personal union of the natures of Christ. And indeed, from hence many wonderful things will arise.

The same Person who was the Creator of all the world was a creature, the very same Person. I do not say He had the same nature, though. This is the wonder in Scripture. And the same Person who is the Lord of mankind is yet the Son of Man. He is the Son of Man and yet the Lord of mankind.

The same Person who is eternal and immortal yet died. So the Scripture says, "They crucified the Lord of glory." What, can God, who is the Lord of glory, who made heaven and earth, the eternal God, whose name alone is excellent—can He be crucified? Yet that Person who was the Lord of glory, whose name alone is glorious, that Person was crucified, but suffered only in His human nature. Whatsoever Christ suffered, He suffered in His human nature. It may be said that that Person who was God suffered, though not the divine nature; the divine nature could not suffer, but the same Person who was God as well as man did suffer. It is the clear Scripture language. And I might give you many texts of Scripture to show you that the person who was God suffered, but this one is enough: "They crucified the Lord of glory" (1 Corinthians 2:8).

QUESTION. To what great purpose is it for us to understand that Christ was God and man in one Person? Is it not enough to understand that He was God and man? Why do we need to look so much at the union of the two natures? ANSWER. My brethren, know that there is a great deal in this, in knowing the union of the two natures. It is of marvelous use to you for helping your faith to know not only that Christ had these two natures, but about the union of those two natures.

But you will say, "How may it help our faith?"

Because hereby you may see that whatsoever Christ did or suffered, though but in His human nature, yet it was of infinite value and efficacy; and the infinite value and efficacy of what Christ did and suffered arises from the union of the two natures because it was that Person who was God who did and suffered such things.

I remember that I once knew a very godly man in the time of his sickness who was in a great agony, under a very great temptation, and at midnight sent for a minister. That minister came to him, and this was his temptation, fearing that he should die: "Why, your sin deserves an infinite punishment; you have sinned against an infinite God and you deserve eternal death. But Christ, in whom you have trusted, being man, and suffering only in His human nature, could suffer only that which was finite. His death was but a few days, a day or two, so how can He, by suffering that which was but finite, by enduring pain for a little while upon the cross, and by being under death but a day or two, how can He deliver you from an infinite suffering, and from eternal death?"

This was the temptation that lay upon him, and he was in a most lamentable agony of spirit upon this temptation. But by recalling to mind that though Christ in His human nature was but finite, and that He suffered could be but finite, yet because His human nature was united in one Person unto the divine nature, hence what the human nature suffered, though finite, came to be of infinite value and worth; and though the death that He was under was but for a day or two, yet it was of sufficient merit to ransom him from eternal death because the Person who was God as well as man was under the power of death. So by recalling what he had heard heretofore about Christ being God and man in one Person, he came to be eased and the temptation began to vanish.

And the truth is, there is no way that I know of to satisfy one's heart and conscience in the sufficiency of Christ's merits but in this, that it was the merit of Him who was both God and man in one Person. It is true, those who do not see the necessity of an infinite merit can easily satisfy themselves and say that they believe in Christ Jesus who died for them. Aye, but how can you tell that this death of Jesus Christ is of infinite merit to satisfy the infinite justice of God that requires satisfaction for your sin?

You might say, "Why, God has so appointed it, and I hope in God that it is so." But if you can see the ground of this, it will be a marvelous help to your faith, that you can look upon your Mediator as God and man in one Person, and therefore you can look upon whatsoever He has done or suffered as being of infinite value, and so you can present it with boldness unto God. This right understanding of Christ will help us to honor

Christ much, and will make Him to be a further object of our faith. Thus Christ is wonderful in His Person, in His Person as relating to God the Father, the second Person in the Trinity, and so in His Person, that is, His human and divine natures united into one Person.

Christ is wonderful in the manner of His incarnation. Third, well may He have this title of "Wonderful," seeing that He is such a one as He is, thus opened unto you. Christ's name is "Wonderful." He is wonderful in the manner of His incarnation. Christ is God and man; but how did Christ come to take man's nature upon Him? It was a wonderful and a strange kind of way in which the second Person in the Trinity came to take our nature upon Him; it was by being conceived by the Holy Ghost and being born of a virgin. Christ was man, and came from man, but not by man; the way of Christ's generation is wonderful. "Oh, who can declare it?" (Isaiah 53:8). We ordinarily can say that we believe that Christ was born of a virgin, born of the virgin Mary. Who cannot repeat his creed? But I appeal to you, when were your hearts ever taken with the wonderful work of God in the incarnation of Christ, that way of being born of a virgin? God says that He will do a great and marvelous thing: "For a virgin shall conceive a son" (Isaiah 7:14). It is such a thing as never was done before since the world began, nor never shall be done again. The ordinary manner of the generation of man was here stopped when Christ came to be born. God said, "I will have a new way of generation." For indeed, there was a great Lord to be born into the world, a great Prince; and He must be born in another way, different from the ordinary way of mankind, in a wonderful way, the Holy Ghost being the cause of the conception, and brought forth by a virgin.

You will say, "Why was this?"

Here indeed consists the wonder that we are to sanctify

God's name in, not only to know that it was after such a way, and not as Adam was, but He must be made man in such a marvelous way.

You will say, "Why could Christ not come into the world after the ordinary manner of generation?"

You will answer to yourselves that God would have it so; but there is something of God's mind that He would have you know as to why He would have it so. If Christ had been made man after the ordinary manner of generation, He could not have been made free from Adam's sin, from original corruption; for the law lay upon Adam and his posterity, against all who would come from him in the ordinary way of generation. Therefore, if Christ had come from him in the ordinary way, if He had been of the seed of Adam, then He must have been under the same covenant that Adam was, for it was so with all his posterity. Adam was to stand as a public person unto his posterity, and in him we were to stand or fall. Now whether there might have been any other way for Christ to have been freed from it, I will not take time to dispute. But Christ was freed from the covenant so that He was not now under original guilt, under original corruption, because He was conceived by the Holy Ghost. He was conceived, but not after the ordinary way of men; whereas you are to know that all your children coming into the world after the ordinary way of generation, coming from man and by man, the first minute that their souls and bodies are together, that the child is alive in the womb, it comes under the guilt of Adam's transgression, and comes to be originally corrupted, immediately full of sin and corruption. But it was not so in Christ, and the wonder of Christ's generation is that He was conceived by the Holy Ghost and born of a virgin, and so was free from all kind of original sin. Had there been the least sin upon Christ, He could never have been a Savior for you or anyone else. Therefore, Christ must come into the world in such a way that there could be no sin upon Him at all. This is the reason why He was born of a virgin, and not after the ordinary course of mankind; and therefore His name may well be called "Wonderful" from the wonderful manner of His incarnation.

Fourth, Christ is wonderful in the wonderful works that He came into the world for. The work that Christ came into the world for is the greatest and the most wonderful work that was ever undertaken since the world began or could possibly be undertaken.

QUESTION. What was the work that Christ came into the world for?

ANSWER. It was, first, to stand between God, the angry God, that God who was provoked with man's sin, and sinful man. It was to be a Mediator between God and His creature; it was to reconcile God and man who had sinned against Him, and who had become an enemy to Him. The work that Christ came to do was to make up all the wrongs that sin had done, all that sin had brought to God. Christ came to make up the vast infinite breach that was made between God and man so as to procure reconciliation for man, as to make amends to God for all the sin that had been committed—this is the work that Christ undertook. He undertook to pacify the wrath of God His Father in such a way that it should be let out upon Him, and He would bear whatever fruits of God's wrath were due to the sin of man, He came into the world to reconcile God and man, to make up all the breach, and to make restitution for all things; not only to make up the breach that was made between God and man by man's sin, but to make up the restitution of all things. By man's sin all the works of God in this world had almost been frustrated and, had man's sin gone on, God would not have had the glory that He made the world for.

Christ came into the world to make up all again so that His Father might have full glory from all His works. Yea, the great work that He came into the world for was that He might bring this to pass, that God His Father would have more glory now from His work than ever He would have had if there had never been any breach made. Here is the great work that Christ came into the world for. Christ beheld that through man's sin all things were brought into confusion. Man's sin had plundered all the world, as it were; it had plundered the works of God and had brought all to darkness, misery, and confusion. So Christ came into the world to make all perfect again, and to raise up for God a name of praise and glory, higher than ever He would have had if there never had been any sin committed against Him.

Now, was this not a wonderful work that Christ came into the world for? We speak much of Christ, and that He came into the world; but what did He come for? Oh, learn to sanctify God's name in this, to look upon Christ, whose name is "Wonderful," in regard not only of what He was in Himself, but in regard of what He came for, the great and wonderful work that He came into the world for and accomplished. And certainly, if we apprehended Christ thus, and looked upon Christ as having such a name as this is, "Wonderful," and knew that upon this ground He is called "Wonderful," it would teach us to adore Him, to honor Him, to magnify Him, and to have high thoughts of Him. This would be a mighty means to draw our hearts to believe in Him.

Seeing Christ as He is in Himself before the soul, as the full object of faith, has a mighty power to draw faith out. As setting a temptation before a man has power to draw corruptions, so setting Christ forth in His glory and excellency, in what He is, and what He came into the world for, has a mighty power to draw forth faith—not only to draw forth faith where faith was before, but it has a power to create faith in the soul. Christ is not only an object for us to work upon when we have a faculty, but such an object as, being set before the soul, has a quickening power to cause life. Therefore we cannot say, "Why should Jesus Christ be preached to a company of people as are dead in sins?"

Aye, Christ indeed is a glorious object. But there must be something to work upon Christ. We must not say so, for Christ is not only an object for the soul to work upon when it has an eye to see, but such an object as setting Him before the soul has a quickening power to work life in the soul, to cause an eye to see Him, and to cause the heart to make after Him, though it was never so dead before.

It should be the work of ministers to set Jesus Christ before the hearts of people, before their eyes continually; and though it may be that nothing comes of it this time, try it again; and though nothing comes of it the other time, but men pass all lightly by and little regard the glory of God who appears in Jesus Christ, yet He is to be set before them again and again. Who knows when the quickening power and life may come from Christ? Now this is the scope of the setting Christ thus before you. This day I have endeavored to set Him but a little before you in opening this title of His.

Let this be the application of it: oh, when you go home, go and meditate of what has been said, and labor when you are before God, which is the time for exercising your faith upon Christ! Labor to set Jesus Christ before your eyes; look upon Him as the great wonder of the world, and never leave meditating until you find your heart come to admire at the glory of God in Jesus Christ. If ever your hearts are taken with admiring anything in the world, let them be taken up with the admiration of Jesus Christ. This may confidently be concluded: the soul that does not find itself taken with admiring the glory of God in Christ never knew what Christ meant; for Christ is such a kind of Savior that if God propounds Christ to the soul in any measure, it is impossible but that the heart must be taken with Him. There is a Savior sent into the world, He who is the object of my faith; and by Him my soul shall be saved. The first work of the heart is to think that this is too good to be true. Do not therefore think that you must be only saved by Jesus Christ, but know what manner of Savior He is. It is He whose name is "Wonderful."

Christ Is Wonderful in His Offices

"And His Name shall be called Wonderful."

ISAIAH 9:6

hrist is further the wonder of the world in His offices: in His natures, in His Person, in the manner of His incarnation, and in the end why He was sent here.

He is wonderful in His offices, in His anointing, as He was Christ. Christ signifies "the anointed of God," and is all one with "the Messiah." He who was the Messiah spoken of in the Old Testament is Christ in the New. The word signifies "anointed." And Christ is the anointed of the Father, anointed to those three great offices of King, Priest, and Prophet. He is great in all these three offices; never did any man in the world have them all before. I say, never was man in the world anointed to these three together, only Christ. We read in Scripture of a king and priest, so Melchizedek was; we read in Scripture of a king and a prophet, and so David was; we read in Scripture of a prophet and a priest, and so Jeremiah was. But of King, Priest, and Prophet together, anointed by God, we read of none but Jesus Christ alone. The Egyptians were wont, out of their philosophers, their wise men, to choose their priests, and out of their priests to choose their kings; and so whosoever was a king to them was eminent first in wisdom, being a philosopher, able to teach, and eminent in his priestly office, and then eminent in his power, so that he might be honored by all people as having those threefold eminencies that were accounted the greatest eminency in the world; for those were the three great eminencies, the eminency of wisdom to teach, and of the priesthood, and of kingly power.

Now Jesus Christ was wonderful in all these. And that is the thing that I aim at, to the show in every particular of the offices of Christ how wonderful He was, and then (though but briefly) I shall set the beauty and excellency of Christ in His three offices before you. That shall be all that I intend to do at this time, and shall be very brief in them too. For I told you in opening the excellency of God that I did not intend to open every particular attribute at large, but only to set the excellency of God before you briefly, and so of Christ.

The Kingly Office of Christ

Christ is King, and wonderful in this office of His; for you cannot understand Christ your Savior aright unless you understand Him in His natures, in His personal union, and also in His offices.

I shall not need to show Scripture for these; the Scripture is full. Read Psalm 45:6 at your leisure: "Thy throne, O God, is forever and ever; the scepter of Thy kingdom is a right scepter." And in Revelation 17:14, Christ is said to be Lord of lords and King of kings. Now Christ is a glorious King, and wonderful in His kingly power.

1. He is King over all, over all kings, over all powers. He has the highest authority of all; take that as the first thing. In Revelation 17 He is said to be "King of kings and Lord of lords." I remember Theodotius, and another emperor, who used to call themselves the vassals of Christ; and so certainly all the kings and princes in the world are but the vassals of this great King. Now He is wonderful in His kingly power who has all the kings and lords, and all authority in the world under His feet; indeed, they all depend on Him, and that will appear from the second point.

2. As His power is the highest, so it is universal over all the world; the government of all the world is committed to Him. 1 Corinthians 15:27: "All things are put under His feet." God the Father has given unto Him the government of all the world. He is not only the King of the saints, though He is their King in a special manner, but He is the King of nations too. Christ is the King of nations, God-man. The government of all the world is given to Him; all the nations of the world are under Him to govern and to judge, and to make use of for the good of His church. He is not only the governor of the world universally, but a heavenly King; even the angels themselves are under Him. Thrones, principalities, and dominions (Ephesians 1:21) are all brought into one under Christ; yea, and the devils themselves are under Him. It is He who has the keys of heaven and the keys of hell. Revelation 1:18: "He that was dead is alive, and hath the keys of hell and death." This kingly power of Christ must be wonderful.

3. But further, Christ is wonderful in His kingly power for

He makes His subjects. His subjects do not make Him. Colossians 1:16: "By Him were all things created that are in heaven and that are in earth." There is no king who ever was in the world but either God from heaven tells people that He would have such a one to be a king, or he is made by the people; for what is one man's flesh more than another man's? At first men agree together to set up such a man or family to have a kingly power, so that the kingly power of the family, and of every one who comes of that family, is by the people at first; none must plead it to be by conquest, for then whosoever can conquer again must be king. If another can conquer he must have the right too, if that is the only right. If the only right that a king had over His people was conquest, then if the people conquer him, they have the right. Certainly the best right of all the kings of the earth this day must be by the first compact with that family; that is their right. Aye, but our King that we have to do with makes his subjects, they do not make him king. Indeed, if kings could give being to their subjects, then their right to rule would be another kind of right than now they have. But the truth is that subjects do give being to their king. Aye, but our King, the Lord Christ, is Wonderful. He is a wonderful King because He gives being to all His subjects.

4. The subjects of this King are for Him, He is not for them; whereas it is otherwise between man and man. Certainly the subjects are not made for the king, but the king is made for his subjects; a kingdom is not made for a king, but a king for the kingdom. But it is otherwise here: Christ was not made for us, but we were made for Him. All the subjects of Christ were made for the honor of Jesus Christ, and Christ, I say, was not set up as King for them.

5. This King, Jesus Christ, is King in another manner than any other kings upon the earth, for it is He alone who makes

laws; other kings have no power themselves to make laws, but only together with their people. But Christ alone makes laws. It is true, the kings of Israel did not make the people join with them in all their laws because God Himself set laws there for the government of the commonwealth. But Jesus Christ, I say, is the only Lawgiver unto His church, and therefore there can be no new ordinances, nor no new laws, nor any new officers in the church that can be invented by man. It is true, in the civil state God leaves laws to human prudence; and we may invent laws and human ordinances, and new officers, so as may be good for the church. One kingdom may have one kind of law and another kingdom another; but when we come to speak of Christ's kingly power, especially as it has reference to the church, there, as He is King of saints, there are no ordinances, nor no laws, nor no officers that can be newly erected, but it must be the same; and it must be the same in all churches in the world; the same laws must rule all, and they must all have the same ordinances and the same church officers. There must be no additions of any kind. Why? Because in spiritual government we wait upon God for His presence; we wait upon the presence of Christ to work spiritually upon the soul, and we expect a spiritual efficacy from Jesus Christ upon our souls to draw us nearer to Him and to draw Him near to us. That is what we do in all church ordinances; and therefore only Christ can appoint laws for them.

QUESTION. You will say, "Can there be no laws, no nothing added in the church for way of decency and order, and such kind of things?"

ANSWER. Briefly, there are some things that belong to those spiritual ordinances, things that are in the church that may be helpful to them in a natural way. For example, if congregations meet they must meet in some place; they must have civil order in their meeting; there may be some civil and natural things subservient unto those things that are spiritual. But that that is properly ecclesiastical whereby I wait upon Jesus Christ to have my heart drawn nearer to Him, or to have Him draw nearer to me therein, there must be no addition of men in any law whatsoever, but only the things of Christ that are merely spiritual. If there is any natural or civil help, as we who are men cannot be exercised in things that are spiritual without some natural and civil helps, certainly there the prudence of man may come in. But this prudence cannot come to set up any new ordinances, to set up any new officers in the church, or to make any new laws that shall concern the spiritual worship of God, to work my heart in a spiritual way unto God, or God unto me.

Here lies the evil of man's inventions: when there shall be any inventions of man that shall come instead of a spiritual ordinance, that shall be set by man's invention, and have more put upon it than it has in a natural and civil way to be helpful, then it comes to be superstition. I say, when anything is set by man in the worship of God that shall have more in it than that which is natural or civil to help, then a thing comes to be sinful and wicked—when I think that by any things of man's appointment God shall come nearer to me, or my heart shall be drawn nearer to God, by virtue of any institution of man. For instance, something that is natural or civil so helps God's worship that man may appoint, but nothing that is spiritual to draw my heart nearer to God, or God nearer to me. As thus: if the church of God meets together for ordinances, it must meet in some place; this is a natural help to have a convenient meeting place. To have a place to keep them from the air, rain, or wind is natural; but if it goes one step higher than naturalness of the place, if I shall make this place by the consecration of man to be used as an ordinance to draw me nearer to God, or God nearer to me, that is, to think that my prayers in that place are more acceptable than in another, that because I perform services in that place it shall be more accepted, here, I say, man raises it higher than natural, and puts a divine instruction upon it, and so it comes to be sinful.

So now you may come to know what the meaning is when we say that Christ only can make laws for His Church, and for the officers for His church. Why? Because whatsoever is spiritual must only be by the authority of Jesus Christ, this great King of His church.

6. Christ is a wonderful King in this that His sovereignty is absolute, which no king's power is. Though they have great power in the world, yet they do not have an absolute power to do what they will; and certainly, no subjects are bound so far to the temperaments of men that they shall do whatever those rulers wish. There is no absolute power that one man has over another; but the power that Jesus Christ has is absolute, an absolute kingly power. His will is the law; no man's will in the world is sufficient to be a law, but the will of this King is sufficient.

7. He has power to bind the conscience. His laws are such as lay obligations and bonds upon the consciences of men; no law that would be made by all the angels in heaven could lay bonds upon the conscience but the law of Jesus Christ alone. All the laws that men can make must receive their power and authority especially from the end of them; and therefore, if they should not conduce to that end for which God sets up magistracy over men, that is, for the good of the place, then the rule will hold that if there is no scandal or contempt, there is no obligation upon a man's conscience merely because it is the will of man. But now the laws of Christ, whatsoever they are, lay bonds upon the conscience, and if I offend them never so secretly, I stand

as guilty before the great God.

8. Christ's kingly power is wonderful in that it rules over the hearts of men as well as their consciences. By His power Christ is able to subdue the wills of men and bring their hearts to obey Him; all the power in the world cannot do this. Why, the kings of the earth, if they were all put together, could not subdue the heart of any one poor man in the world. The will of the poorest creature in the world cannot be subdued by all the powers of all the potentates and emperors on the face of the earth. They may beat his body or kill his body, but to subdue his heart, to make his soul to be subject and obedient to them, that all the powers of all the potentates in the world, nay, all the angels in heaven cannot do it. The will of a man or woman is such that all the angels in heaven cannot bring it down, only God Himself. You many times say that you will break the will of such a one; that is, you will make them not to do such a thing, but you are never able to break their wills. Kings may prevail over their subjects, to make them to do what they would have them do, and their estates and liberties may come to be at their dispose; but all this while it may be that he has never a one of their hearts. And that is but a very mean kind of kingly power only to rule over men by fear, and they not to love him.

But Christ in His church has no subject who is truly under His kingly power but he rules His very will, and never has a subject but who loves Him. Where Christ rules spiritually in the hearts of His people, though they were so stubborn and rebellious before, yet when Christ comes and brings them under His power, He brings their wills and their hearts to Him; and that is the glory of the kingly power of Christ.

9. Christ is a wonderful King in that He has perfect knowledge of all His subjects and of their wants. Alas, kings and princes in great states know but very few subjects that they

have. But Jesus Christ takes notice of every subject who is in His kingdom, and knows all their thoughts, all their ways, all their wants, and all their conditions. He knows them all perfectly. Oh, this is the glory of this King, and He is wonderful in His kingly power in this.

10. He is present with them all in all the administrations of justice; the king cannot administer justice, but he uses instruments to do it, and he cannot always be present. But Jesus Christ is always present in the administration of whatever is administered to any of His subjects. He stands by and looks upon them all.

11. Christ is such a King as has no need of any instruments at all. He may make use of them sometimes, but He has no need of any. Kings can do very little without some instruments. What can a king do for the ruling of a kingdom but with such and such instruments? But Jesus Christ is wonderful in His kingly power in that He has no need of any instruments for the administration of any justice. He can do it all immediately Himself if He pleases.

12. Christ is glorious in His kingly power in that He overrules all the plots and counsels of all the enemies of His subjects, for the furtherance of the glory of His kingdom and the good of His subjects. Now, my brethren, look upon these things as real; and certainly by faith they are made real to the hearts of the saints, and the saints rejoice in this. If we had such kind of governors who had power over all the plots and designs of the enemies, what a happy condition would we think ourselves to be in? Now this is in our King, the Lord Jesus Christ. He has power over all the plots and endeavors of all adversaries, to work them all for the good of His church.

13. Further, the Lord Christ is wonderful for His kingly power in regard of His righteousness. "Thy scepter is a righ-

teous scepter." He is King of righteousness, and so King of peace, as Melchizedek was. It is a happy thing when people live under righteous governors, that they shall be sure never to have any oppression, or any wrong at all done by them, but they shall enjoy all in a righteous and just way. Jesus Christ is such a King. You shall have nothing but righteous dealings from Him. Aye, but there is something more in this. He is not only righteous because He makes righteous laws and has righteous administrations, but this is a King who brings everlasting righteousness to His people, yet He Himself is the righteousness of His people. It is He who clothes His people with righteousness. Indeed, it is said that Saul clothed the people with scarlet. By a good governor people may come to be clothed with fine raiment, and enjoy glorious prosperity, and the like. But this is that King who clothes His people with everlasting righteousness so as to make them all to stand righteous before His Father. This is the glory of this King.

And then He brings peace by righteousness. He does not bring peace to them by the sword, but by His righteous administrations. So He comes and brings peace to the conscience, peace to the soul, which no kings can do. What can kings do? They may talk about peace; and if they are righteous they may be the cause of an abundance of outward peace. Aye, but they cannot bring peace of soul. Christ is the King of Righteousness, and the King of Salem, for so Melchizedek signifies. He was king of righteousness and king of Salem, that is, king of peace. This is the glory of this our King.

14. Other kings are born to be kings, but Christ died so that He might be a King. It is true, He was a King when He was born, and He was born as others are to be a King; but especially Christ had His power upon His death. "It behooved Him to suffer, and so to enter into His glory," so to enter into His glory,

that is, upon His sufferings, and it behooved Him to do so. And so the apostle tells the Jews in Acts 2 that they had crucified Christ, and upon their crucifying Him Peter there stood up and told them in verse 36 that God had made that same Jesus whom they had crucified both Lord and Christ. By His death He came unto His glory. Others come to glory by their lives, but Christ comes to His glory by His death, and was raised to sit upon the throne of Majesty and glory upon His death, and in that He is wonderful in His kingly power.

15. Christ is King from everlasting to everlasting, forever: "Thy throne, O Lord, endures forever and ever." Other kings are but of yesterday, and they are dead and gone; but it is not so with our King: the Lord is King forever.

16. He is wonderful in that He now sits upon His Father's throne at this time. You have such a place in Revelation 3:21, where Christ promises to those who overcome that they shall sit upon His throne, even as He overcame and has sat down with His Father on His throne. The administration of all things in the world now, I say, is given to Christ jointly with His Father. Jesus Christ, the God-man, sits upon the throne of His Father, not only as the second Person in the Trinity, but as Christ the God-man He sits upon the throne of His Father, and together with His Father orders and governs all things. Here is a height of glory that no other creature can be capable of: the human nature of Christ being joined in one Person with the divine nature so that it comes to have the glory of this kingly power upon it, so that it may be said, "That Person who is man now at this time sits upon the throne of His Father, and together with His Father administers His power." So the apostle speaks in 1 Corinthians 15:25 of a subjection of Christ that shall be afterwards unto the Father more than is now. It is a text that certainly has a great mystery in it, and is very hard to under-

stand: "For He must reign till He hath put all enemies under His feet; the last enemy that shall be destroyed is death, for He hath put all things under His feet. But when He saith, 'All things are put under Him,' it is manifest that He is excepted which did put all things under Him. And when all things shall be subdued unto Him, then shall the Son also Himself be subject unto Him that put all things under Him, that God may be all in all" (1 Corinthians 15:25–28).

When all things shall be subdued unto Him, then the Son Himself shall be subject. It seems there is not that subjection now as shall be hereafter. Christ now sits upon the throne of His Father, and rules together with His Father; but there is a time when Christ shall give up the Kingdom that He now has. And He Himself shall be subject, that is, He, when He has subdued all the enemies of the church, He shall in a visible and a more glorious way rule over His own saints, and that eternally. And then He together with His saints, He as the head of His saints, shall in another way be subject unto God than now He is for the present. There shall be another administration of things than now there is. Now Christ sits upon the throne of His Father; here Christ makes His throne and His Father's throne distinct, so that there is yet to come another kind of throne that Christ has besides the throne that He now sits upon. But this, I say, is a great mystery; only the Scripture holds such a thing as this, that hereafter Christ shall have another throne than this one He now has.

17. Yea, Christ is wonderful in that He will not only subject all enemies in the conclusion, but He will put down all rule, and all authority and power. 1 Corinthians 15:24 is a very notable text often read (but little observed): "Then cometh the end, when He shall have delivered up the Kingdom to God, even the Father, when He shall have put down all rule, and all authority and power." Though our condition is that, for the present, we

have a great need for human rule and authority, yet it is certain that there has not been any such enmity unto the Kingdom of Christ as the rulers, kings, and princes of the earth, for the greater part; I say, Christ has had no men who have more kept under His Kingdom than the rulers, great ones, and princes of the earth. Therefore it seems that His Kingdom cannot be full till He has put down all rule and power, and He Himself reigns wholly without any such help of man as there is now.

But now, in regard of our necessity, it is true that if all rule and authority should be put down while we are in such a condition as we are for the present, certainly we would all be in confusion; therefore, though Christ sees that so many of the rulers and great ones of the world have been and are enemies to His kingdom, yet to keep things in a civil order Christ would have rule and authority for the present. But there is a time coming when His people shall be made so subject that they shall have no need of these things. Christ will put them all down here in the world, and He only shall reign. So you have it in Revelation 11:15: "There were great voices in heaven, saying, 'The kingdoms of this world are become the kingdoms of our Lord, and of His Christ, and He shall reign forever and ever.'" It seems that Christ has not yet taken His power. He had not then, and neither has He since. But there is a time coming for the kingdoms of the earth to be the Lord's and His Christ's in another way than now they are.

18. Last, Christ is such a King as in a spiritual sense makes all His subjects kings. He has a crown of glory for every subject, for every one of those who are His subjects in that near relationship of His being King of saints. I say, He will put crowns of glory upon them all. You have it in Revelation 5:10: "And hast made us unto our God kings and priests, and we shall reign on the earth"—not only in heaven, but on the earth. Now how

wonderful is Christ in His kingly power, that He is able to make
every subject that He has a king. And He will do it.

Now then, if we should put all these together that have been
named, you see how wonderful Christ is in this kingly power:

1. He is high above all, King of kings and Lord of lords.
2. He is a universal King over all the world, a heavenly
   King, over angels, yea, over powers, over the devils
   themselves.
3. It is He who makes His subjects, not they who make
   Him.
4. His subjects are here for Him, and not He for them.
5. He alone is able to make laws for His church.
6. He has absolute sovereignty.
7. His laws bind conscience.
8. He rules in the hearts of man.
9. He has perfect knowledge of all His saints, and all their
   conditions.
10. He is present in all administrations.
11. He is the King of righteousness and of peace.
12. He has no need of any instruments to do anything.
13. He overrules all the plots, counsels, and endeavors of
    His enemies.
14. He was not only born to be a King, but He died to be
    King.
15. He is an everlasting King. His kingdom endures from
    generation to generation.
16. He sits upon His Father's throne as equal with Him.
17. He will certainly subdue all enemies, and will put down
    all rule and all power.
18. And He will put a crown of glory upon every one of His
    subjects.

This is our King. "Rejoice therefore, O daughter of Zion, for thy King cometh." Oh, if we but apprehended these things by faith, that we have to do with Christ as such a King, certainly our hearts could not be troubled whatever stirs there are in the world, whatsoever kings and princes do in the world. Yet when we look up to this King, and by faith make all this real to our souls, oh, what manner of infinite joy it is! I beseech you, do not think that these are mere notions that I speak unto you; those who exercise their faith aright upon Christ exercise their faith upon Him as such a King.

You say that you believe in Jesus Christ, but what do you mean by Jesus Christ?

Why, you will say, He was the Son of God. Christ, who is anointed.

Anointed to what?

To King, Priest, and Prophet, you will say.

King, what kind of King is He? Here I have presented to you what kind of King Jesus Christ is who has been anointed by the Father. And thus you must present Him before your souls when you exercise your faith upon Him. Certainly there are few people who know what it is to exercise their faith upon Christ, because they never knew Christ to be thus. Well might the psalmist say in Psalm 97:1, "The Lord reigneth; let the earth rejoice; let the multitude of isles be glad thereof." Oh, it is well for us that the Lord reigns. Certainly, if Jesus Christ did not reign in His church, yea, if He did not reign in the world, all things would come to confusion immediately. Were it possible that such a handful as His church, that is a despised company, a poor people that lives in the world, and is so hated by the world, and all the devils in hell, and their instruments, which labor to extirpate them, and yet that they should continue—

certainly it is because the Lord reigns, and so orders all things that seem to be against His church for the good of His church; otherwise, it could not continue in the world. Oh, let the earth rejoice, because the Lord reigns!

Again, in Psalm 99:1, mark what use is made of Christ's kingly power: "The Lord reigneth, let the people tremble." Oh, the Lord reigns; let the people tremble. Certainly all wicked and ungodly men who are rebels against this King have cause to tremble, such men as say of Christ, "We will not have this man to reign over us." They have cause to tremble, for the Lord Christ will overcome them. Certainly His garments shall be dyed in blood. And what will become of them when He shall come to take His Kingdom to Himself?

"Moreover, those enemies of Mine that would not have Me to reign over them, come and bring them, and slay them before My face." All wicked and ungodly men in their sins do as if they should say thus, "We will not have this man to reign over us"; you who cast off Jesus Christ as a King, certainly you cannot expect good from Him as a Savior.

Christ's Priestly Office

Christ is wonderful in His priestly office. He is a great High Priest. In Hebrews 4:14, Christ is called a great High Priest: "seeing then that we have a great High Priest that is passed into the heavens." And so it is in Hebrews 7:26: "For such a High Priest became us, who is holy, harmless, undefiled, separate from sinners, and made higher than the heavens." A great High Priest, a High Priest made higher than the heavens—this is the High Priest that we have upon whom we are to exercise our faith.

Christ is wonderful in His priestly office for these reasons:

1. He has a royal priesthood, for it is joined with kingly power; and therefore Melchizedek was His type. He was not after the order of Aaron, but He was after the order of Melchizedek because it is a royal priesthood; and so the saints are called a royal priesthood. And Melchizedek is said to be without father or mother. The meaning is that he was not so as he was a man, for he had father and mother, beginning and end, but in his typical relationship he was so; they were concealed to typify that Christ, as He was man, had no father, and as He was God He had no mother, and He had no beginning in His priestly office. It was from everlasting, and it shall endure to everlasting. So He is a priest forever after the order of Melchizedek, and not after the order of Aaron.

2. All the priests under the law were a type of Christ, and all ceased in Him. Certainly He must be a great High Priest who was typified by them, and in whom all ceased and vanished. As when the sun arises, the light of the stars no more appears, so there was no further priesthood when Jesus came and took that office to Himself in His human nature in this world.

3. Christ is wonderful in His priesthood in that He had no need to offer for Himself, as others had; for He was blameless and without sin.

4. Yea, and consider what Christ offered, and there you shall see Him to be wonderful. The offering that Christ offered was the blood of God. I say, it was what we may safely call, according to Scripture language, the blood of God; and that will not seem to be a hard expression if we understand what the personal union of the two natures is. In Acts 20:28, the apostle says to the church at Ephesus, "Take heed therefore unto yourselves, and to all the flock over which the Holy Ghost hath made you overseers, to feed the church of God which He hath purchased with His own blood." These kind of phrases we have that come

from the personal union of the two natures; so that the blood that Christ shed and offered unto God as a sacrifice for the sin of man is what the Scripture calls "the blood of God." Now the blood that other priests offered was the blood of goats, bulls, lambs, and kids. But what a wonderful Priest we have who comes to offer sacrifice to the Father for us, and comes to offer blood that is the blood of God. He is wonderful in His priestly office in regard of His offering.

5. From this follows that Christ offered a sacrifice unto God that was sufficient to satisfy God for all the wrong that ever was done Him by man's sin. They offered poor things unto God, you know, in the time of the law, things that were worthless. But now the sacrifice that Christ that High Priest offered unto the Father was a sacrifice that satisfies God's infinite justice and made up all the wrong that all the sins of the elect had ever done to God; it was that with which infinite justice said it was well-pleased. It was worth all that Christ rendered it up to His Father for, not only a sacrifice that was a sweet savor, because God would be pleased to accept it, but a sacrifice that had in itself such a savor that could not but be sweet in the nostrils of God the Father. For it fully satisfied the justice of God the Father for the sins of mankind. Here is a wonderful High Priest, that He should come and offer such a sacrifice that would be of such infinite merit and worth as it was.

6. Yea, and He was wonderful because He offered Himself—not only His blood, but Himself, soul and body. He made Himself a sacrifice. None of the priests did so. In the time of the law, never was there heard of such a priest who came to offer sacrifice who offered himself for such as he would make atonement for. Jesus Christ was anointed by God the Father as a Priest of His church to offer sacrifice. Now He must have something to offer, and Christ saw that whatsoever He could offer,

if so be that He had offered that which had been the worth of heaven and earth, whatsoever it had been, it could never have been an atonement for those souls whom He undertook for. Therefore Christ offered Himself. Since nothing but God can be a satisfying portion to an immortal soul, so no sacrifice but Christ Himself could be a sacrifice to pacify God's wrath for the sins of mankind. If Christ should have said, "Father, Thou hast made Me Lord over all the world, and I will give it all as a ransom for the soul of this poor sinner," God would have said, "It will not do; it must be Thyself." Aye, and Christ yielded to it. "A body hast Thou prepared Me." And He made His soul an offering for sin (Isaiah 53:10). Both the body and soul of Christ were offered to God the Father for a sacrifice so that He might smell a sweet savor of rest, even concerning us who are wicked and wretched sinners. Either Christ must offer Himself soul and body to be a sacrifice for your sin, or else your soul and body must be offered as a sacrifice to God's justice; and then it must eternally be under the stroke of God's justice. But to free that soul and body of yours, if you are a believer, to free you from the eternal justice of God, therefore Christ offered His soul and body as a sacrifice to His Father.

7. Christ was wonderful in His priestly office, for He was not only the sacrifice, but the altar. It would be wonderful to hear of priest who would offer himself, but for the priest to be both the sacrifice and the altar that would sanctify the sacrifice is a greater wonder. And because this expression seems to be very hard, I take this out of Hebrews 9:14: "How much more shall the blood of Christ, who through the eternal Spirit, offered Himself without spot to God...." He offered His body and soul, as it were, upon His divine nature, so that, as the altar sanctified the offering, so the divine nature of Christ sanctified the offering of His human nature. So He indeed became both the altar

and the sacrifice.

8. Christ is wonderful in His priestly office in that He offered but one sacrifice, and at one time. The priests in former times offered many sacrifices, and they offered them often. But if you would read about Christ's priestly office, read especially Hebrews 7–9, and there you shall have almost as much as in all the Scripture besides of the priestly office of Jesus Christ. The priest in the law they offered often, but Christ offered but once; and having but once offered Himself He sat down in glory. After offering Himself but once before the Father, that offering was available forever, for so the Scripture tells us in divers places in Hebrews. And He was able to save to the uttermost upon His once offering Himself.

9. Christ is wonderful in His priestly office in this, which is as much as in anything, and that is that He now exercises it in heaven at the right hand of the Father by His intercession; for so the Scripture says in Hebrews 8 that "we have such a High Priest, who is set on the right hand of the throne of the Majesty in the heavens," and there He makes intercession. The priest in the time of the law exercised his priestly office not only by offering sacrifice, but by going into the holy of holies, and there had the names of the tribes engraved upon his breast. And so he presented them before God and made intercession for all the tribes.

Also, Christ is our wonderful High Priest for He, having offered Himself as a sacrifice to the justice of His Father, has gone to heaven and has the names of all believers upon His breast, and there presents them all before His Father. He is their Advocate and makes intercession for them. He is always holding before the Father all His sufferings, pleading, as it were, before God the Father for them. You may be a poor creature here, and have, it may be, fallen down in your closet pleading with God for mercy; you may be discouraged for the coldness of your heart and the like. But learn how to make use of your faith; look upon Jesus Christ. He is the object of your faith, aye, but you must believe in Christ as the High Priest who has gone before into heaven, and now is at the right hand of the Father making intercession for your soul. It may be that you are discouraged because your prayers are poor and weak; aye, but your faith must be exercised upon that God-man who is pleading with God the Father for you, and that by His own merits, that are worth more than ten thousand thousand worlds. And unless you exercise your faith upon Christ as a Priest thus, you do not exercise your faith aright. Oh, what strangers are most people in the world to the exercising of faith! I appeal to you, when did you exercise your faith upon Christ as such a High Priest? You would see Him to be a wonderful Savior indeed, if by the eye of faith you beheld Him to be thus.

Thus He is wonderful in His priestly office. Oh, what wonderful things would these be if they were made real to us by faith! How wonderful would the comfort and joy of the saints of God be in exercising their faith upon this that I now name unto you; whereby as we go along you may see how far short you have come from exercising your faith upon Christ as such a Savior, as the Scripture presents Him to you.

10. Again, His priestly office endures forever. He lives forever to make intercession. The priests in the law died, but Christ is a Priest forever, and He makes intercession Himself. He has no deputy, nor any successors, as others had; but He Himself makes intercession forever for His people, and His priesthood is confirmed by an oath. "The Lord sware" (Psalm 110:4). The Lord by an oath confirmed the priesthood of Christ after the order of Melchizedek, to the end that we might be more sure of such a wonderful mercy of God to mankind; that is the rea-

son that He added an oath to the priesthood of Christ because that aimed a higher things than the priesthood of Aaron did; that was but an external priesthood. But this aims at such high things, yea that sacrifice that must be tendered up to God for a full atonement for the sin of mankind; therefore God confirmed this by an oath. For when believers hear such things (those who are weak), they think, "Aye, but Lord, are these things so?" Is it possible that God should have such thoughts of mankind, to work so wonderful for man's salvation! Therefore, says God, I have confirmed this by an oath.

11. And then this priesthood of Christ is a priesthood of a better covenant. The other was but after a carnal commandment; and in comparison of this it was but an external covenant, for there was certainly a covenant of works besides that of grace that God renewed with the people of Israel, even when He gave the law. The ceremonial law not only typified the covenant of grace that would be revealed hereafter more fully, but it was annexed to the covenant of works, as appears plainly in the Epistle to the Hebrews; but still, I say, they had a covenant of grace that was couched darkly in the ceremonial law—therefore Christ is said to be a Mediator of a better covenant. He comes to deal between God and man in a better covenant than was before.

And then further, the priesthood of Christ comes to have more efficacy than that of Aaron had, for it prevails to the purging of conscience, which that could not do.

And it brings the saints into the Holy of holies, and that with boldness, and for that you have a most excellent Scripture of the saints being brought into the Holy of holies in the priesthood of Christ, in the chapter to the Hebrews, "Having therefore boldness to enter into the holiest by the blood of Jesus" (Hebrews 10:19), by the sacrifice that this our Priest has offered to the Father, we come to enter into the holiest of all, and that with boldness.

It was not so in the time of the law; no, but after the high priest had offered sacrifice, he alone goes into the Holy of holies. But now mark, here not only Christ our High Priest, but we may come with boldness, which none of the people could do under the law. That is, there is such an efficacy in the sacrifice of our High Priest that every believer may come. Though he has never so many sins of his own, he may come with boldness into the Holy of holies, into the most immediate presence of God the Father, through the sacrifice of our Priest, who has made such a way by His blood for us to come and enter into the Holy of holies. The people in the time of the law were to stand at a distance, for this sacrifice was not actually offered; but since Christ's coming, and His actual offering of His sacrifice, now the saints of God may come with boldness into the holy, immediate, and glorious presence of God that can be. Let God appear never so gloriously, yet the saints have liberty and boldness to come into the most glorious presence of God. And therefore Christ is wonderful in this priestly office of His.

Since Christ has made us priests unto God, we have the glory of His priesthood upon ourselves if we belong unto Him. We are priests, so that we may offer up sacrifice to God that is now acceptable; were it not through the virtue of this priestly office of Christ, we could not do it. But it is by the priestly office of Christ that all believers are now made priests unto God, so that they may offer acceptable sacrifices to God. It may be that you go to God in prayer, offer up a sacrifice to God, and think that God will be well pleased with it. I pray now, on what terms do you offer them up? Your prayers should be sacrifices; but in the time of the law none were to offer a sacrifice but a priest. Do you have an interest in the priestly office of Christ, and do you go to Jesus Christ by faith and give your sacrifice into His hands, desiring that He would present it to the Father? Certainly, unless you do so, all your sacrifices are cast in your face as dung and filth, and are an abomination unto God.

In the time of the law, we know that, let a man offer never so good a bullock, or sheep, though they were worth never so much, yet if he did not offer them by the priest, they were an abomination unto God. So our services are as our sacrifices, and they must be offered up unto God by this High Priest. And in this Jesus Christ is wonderful in His priestly office, for by virtue of that sacrifice of His that He offered to the Father, all the sacrifices of all the elect ones are tendered up to the Father, and so come to be accepted. And then we exercise our faith upon Christ aright when we can look upon our High Priest, and tender up our sacrifices by faith unto the Father through Him. To believe in Christ is to have your faith entirely upon Christ in His various offices. Oh, what strangers are most unto the glory of Jesus Christ! What little glory has Christ from you, when you do not understand Him in those things that are His glory. Or you who do understand Him, how seldom has your faith acted upon Him, according as He has been set out to you in these several things?

The Prophetic Office of Christ

Christ is wonderful in His prophetic office. I will name one or two particulars that are exceedingly comfortable:

1. He must be a wonderful Prophet, for He is one who knows all the mind of God the Father perfectly, which certainly all the creatures in the world do not. Take all the angels in heaven and all the men in the world, and they do not know all that is in the heart of God the Father. Now Christ knows

all that is in the very heart of the Father, and whatsoever the Father does, Jesus Christ knows it. John 5:20: "For the Father loveth the Son, and showeth Him all things that Himself doth." There is nothing that God the Father does but He shows it all to Jesus Christ. And John 1:18: "No man hath seen God at any time but the only begotten Son, which is in the bosom of the Father." This is a wonder Teacher indeed, a glorious Prophet. We may well call Him wonderful in regard of His teaching. He is called Prophet, and that in Scripture because He is one who came from the bosom of the Father and lives in the bosom of the Father; and whatsoever the Father has done or will do, He shows it unto Him. Therefore He knows all the mind of the Father, and knows all the things that in any way concern His Church, or whatsoever shall befall His Church. It is He who knows it, and is able to make it known as He pleases; and He is anointed by God the Father to be the teacher of all those who are elect ones, who belong to Christ. He has taken charge of every one of them, to teach and instruct them in all the mind of His Father.

Next to the sacrifice of Christ, there is no one thing in Scripture of greater use than this to the servants of God. Believers many times go away and say, "Oh, I have heard of great and wonderful things, but I cannot understand them." Oh, do not go away discouraged, but remember the last thing that is said in this sermon, that Christ is wonderful in His prophetic office, and has undertaken the charge of your soul to instruct it in all the mind of His Father. And so far as is necessary for your salvation you shall be instructed, or else Christ must be unfaithful in His office. Now that cannot be; but unless you are instructed this must be, for Christ has the charge of you. In Scripture this is made out to be a fruit of His being slain. Revelation 5:6: "And I beheld, and lo in the midst of the throne, and of the four beasts, and in the midst of the elders, stood a Lamb as it had been slain, and He came and opened the seals." He opened the prophecies, and so foretold what would befall the church to the end of the world. It was a Lamb slain that did it, noting that it is a fruit of the death of Christ that those things that concern the saints come to be opened and made known unto them. And Christ cannot plead to His Father and say, "Thou gavest Me the charge of such and such, but they were dull and could not learn."

2. The dullness cannot hinder, whether they have strong parts or weak parts; it is all one to the teaching of Jesus Christ. It may be a hindrance to a minister's teaching, but if persons come under the teaching of Jesus Christ, it makes no difference at all whether they are strong-parted or weak-parted. There is one Scripture that declares the faithfulness of Christ in His office, and it is an infinite treasury of comfort to the saints. In John 15:15 there is an expression of the prophetic office of Christ: "Henceforth I call you not servants, for the servant knoweth not what his Lord doth; but I have called you friends, for all things that I have heard of My Father I have made known unto you." Jesus Christ knows the counsels of His Father perfectly, and all His will and mind. "Now," He says, "all things that I have known of the Father," that is, that concern you to know, "there is nothing that I have known of My Father from eternity that in any way concerns you to know but I have revealed it to you." Christ is the Prophet of His church to reveal to your soul if you are a believer; whatsoever He knows of His Father—all those treasures of wisdom and counsels of His Father concerning your eternal estate—Christ is designed by His Father to make these things known to you. First or last you must come to know what you are capable to know. Oh, how wonderful Christ is in His prophetic office to undertake to teach all the elect

from the beginning of the world to the end. This indeed is the reason why many poor, weak people understand more of Christ than many learned men do.

OBJECTION. You will say, "We never can believe that such poor, ignorant people should understand things of religion better than learned men, and great rabbis."

ANSWER. You speak ignorantly and carnally. You do not understand what the prophetic office of Jesus Christ means, for God the Father has anointed Jesus Christ to come to instruct His elect ones in all the mystery of godliness, and whatsoever He has heard from the Father He tells them. When God the Father sent Christ into the world, He said, "Go Thy way. And this is the charge that I lay upon Thee, that whatsoever Thou hast heard of Me from all eternity, first or last, reveal it to those souls." It is a wonderful benefit that the saints have by this prophetic office of Christ; and this is spoken to His disciples not as eminent only, but He calls them friends in the fourteenth verse: "And all things that I have heard of My Father I have made known to you." Here is the fruit of Christ's friendship: "You are My friends; and here is the fruit of My love for you." He does not say, "I have called you friends, therefore I will give you great possessions in the world." No, but, "I have called you friends, for all things that I have heard of My Father I have made known to you." For Jesus Christ to make known these blessed things that He has heard of the Father, that are kept from the wise of the world, this is the fruit of Christ's friendship. Therefore, though Christ does not give you possessions in the world, though you are poor and mean, yet you may be dear friends to Jesus Christ.

QUESTION. "How shall I know this?"

ANSWER. Why, if Christ reveals to your souls those great things of eternal life that He has heard from the Father, certainly you are the friends of Jesus Christ. Oh, that we could exercise our faith in this prophetic office of Christ, in which He is wonderful! When you would exercise faith upon Christ, exercise your faith upon Him as a Prophet: "Lord, I am weak and dull, but, Lord, Thou hast anointed Thine own Son to reveal unto me Thy will, as much as concerns my everlasting good." Look upon Jesus Christ as the wonder of the world in all these things, in His kingly, priestly, and prophetic offices; and then you honor the Son of God when you look thus upon Him.

Another Scripture we have in John 17:8: "I have given unto them the words which Thou gavest Me, and they have received them, and have known surely that I come out from Thee, and they have believed that Thou didst send Me." That is to say, "When I was in Thy bosom from eternity, Thou gave Me such words, and put upon Me that I should reveal Thy will to such and such." And every particular one was mentioned unto Christ, to whom such words should be made known. So Christ says, "I have done it. I have given unto them the words which Thou gavest Me." and therefore Christ is called the Word, especially in regard of His prophetic office. "The Word was made flesh… the Word was God."

Christ came to reveal the mind of His Father unto the children of men. As by the words of a man, the mind, counsels, and thoughts of a man come to be made known, so Christ was the Word of God (though I do not say that this is all the sense from that, but there is a higher sense); but this is one thing aimed at, that by Him the counsels of God come to be made known to the children of men. Therefore Christ said that no man knows the Father but the Son, and him to whom the Son shall reveal Him." He came to reveal God to the children of men.

3. The wonder of Christ's prophetic office is in the great things that He was sent to reveal, in the high things, the supernatural things, things that are so infinitely above the reach of reason, Let a man be elevated unto the greatest height of reason, he is not able to reach into the mysteries of godliness. No, as the apostle says, it must be the Spirit of God who searches the deep things of God. Now this is the Spirit of God who was sent from the Father and the Son, who searches the deep things of God. They are deep, high, supernatural, glorious things that Jesus Christ reveals. Oh, there are unsearchable riches! The apostle calls the gospel, "unsearchable riches," rich things that have no footsteps at all in the creature. We can never come, by any knowledge that we can have from the creature, to understand those things. There in nothing written in the book of nature, in the great book of God's creation and providence, not one letter written of the glorious things of the gospel.

Now these are the things that Christ is wonderful in, to reveal things that are so high, so wonderful and glorious. Therefore, in Luke 4:22, when Christ was performing that prophetic office of His, the text says that "all wondered at the gracious words that proceeded out of His mouth." It is as if they should say, "Oh, here are wonderful things indeed! These are secret things indeed that we were not taught." They all wondered at the gracious things that proceeded out of His mouth. It is true, before Christ was incarnate there was something of the mystery of the gospel; and our forefathers who were saved were saved by the same gospel, but the knowledge of the glorious mysteries of the gospel were kept hidden till that great Prophet came into the world. And that is a special reason why all the time, before the incarnation of Jesus Christ, there was so little knowledge. God, and the way of eternal life, was known so little because the Lord would reserve the revelation of Himself, and those great counsels of His will concerning man's eternal estate, for the great Prophet to come to reveal. And when Christ came, then broke forth light into the world. And when Christ comes to any place, there breaks forth the light of those glorious supernatural things that are above the reach of reason, yet such things as angels could never have understood. Therefore it is said in one passage that those things are made known to angels by the gospel. The Lord sends His ministers in His Name to preach those things from Christ, so that the angels came to understand further things in the mystery of the gospel than they did before. Therefore they are things above the reach of any man's understanding whatsoever.

4. It will especially make the prophetic office of Christ wonderful if we add to this a fourth consideration, that these things are not revealed to the wisest and the great ones of the world, but to such men and women who ordinarily have the least understanding in the things of the world, those men who have the dullest capacity to understand the reason of things in the world, those who are the most ignorant people in the world. Why, Jesus Christ chooses them, and makes them to be apprehensive of the mysteries of the gospel, such things as angels themselves desire to pry into. Here is a wonder, that such poor, weak, dull, ignorant creatures, who sometimes are scarcely able to speak two or three sentences in good sense together to a man, yet have the clear understanding of the chief mysteries in the gospel, such things as angels desire to pry into. This is a wonderful work; and therefore we read in Matthew 21:15 of when the poor children came to understand something of Christ: "When the chief priests and scribes saw the wonderful things that He did, and the children crying in the temple and saying, 'Hosanna to the Son

of David,' they were sore displeased." Mark how this is joined
to the wonderful things. They saw the wonderful things that
Christ did, and the children crying in the temple, "Hosanna
to the Son of David," and they were displeased. It is one
of the most wonderful things in the world to see that sometimes poor young children, and such as understand but very
little in the matters of the world, yet shall come to understand
the deepest mysteries of godliness. Those things that exercise
the understanding of angels, and shall exercise them to all
eternity, yet poor children and youths shall come to understand these things further than the great rabbis and doctors
of the world. Is not this a wonderful thing in the dispensation
of the prophetic office of Christ?

When you see poor youths come to have understanding
in the great things of the gospel, you think that surely it is
but a fanciful thing. Oh, but rather let your thoughts be carried
to admire the wonderful dispensation of the prophetic office
of Jesus Christ. In Matthew 11:25–27, you see what a wonderful thing is made of this dispensation of Christ's prophetical
office: "At that time Jesus answered and said, 'I thank Thee
O Father, Lord of heaven and earth, because Thou hast hid
these things from the wise and prudent, and hast revealed them
unto babes.' " Now that the Father hid them from the wise
of the world and revealed them unto babes was by Christ, though
He thanks the Father. And that it was done by Christ appears
in verse 27: "All things are delivered to Me of My Father, and
no man knoweth the Son but the Father; neither knoweth any
man the Father save the Son, and he to whom the Son will
reveal Him. All things are delivered to Me." So Christ here
makes the revelation of God unto babes to be the fruit of God's
delivering up all things to Him. "All things are delivered to Me;

and no man knoweth the Father but the Son, and him to whom the Son will reveal Him." So Christ has received all power from the Father, and it is upon this that these babes come to have such understanding in the mysteries of godliness, and the wise of the world never come to understand.

It is very remarkable as we go along that upon this ground Jesus Christ invites souls to come to Him: "Come unto Me all ye that labor and are heavy laden, and I will give you rest." Conceive now as if Jesus Christ were preaching personally to you, and He were saying this to you: "All power is committed to Me by the Father and, as a fruit of what the Father has committed to Me, I reveal Him to whomever I please; and none can know the Father but by Me. I have the dispensation of all the treasures of wisdom, and the revelation of all the mysteries of eternal life from My Father. Oh, therefore, come to Me; come to Me all you who labor and are heavy laden. You labor under the burden of your ignorance. Perhaps you complain that you do not know God, that you do not understand the great mysteries of salvation. You pray and hear, and yet you cannot come to understand what God is. Why, come to Me, for all things are given to Me; and if I reveal the Father, you shall know Him. Therefore all you who labor and are heavy laden, all you who see the need you have of the knowledge of My Father, and of the way of eternal life, come to Me, and I will reveal these things unto you, and so will bring rest unto your souls." Christ is wonderful in the way of His administrations, and that is another consideration in the prophetic office of Christ.

5. Christ is a wonderful Prophet in that He reveals things many times suddenly. He is not bound to those ways that any

man or angel is bound to; if a man or angel came to instruct others in the truths of the gospel, they must instruct them by degrees, to understand one thing at one time, and another at another time, and so deduce one thing from another in that way. But Christ can make known the things of eternal life in an instant to the soul. Whosoever comes to Christ must be convinced of sin, and be emptied of himself and be humbled. All these things are in every soul that comes to Christ. Now all these things may be wrought by one beam of light that Jesus Christ shall let into the soul. As an apothecary may get the very quintessence of all herbs in one drop, though you cannot see the herbs, so Jesus Christ, I say, sometimes by one beam of light, lets in a hundred truths into the soul, so that the person apprehends the substance of all those particulars that are spoken of. And there is a proportionate work upon men's hearts to bring them to Christ. Is this not a wonderful work of Christ, that a man who has been an ignorant, sottish, blind creature, a profane, ungodly man who hates all godliness, perhaps comes to hear a sermon merely to scorn, as many have done; and that this man comes in the very heat of his wickedness, so that a man would wonder that some fruit of God's wrath did not come from heaven to strike him into the bottomless pit; and yet, it may be, at this very sermon there shall be some one beam of light darted into his spirit that may work his soul to heaven if he should die at that instant? Is this not a wonderful work of Christ? Though it is true, ordinarily God begins to stir first, and does not do it all at once; yet sometimes some who come into a congregation most ignorant and sottish, and know no other god but mammon and lusts, yet come to the Word and in one instant God darts in that light into their spirit so that this man comes to have his heart turned to God, comes to know his misery, to know the way of salvation and the covenant of grace, but not distinctly. It may be after this beam of light is darted in God may come over again distinctly, and reveal to him his miserable estate by nature, humble him more, and so he may have a little glimpse of this at one sermon and a little more at another. But at that very instant there may be that let into that heart that which may possibly unite the heart to Jesus Christ, and save it if it should die at that moment. Here is a wonderful work in the prophetic office of Jesus Christ.

6. Christ is wonderful in His prophetic office in that He teaches the heart. No men or angels can teach the heart, only Jesus Christ. Though men or angels may present truths before another man, and so convince the understanding, yet no men or angels can be able so say, "I will so make known such a truth to this man or woman as I will gain his heart by it; it shall transform his heart into the very image of that truth that I shall present unto him." No man or angel can do it; but Christ teaches so as no man teaches. Job 36:22: "Behold, God exalteth by His power; who teacheth like Him?" Now God teaches by Christ in the administration of His prophetic office. Man may come and tell us that this and the other thing ought to be done, oh, but who teaches like Jesus Christ? None teaches the heart but Jesus Christ. Job 38:36: "Who hath put wisdom in the inward parts, or who hath given understanding to the heart?" Certainly no one living. No angel can do it, nor can any man do it; it is only Jesus Christ in the administration of His prophetic office who teaches, and prevails with the heart when He comes with truths.

Therefore, when you see people come to hear many truths, and sit under a clear and distinct ministry that opens many truths unto them, it may be that many will get brain-knowledge that shall make them to confer about those truths, but yet not be changed. You will ask, "What is the reason why they who have so much knowledge live wickedly?" Why, here is the ground: Jesus Christ has not exercised this prophetic office of His so far upon them as to overpower their hearts. Here is the reason why such men have had knowledge in the brain, and yet lived wickedly a long time. Yet if they belonged to Christ, at some other time they shall come to hear the Word of God, they shall hear the very same truths they heard before, and perhaps delivered in a weaker manner than they have heard it, and yet their hearts shall be a hundred times more wrought upon at that time than ever they were wrought upon before. Sometimes a man comes by accident into a congregation, and hears a minister upon such a subject. And it may be that a minister by the by speaks of something that he little thought of before he came. This man had heard the same truth largely handled, perhaps read many tracts about it heretofore, and his heart was never touched. But now, hearing it mentioned by the by his heart is mightily wrought upon, and he goes away and says, "Verily God is in this place." What is the reason? Why, here Christ speaks to the heart; before man only spoke to the ear. This is a wonderful thing in the prophetic office of Christ, that He speaks to the heart.

And thus should we exercise our faith upon Christ in this: when we come to the Word, look upon Christ by the eye of faith as the great Prophet of the church, who teaches as no man teaches, who not only speaks to the ear, but to the heart.

7. Christ is wonderful in His prophetic office in that

He teaches immediately Himself. Indeed, He teaches mediately, that is, by His ministers. Therefore you find in Acts 1:1 Luke speaking of Christ's teaching when He lived here upon the earth: "The former treatise have I made, O Theophilus, of all that Jesus began both to do and teach." Why, Luke is the one who wrote the gospel and Acts; he wrote the sum of what Christ taught in the whole course of His life. Yet here he tells us that he made a treatise, and related what Jesus "began" to do and teach. If one should have said to Luke, "Why did you not relate all that Jesus did and preached? Christ is dead now." But the meaning is that indeed all that Christ preached personally when He was here in the world was but a beginning, Christ was to teach afterwards to the end of the world, and that He was to do partly by His ministers who would be to the end of the world. He exercises His prophetic office by them.

And by the way, whenever you come to hear any minister of God reveal anything of the gospel to you, you are to look upon it as Christ exercising His prophetic office in this way. He is wonderful in teaching in that He not only teaches by His instruments, but immediately Himself many times. Where there is a want of means, we may there expect Jesus Christ immediately to reveal the will of His Father to those souls who belong to His election.

8. And then Christ is wonderful in teaching for He teaches infallibly, which none can do. Many other particulars might be named in the wonder of Christ's prophetic office, but time slips by me. Therefore I will proceed to the next thing in the wonder of Christ. Only take this alone with you, that in your believing in Jesus Christ you must believe in Him

as Christ, who is anointed by the Father to be King, Priest, and Prophet. And when you exercise your faith upon Him in all three of His offices, then you will know what it is rightly to believe indeed.

Christ Is Wonderful in His Miracles

"And His name shall be called Wonderful."

ISAIAH 9:6

hrist is wonderful in the miracles that He wrought here in the world while He lived. Acts 2:22: "Ye men of Israel, hear these words: Jesus of Nazareth, a man approved of God among you by miracles, wonders, and signs which God did by Him in the midst of you, as you your-selves also know." Never did anyone come into the world to work such great miracles and wonders as Christ did; and indeed, all who ever did miracles and wonders did them by Jesus Christ. Josephus, who was no great friend to Christ, was a Jew, and did not acknowledge Christ to be the Messiah, yet writing the story of those times, he could not but take notice of such a one as Christ. He professed that at such a time there was a wise man who arose, whom they called by the name of Jesus, who worked a great many miracles. And, he says, "If it is lawful to call Him a man." He was afraid to call Him a man because of the wondrous things that He did.

QUESTION. But if any of you say, "How shall we be able to know certainly the truth of all those miracles that He did? We read in the gospels how great things Christ did—how He cast out devils, cured the blind and the lame, raised the dead, and the like—but how can we know the truth of them?"
ANSWER. Augustine said this: Either all those things are true or they are not; if they are, then He is confirmed to be the Messiash. But if they are not true, then this is the greatest miracle of all, that such a supernatural doctrine as this is, to believe in Him who was crucified to save the world, and for men to venture their souls and eternal estates upon this without having this to be confirmed by miracles first—this is the greatest miracle of all.

But we will pass by that, only note it as we go, that Christ was wonderful in all the wonders that He wrought while He lived.

Christ is wonderful in the glorious endowments and excellencies of His Person.

Further, Christ is the wonder of the world in regard of those glorious endowments and excellencies of His Person; and herein He is the wonder of the world. The endowments and excellencies of Jesus Christ are great and glorious. "Thou art fairer than the children of men." It is He who received the Spirit without measure; it is He who had the treasures of wisdom and knowledge dwelling in Him bodily—and He must be the wonder of the world. That Scripture in Colossians 2:3 shows us what a wonderful Savior we have. It is such an expression that, if we did not have it from the Holy Ghost, we would never have dared to have ventured upon it: "In whom are hid all the treasures of wisdom and knowledge." And then in verse 9: "For in Him dwelleth all the fullness of the Godhead bodily." What a high expression is here! All the fullness of the Godhead dwells bodily in Jesus Christ. Surely He has excellent endowments then. He is filled with glorious things. His human nature is elevated and enlarged to the highest capacity that a creature can have to receive excellency. And God has raised up the human nature of Christ to show how high He is able to elevate a creature, and make it capable for the receiving of glory, so that He might declare it to angels and saints for all eternity.

I say, man's nature is raised to that height so that God might, to all eternity, make known to the angels and saints this thing, and say, "Behold to what a height My infinite power is able to raise a creature to be capable of happiness." Therefore Christ's human nature is so raised, and our nature in Him, which should be a wonderful comfort to us, that our nature should be raised to so much glory in Christ.

This is a great argument to us to take heed of the abuse of human nature, of your body and your soul. Oh, that ever anyone should be given up to that sottishness, that is, that a man who has human nature in him should look after no greater good than merely to eat, drink, play, and satisfy his lusts. Do you know, O creature, that your nature is raised to such a height of excellency so that God might declare to angels and men what His power was able to do? And shall you who has the same nature, who is a kin (as it were) to Christ, shall you be so base and vile as to mind your filthy and base lusts, and to mind no higher good than this?

The very thought of raising our nature in Christ is a mighty argument to raise the thoughts of one who is a man to a higher pitch than ever they have been. Think thus: "Certainly my nature is capable of some higher good than merely to eat, drink, play, and have a little money here for a while." Why, no one who shows the personal excellency and endowments of Christ in general, that all the fullness of the Godhead dwells bodily in Him; and therefore Christ is called the character, and the engraven form of the image of God, in Hebrews 1. This is not said of man; though man is said to be made according to God's image, yet it is never said that he is the brightness of God's glory and the express image of His person, as it is said of Christ.

In Colossians 1 you have mighty, high expressions about the personal excellency of Christ. In 1:15: "Who is the image of the invisible God, the first born of every creature, and then He is the beginning of all things." Verse 15: "He is the image of the invisible God," as God and man, for so I must speak of Him. He is the image of the invisible God in another manner, and more fully, than any creature is or possibly can be; for Jesus Christ, God and man, has the very character and engraven form of whatsoever glory there is in the Father. I say, take Him as God and man. He has an omnipotence in Him; therefore in it is said Philippians 3:21: "Who shalt change our vile body that it may be fashioned like unto His glorious body." How? "According to the working whereby He is able even to subdue all things unto Himself." Now this is a great mystery of godliness, that God-man should have an omnipotence in Him.

And then, likewise, He has the express image of all the knowledge of God; for as He is God-man He is made the Judge of all the world. And He will be the Judge not merely as He is God, but as God and man. Now seeing that He is the Judge of all the world, He must have an infinite knowledge. He must know the hearts of men, and all the works of men. He must have an infinite holiness and justice who must judge all the

world. And thus God-man has an express character of the attributes of God, which no one else has.

And then He has an express character of the immensity
of God. If you speak of His body, it cannot be everywhere; but
God-man is in all places. Thus you have it in John 3:13; it is a
very strange expression, and it can never be understood but by
understanding the personal union of the two natures. At that
time He was speaking to them there upon the earth, and yet
He said, "The Son of man which is in heaven." At this time He
who is the Son of man is in heaven. His body could not be in
two places at once, but God-man was then in heaven. Thus you
see the excellency of Christ in being the character of the Father,
and having the divine attributes in Him in another manner than
any creature in the world could have who is a mere creature.

This personal excellency of Christ will appear when we consider how Christ comes to have those excellencies, that He has
them all by virtue of the personal union. The human nature
alone is but a creature if you take it as being distinct. But this
human nature is filled with all excellency from the Father; and
indeed the Father is the Fountain of all first. These excellencies
that Christ has come from the personal union immediately. Now
God, unto other creatures, gives them, as it were, out of Himself
and His bounty. He confers them from Himself. He puts forth
an act of power for bestowing such and such excellencies upon
such creatures; but when the human nature of Christ was to be
filled with such excellencies, it was by taking the human nature
of Christ into Himself, as we say concerning sight.

Philosophers have a dispute whether it is by taking in the
species, or by sending something out from the eye. This may a
little resemble this great mystery. There are some things that
God bestows by sending them out from Himself; other excellencies He bestows by taking them into Himself. Now all other

creatures, angels and men (but only the human nature of Christ) have all the excellency that they have by God's sending it out from Himself; but all the endowments of Jesus Christ, and all His excellencies, He has them all from God taking Him into Himself, that is, in a personal union, not taking Him into communion with Himself as His saints, but taking Him into a personal union. And so He comes to have all excellencies in another manner than any other creature can possibly have.

Christ is wonderful, take Him as God and man, in that all the personal excellencies that He has depend upon Himself. He is independent; the excellency that Christ's human nature has is, I say, independent in that it depends upon His own person. There is no dependence of the excellency that Christ has but upon the very person of Christ Himself; all depends upon Him, for He says of Himself that He has life in Himself. In John 5:26, it is said concerning Christ's excellency, "For as the Father hath life in Himself, so hath He given to the Son to have life in Himself." Indeed, the Son is from the Father by an eternal generation; but now, though He is first from the Father, yet the Son has life in Himself, yea, and eternally He had life in Himself. And so what excellency the human nature has, it depends upon its own person, which is a higher and a more glorious way of having excellency than it is possible for anything else to have.

Hence Christ, even God-man, comes to be worthy of divine honor. Divine honor is due to Jesus Christ who is God-man; no creature can partake of divine honor by coming ever so near to God, but only by the human nature of Christ being personally united. Let a child of God, a saint, be never so holy because he comes to partake of so much excellency of holiness, he is not therefore to partake of divine honor, nor are angels. But Christ, being God and man, the very human nature joined with the divine in one personal union, comes to share in the divine honor that is due to Him both as God and man. And it is a wonderful work of God to bring that which is in itself but a creature, to come to have a share in divine honor.

Christ is wonderful in that hence He is an infinite object of the delight of His Father, not only as He is eternally begotten of the Father, but as He is both God and man. "This is My beloved Son in whom I am well pleased" (Matthew 3:17). "I am pleased fully in Him." Jesus Christ is an object adequate to the very heart of God the Father. Oh, how we should be content in Him! Certainly if He is as excellent as He is, so as to give full satisfaction to God the Father, then He may very well give full satisfaction to your souls.

Yea, and God the Father manifests His satisfaction so fully in Him that He has made Him to be heir of all things (Hebrews 1:2); and therefore He is said to be the beginning of all things, so that all subsist by Him. Yea, further, there is that satisfaction that the Father has in Him that God the Father made all things for His sake. I say, all things in the world are made for the sake of Jesus Christ: angels are made for His sake; this world, the seas, all the work that God ever did or will do to all eternity was for the sake of Jesus Christ, so that God the Father might honor Himself in Jesus Christ. Colossians 1:16 is very full for that purpose, and we need no more: "All things were created by Him, and for Him." God had a higher end in creating the world than you think. God not only created so that He might manifest that He was a mighty God, merciful, bountiful, and the like, but God had a higher end when He made the world—it was to advance His Son. When God made the angels, He would never have made them but for the honor of His Son.

Oh, what infinite cause we have to honor Jesus Christ! Oh, how happy are they who live for the honor of Jesus Christ, by whom God may have glory beyond a natural way! Consider that you were made for the honor of Jesus Christ. The honor that God the Father would have from you is this, that you would live for the honor of His Son; and all other honor that you give to God, unless it is for His Son, is not accepted. I say, whatsoever honor any man or woman endeavors to give to God is not accepted by Him but in relation to the honor of Jesus Christ. Therefore, if you look at God in a mere natural way, and honor and worship Him never so much, as the heathens did, all this would not do, only the honor that God has in reference to His Son. When a poor sinner is sensible of the breach that sin has made between him and the infinite God, and when he comes to see Jesus Christ, seeking to advance Him by faith, God says, "Here is the honor that I would have." And therefore, when all the elect ones who were given to Jesus Christ to redeem are all converted and brought to Him, the world will fall about our ears. Why? "Because," says God, "I have the end that I made the world for. Now I have brought in all who belong to My Son; and all those works by which My Son will come to have His honor eternally are done."

Let there be an end of the world (and the end of the world is likely to be sooner now because what we see is doing much to set up Jesus Christ in this latter age). When a man's time is almost at an end for his work, then he works more speedily than he did before. "And now," says God, "I have made the world for the honor of My Son; yet to this day how little honor has My Son had from the world? And there is a time when I will manifest to all the world that I made it for Jesus Christ." He did not make it for a company of tyrants to do what they would in, nor for a company of profane people, to eat and drink, and follow their lusts in. But here is the end at which God aimed in making the world: "I will set up My Son in the world, and all the works that ever have been done in the world, shall at length come in to conduce to the honor of My Son." And this shall be the great work that shall be done on the Day of Judgment: He will show to all the world how all those works that seemed to go most against Jesus Christ were brought about for the honor of Jesus Christ. Oh, blessed are those souls who come to see that all things were made for the honor of Jesus Christ, and so give glory to Him accordingly! Thus you see what a wonderful Savior we have, that God has made all things for Him. Surely our Savior is glorious and wonderful.

There is one thing more. He is wonderful in His endowments and excellencies in that His excellencies are in Him to be conveyed to His people. "Out of His fullness do all we receive, and grace for grace" (John 1:16). Out of the fullness of all excellency that is put into Him the saints of God and elect ones draw all the excellency they have here, or shall have to all eternity. For you must know this, though the divine nature is the fountain of all excellency, yet it is not to be conveyed but through Jesus Christ. This is the great mystery of godliness; and this is the wonder in the gospel that is so much above nature, that though God is the Fountain of all in Himself, yet He has determined that this goodness of His shall be first let out to His Son, and so shall be conveyed through Him to the saints. So that we must not only look upon all the gifts and graces we have as coming from God the Creator of all things, but as coming from God through Christ, who is God and man, in this mystical way. Therefore, if you say that you look at God and believe in God's mercy, without understanding the way of God's communicating Himself, you may utterly be mistaken. It must be in Christ that we must receive grace for grace.

Now that there should be such a thing revealed, that God should say, "I will set up My Son, the second Person in the Trinity, to take your nature, and to be God and man; and He shall be as a conduit, to be filled with all things whatsoever; and you shall have, as it were, your pipes joined to Him; and through Him you shall come to partake of whatever good I intend for you"—this is the wonder of the world.

And hence it is that Christ is compared to all things that have any excellency in them. Is there an excellency in light? Christ is called light (John 1:9). Christ is called pearl (Matthew 13:46), gold (Revelation 3:18), raiment, the sun (Psalm 84:11), and living water (John 7:38). He is anything that has any excellency in it: bread (John 6:50), wine (Isaiah 55:1), milk. Whatever in the created realm has any excellency in it, Christ is called by that name, to show that all excellencies are in Him as one. As I told you that God's excellency was such an excellency since the very quintessence of all excellencies was united in one in Him, so Christ has the quintessence of all excellencies in Him, and in Him as in a conduit to be conveyed to all to whom God intends eternal good.

Oh, what a Savior we have, my brethren! I think that this should be a very strong argument to draw your hearts to Jesus Christ, or at last to say as Philip said, "Let us see but Jesus Christ, the wonder of the world, and we will never wonder at anything in the world." Oh, let us understand what Jesus Christ our Savior is. Here you may see what a full object for your faith Jesus Christ is, how you may venture your souls upon Him, and your eternal estates. Here is enough to draw faith, to encourage faith, and to enlarge faith. Oh, that God would be pleased, by presenting what Christ is, to work faith in some soul that has not had it before. But now, where faith is before this, look beyond your own worth and your own enlargements. And thus in these things you see how wonderful Christ is. Two more things remain.

Christ Is Wonderful in the Glory of the Father, Part 1

"And His name shall be called Wonderful."

ISAIAH 9:6

*I*t is in Jesus Christ that God reveals Himself and appears to both men and angels. It is true, we might know something of the invisible things of God by the things that are seen, as the apostle says in Romans 1:20, by His great works of creation and providence: but there is as much difference between the glory of God that shines in all His works of creation and providence, and the glory of God that shines in the face of Christ, as there is between the glittering of a glow worm on a dark night and the glory of the sun in its full strength. Now take this along with you: God expects that those who see His glory in Christ should glorify Him in another manner than those who only see His glory shining in the works of creation and providence. As there is much difference between the shining of the sun in its full strength and a glow worm, even so there should be as much difference between believers glorifying God and heathens as there is between the glowworm and the glory of the sun.

You should not satisfy yourself unless you find that there is some such proportionable difference; for certainly, if you have seen God in Christ, you have seen Him wonderfully indeed. Therefore, in 2 Corinthians 3:18, the apostle says, "But we all, with open face, beholding as in a glass the glory of the Lord, are changed into the same image, from glory to glory, even as by the Spirit of the Lord." This Scripture has much in it. The apostle is speaking of the gospel, and compares it to a glass wherein the glory of God shines, so that we may behold it with open face, and so behold it that we are changed into the very same image of it, from glory to glory, from one degree unto another. We may behold the glory of God in the glass of the creature, and never be changed into the same image; but when we behold the glory of God in the glass of the gospel, we then come to be changed into the same image, and still to be changed more and more—and with open face we behold it. In chapter 4:6: "For God, who commanded the light to shine out of darkness, hath shined into our hearts to give the light of the knowledge of the glory of God in the face of Jesus Christ." Mark it, He is the knowledge of God, the "light of the knowledge of God, and the light of the knowledge of the glory of God." And all this is in the face of Jesus Christ. In the face of the creature there may be the knowledge of God, but the light of the knowledge of the glory of God is in the face of Jesus Christ. "He that hath seen Me hath seen the Father," Christ said to Philip.

It was a maxim among the fathers in the time of the law

that no man could see God and live. God was so glorious that they thought He could not be seen, but it would overwhelm any creature that was in the flesh that should see Him. But mark the prophecy that we have of the times of the gospel in Isaiah 40:3. There is a clear prophecy of Christ: "The voice of him that crieth in the wilderness, Prepare ye the way of the Lord," which is in express words applied to John the Baptist, the forerunner of Christ. And in the very same words, "make straight in the desert a highway for our God; every valley shall be exalted, and every mountain shall be made low, and the crooked shall be made straight, and the rough places plain." Then it follows in verse 5: "And the glory of the Lord shall be revealed, and all flesh shall see it together." Before, no man could see God and live. Flesh was not able to behold God, but when the Word was made flesh, when the times of the gospel came wherein God would make Himself appear through His Son more clearly and fully, now all flesh shall see it, shall see the glory of the Lord.

Now the glory of God appears wonderfully in Christ in these particulars:

1. The power of God appears in Christ. The glory of God's attributes shine more brightly in the face of Christ than in any other ways. For instance, the power of God appears infinitely more in Christ than in making heaven and earth. For God to unite God and man together in one Person is a greater work than making heaven and earth; there is more power of God put forth in the hypostatic union of the natures of Christ—besides all the power of God that appears in the great works that Christ did, and in carrying Christ through all those great works that He was carried through—than in making heaven and earth. There is more power of God appearing in the conversion of one soul to Christ than in making heaven and earth. Then what

power of God appears in Christ Himself?

2. The wisdom of God appears in Christ. The wisdom of God appears more in Christ than in the creation of heaven and earth. Now for God to find out such a glorious way of reconciliation as He has found out in His Son, in this the wisdom of God is infinitely more glorious than in all His works. The glory of God's wisdom in other things is darkened in comparison to His wisdom in this. If God had put it to angels to find out a way of reconciliation, they could never have guessed at such a way as this is, that we should be reconciled in Christ. Here is the glory of wisdom.

3. The holiness of God appears in Christ. There likewise appears the glory of God's holiness more in Christ than in any other way. It is true, the law is a glass of God's holiness; and those who cast reproach upon the law spit in the very face of God's holiness. Aye, but the law is no such glass as Jesus Christ is; there we see the holiness of God in another manner than we can in the holy law that God has made.

God never showed His hatred of sin so much as He did in Christ; and it cannot be devised by all angels and men how it would be possible to have such an argument to manifest the hatred of sin so as it is manifested in Christ; that God should so deal with His Son as He has done for the sin of man. I say, if an infinite wisdom should set itself to work never to much to find out an argument to manifest the hatred of sin, there could not be a greater argument. So when God sent His Son into the world to die for man's sin, He said, as it were, "I have many ways to manifest My holiness to the children of men, how infinitely I hate sin, but here is a way that it shall appear to the uttermost. They shall see it in My dealing with My Son."

Certainly in Christ God's wisdom has found an argument to make us all to be convinced of the infinite holiness of God, that

God hates sin more than hell itself, and that we should too.

4. The justice of God appears in Christ. The justice of God appears in Christ more than in anything else. It appears not so much in all the torments of the damned as in God's dealing with Christ, in that He required such satisfaction from Him as He did. When we hear of the dreadful curses of the law, and of the torments that are in hell, we may thereby be put in mind of an infinite justice. Oh, how righteous God is in His ways there, and His justice seems to be wonderful unto us. But when you behold God's justice in this red glass of the blood of Christ, it is a great deal more glorious here than in all the damned in hell. If God should grant to any of you to stand upon the very brink of hell, and there to look into the pit, to see all the torments and tortures there, and to hear all the cries there, then you think your hearts would be so affected with the justice of God as to fear it. Aye, but when God makes Himself known to you in Christ, when you hear of the sufferings of Christ for sin, God would have you to be more affected with His justice, and to fear it more, than if you saw all the torments of hell. The truth is, there is no such way to set out the justice of God as to show the dealing of God with His Son for the sin of man. If I were to preach but one sermon that would be my last, it would be on the terribleness of God's justice; and I would speak on some Scripture that would show the terribleness of the dealing of God with His Son—and that would set out the justice of God to be a great deal more glorious Christ than anything else.

5. The glory of God appears in Christ. And so the glory of God's mercy and goodness is more in Christ than in any other thing. We enjoy these outward comforts as a fruit of the bounty and goodness of God; aye, but what are all these to all the love of God in His Son? I remember a learned man compared all the good things we receive from God, from His general bounty

and providence, and His love and mercy that appears in Christ, with a few sparks that come out of a burning furnace, and the heat of it within. Look what difference there is between them, and such difference there is between the love of God to us in all the comforts in this world, and the love of God in Jesus Christ. God would have an argument to manifest the infiniteness of His love unto His creatures; and there is no such argument as this: "So God loved the world that He sent forth His only begotten Son" (John 3:16).

6. The glory of God's truth appears in Christ. The glory of God's truth that is manifested in fulfilling promises, any promise that is fulfilled, manifests the glory of God's truth and faithfulness. But in fulfilling that great promise of God in sending His Son into the world, here the truth and faithfulness of God appears more gloriously than in all other; for there was never a promise so difficult as this promise. Many men can be content to fulfill promises of smaller importance when there is no great difficulty in fulfilling them, aye, but here is the greatest promise that ever was, and there was the greatest difficulty for God to fulfill this promise of anything that God ever promised. Indeed, when we hear that Christ was promised some four thousand years before He came into the world, and yet at length He came into the world, it is a good argument to teach us never to doubt the fulfilling of God's promises. Indeed, the right apprehension of God's faithfulness in this great promise regarding His Son will mightily strengthen the faith of the people of God to believe any smaller promises, and not to stagger in them. The reason why people are so ready to stagger in their belief about smaller promises is because they have not been acquainted with the work of faith in believing the great promise that God made with His people in sending His Son into the world.

So these attributes, with all others, shine gloriously in Christ. No marvel then if the angels, upon the birth of Christ, cried out, "Glory be to God on high." It is as if they should say, "O Lord, here is one come into the world wherein Thy glory appears, and by whom Thou shalt have glory to all eternity." Though Christ was but a babe in a manger, yet the angels saw more glory in Him than in the highest heavens; they did not see so much cause to cry, "Glory be to God on high," from any object that ever they saw as when they saw the babe in the manger. Then it was, "Oh, glory be to God on high. We behold Thy glory shining here."

And blessed are those who shall be enabled to behold the glory of God in the face of Jesus Christ. Who would not have beheld the glory of God in His great works? What man or woman who has any knowledge of God at all would for a world but have beheld so much of the glory of God as appears in the great works of creation and providence? Oh, what comfort have the saints in beholding the glory of the great God when they look up unto heaven, upon the earth, and on the seas! Oh, but then the sweetness and soul-satisfaction that there must be in beholding the glory of God in the face of Jesus Christ!

This, by the way, would be a good evidence of your faith. Have you beheld more of God's glory in the face of Christ than ever you did in all the world besides? Yea, and has the glory of God in the face of Christ darkened all the glory of the world besides to you? Have your hearts been taken with that glory more than with all the glory there is in the world? Why, here would be a good evidence of faith indeed, that you have had a true and real sight of Jesus Christ. We cannot have a real sight of Jesus Christ but we must certainly see more of God in Him than in all things else.

The glory of God's great works in bringing man to his eternal estate appears in Christ. As the glory of God's attributes, so the glory of the great counsels and works of God, especially in the governing of man unto his eternal estate, appears in Christ above all, such as the great counsels of God in election. "We are chosen in Christ" (Ephesians 1:4). The great counsels and works of God in vocation, justification, adoption, reconciliation, sanctification, and glorification are the great works in which God glorifies Himself. These are the great things that the thoughts and counsels of God have been exercised about from all eternity. Whatsoever your thoughts are exercised about, yet I say, the thoughts and counsels of God have been exercised from all eternity about these great works of His—election, vocation, justification, adoption, reconciliation, sanctification, glorification—all these works whereby He orders and guides mankind to an eternal estate.

Now the glory of God in all these works is in Christ. Christ is the Head of our election, and all are chosen in Him. What is vocation but a calling unto Christ, and revealing Christ to the soul? And so justification is in Christ; and we are made children, adopted in Him, reconciled in Him, sanctified through Him, and are to be glorified through Him. All these great works, about which the heart of God is so busied, the glory of God in all these shines in the face of Christ—and without the knowledge of Christ we could never come to know any of these things. What could the heathen know of God's eternal election, vocation, justification, adoption, or glorification? To speak such words to the heathens as these are in reference to God would be barbarism. But these are the great things of God that are revealed to Christians by Jesus Christ. We come to have all these glorious counsels of God in these great works of His to be opened to us; and Christ is wonderful in all them. And all who know what these things mean see the glory of God wonderfully in them.

The glory of God is wonderful in Christ in that all the good
and mercy that lead to eternal life, that God communicates to
the children of men, are through Christ.

Now I mentioned something like this when I showed
Christ's endowments, that from Him we have all excellencies.
But I only mention it now to show how the glory of God the
Father is in Him, because God has appointed Him for the communication of all the good He intends towards the children
of men in order to eternal life. Now the glory of God must be
eminent in Him this way; for God accounts it a great part of His
glory to communicate Himself to His creatures. Therefore, that
through which He communicates Himself must be a partaker
of an abundance of glory.

God has honored Christ in that He has chosen Him to be
the instrument of the conveyance of all saving good to all the
elect. Now suppose that there was a glass, and that all the beams
of the sun that ever could shine upon the world were contracted
in it, and no beam of the sun could shine upon the world but
through that glass. First it must come upon that glass and shine
through it, and then it could shine upon the world. Surely this
glass would be very glorious.

You may conceive of Christ thus. Conceive of God the
Father as the sun, of all His elect ones as the world, and Jesus
Christ as the glass between the Father and all the elect. Now
all the beams of the love, mercy, and goodness that ever shall
come from God upon all His elect ones all come through this
glass, through Jesus Christ. Oh, how glorious is Jesus Christ!
How wonderful is He then in that glory of the Father!

The glory of the Father is wonderful in Christ in that God
the Father attains unto His greatest design, the great design
that God had in making of the world, and in the preserving of

the world. I say, God attains to it by His Son, by Jesus Christ. And that design would be lost if Jesus Christ did not bring things about for the glory of His Father. God has made a world for His glory, and He preserves a world for His glory. But the main design that God had in making the world, and that He has in preserving the world, He has only by Jesus Christ. And therefore, it is that the Father is so well-pleased in His Son, because by Him He comes to attain the great design that He has in making the world.

QUESTION. You will say, "What is that?"
ANSWER. The truth is, we understand but little of it for the present, but we know in general that it is so that He might have His elect ones eternally with Himself to behold His face, and magnify Him together with angels for His mercy in Jesus Christ. That is the great design that God had. Other men have great designs in their heads, but the greatest design that God has of all is to fetch about His honor in His Son, and to glorify Himself in His elect ones to all eternity. That is the great design for which He made the world, without which He would never have made it. And God, if I may so say, is well enough satisfied in the midst of all the dishonor that is done to Him in this wicked, corrupt world, with this consideration: "Well, My Son drives on My design, and this pleases Me. No matter if I am dishonored, if My name is never so much blasphemed in the world, yet My Son carries on My great design. And the glory I foresee I shall have in the accomplishment of that great design of Mine. It so pleases Me that it is no great matter to Me what wicked men, who do not belong to My election, do." Christ is wonderful in that He carries on the great design that God had from all eternity in making the world.

Then, the glory of God is great in Christ, and is therefore

wonderful because it is through Him that all the services and
praises that God has from His elect ones come. As there is a
reflection of the glory of God in the descending of it, when it
descends to the elect through Christ, so in the ascending of
it again from believers it ascends through Christ. There is as
great a necessity that when we tender up any honor to God
that it should come through Christ as, when God lets down
any beams of His glory, that that should come through Christ.
Christ is as Jacob's ladder for God to come down, as it were,
from heaven to us, and for us to ascend up to heaven through
Him. (Ephesians 3:21: "Unto Him be glory in the church by
Christ Jesus throughout all ages world without end." Unto Him
be glory in the church. But how? By Christ Jesus. Unless the
glory that you tender up to God goes through Christ, God does
not account Himself to be glorified in it. For whatsoever comes
from God to you, unless it comes through Christ, it will be to
little purpose. So whatsoever comes from you unto God, unless
it comes through His Son, it is not accepted by God. Therefore, oh, how wonderful is Christ in this, that such glory of the
attributes of God shine in Him? The great counsels and works
of God about man's eternal estate are all in Him. All the good
that God communicates to His elect ones is through Him. And
the great design that God had from all eternity He attains it by
His Son. Last, all the honor that He has from all His elect ones
is through His Son. How wonderful is Christ, then, in regard of
the glory of the Father in Him? Only as we go along, remember
that when I set Christ thus before you, I do it not merely to your
understandings, so that you may conceive thus of Christ, but
as an object of your faith. You must exercise your faith upon
Christ as such a Christ in whom the glory of the Father so much
appears.

Christ Is Wonderful in His Humiliation

Christ is wonderful in His humiliation; and indeed this may seem to be the greatest wonder of all, at least to our sense it is, especially if we understand what has been said before of Christ, and what a Person He is. Now what we shall hear of His humiliation will appear to be an amazing and an astonishing wonder.

1. The wonder of His humiliation is in that Christ, God and man, as you have heard before, should have all the sins of all the elect ones from the beginning of the world to the end of the world laid upon Him. Such a one as Christ is, infinitely beloved of the Father and equal with the Father accounted it no robbery to be equal with God (Philippians 2:6), yet He stood before God the Father with all the sins of the elect charged upon Him. So the Scripture tells us in 2 Corinthians 5:21: "For He hath made Him to be sin for us, who knew no sin." God has made Him to be sin for us. For Christ to be made a worm was a wonderful humiliation, but for Christ to be made sin was a greater humiliation than to be made a worm. Surely this must be a wonder to all the angels in heaven, for them to see such a one, whom they knew to be the eternal Son of God, equal with the Father, to stand before the Father clothed, as it were, with all the sins of the elect.

We read in Zechariah 3:3 of a kind of type of this. Joshua the high priest was "clothed with filthy garments, and stood before the angel." So Jesus Christ stands clothed with filthy garments. He who is clothed with majesty and glory, He must come and stand clothed with filthy garments before the Father. For one to be clothed with filthy garments, and yet to be in some room alone, so that nobody should see Him, is no great matter; but to see a great prince come out before the world clothed with filthy garments is a very great humiliation. But Christ, who was infinitely above all the princes in the world, comes and stands before men and angels, yea, before God Himself, clothed with these filthy garments.

For a man to have sin upon him before other men is no great matter, but for him to come into the presence of God with sin upon him is a terrible thing—but the Son of God must do it. He comes into the presence of the Father and stands with all the sins of the elect upon Him. What an object of wonder this is! Luther called Christ the greatest sinner who ever was in the world. I confess that this is somewhat hard, for sin was but charged upon Him; but his meaning is only what I am speaking of. Christ had not only the sins of David—his murder and adultery—and the denial of Peter, and the like, but all the sins of all the elect ones from the beginning of the world to the end of the world, that they were or should be guilty of, charged upon Him.

2. The wonder of Christ's humiliation is that He who was so high should now be brought down so low for the sin of man. Is this not a wonder, that He who thunders in heavens should be crying in a manger? Is it not a great wonder that He who framed the heavens and earth should work with a carpenter in his trade; that He who is the great Judge of all the world should be accused and condemned as a malefactor, and crucified among thieves; that He who is the Lord of life should die; that He who dwelt in that light that is unapproachable should have darkness to cover Him; that He who is the blessed God should be made a curse for the sin of man—are not these things wonderful in the Christian religion? And yet all these are things that may be said of Christ; for the Lord of life to come and die that accursed death was a wonder that all the world seemed to be affected with, even the very senseless creatures. At the death of Christ the sun withdrew its light, being amazed with this wonder, not

able to behold it. The earth shook and trembled, the graves opened at this wonder, and the very stones broke asunder at this wonder. There was such a mighty concussion of things at this time that it made one who knew nothing of the cause of it (one Dionysius, seeing the darkness at that time, and such great things as were done) cry out, "Certainly either the God of nature suffers at this time, or the world is at an end." So great a wonder was it that the Lord of life should thus die an accursed death. Angels, yea, all insensitive creatures, stood amazed at it, and seemed to be exceedingly affected with it.

3. There is a greater wonder in Christ's humiliation than in the sufferings of the servants of God, because though their bodies suffered, yet they had much freedom in their souls; they were fitted with joy and comfort in the time of their sufferings. So it was in the case of the martyrs. Oh, but it was otherwise with Christ. Though He was the Fountain of all consolation, yet Christ suffered in His soul. He was sorrowful in His soul to the very death, He gave His soul to be an offering for sin. And indeed the suffering of Christ's soul was the soul of His suffering, the chief of His suffering. When Christ was in the garden, there He acknowledged that His soul was compassed round about with sorrows. "His soul was very sorrowful" (Matthew 26:38). He began to "be amazed" (Mark 14:33). Another of the gospels says that He "began to be filled with sorrow in His soul." The very trouble of His soul was that which drew forth from Him such a wonderful sweat as never was heard of in the world before, nor ever since, nor ever is likely to be, that a man, from distress and trouble of his soul, should sweat so. Many a man, when he is in fear and trouble of mind, may sweat; but when did you ever hear of a man out of trouble of mind who sweat blood; that blood should come and break through his skin and

run down upon him, and this through the trouble of his mind? There was no bodily affliction upon Christ then, merely the trouble of His Spirit. And knowing what cup He was to drink, and the trouble that He suffered in His soul, caused the blood to break through His veins and come to trickle down—and not some thin blood, for so I have read of one in Paris who was condemned to die, and the very trouble of his spirit caused some blood to come out of his body, but it was thin. But the Scripture tells us that there were clods of blood. And when was this blood sweat? When He was abroad in the nighttime, and lay upon the ground; and this in the winter season. This took place on a winter's night, when He was abroad and lay upon the ground. He sweat this sweat, and all from the trouble of His Spirit.

A man may sweat in summer, and in winter in the daytime, in a warm room, or in a warm bed; but for Christ to sweat such a sweat on a winter's night, while lying upon the ground, so as for clods of blood to trickle down—never was a garden watered like this garden. Now who would not account this a wonder of all wonders?

Here upon this ground lies groveling the Son of God, the same God who made the heavens and earth. He lies here in trouble and anguish of His Spirit, while He sweat clods of blood. Certainly there was some great matter upon the Spirit of Christ at this time. We know by experience that when someone carries a great burden upon his back, he carries it while he sweats still. Oh, when you see men sweating under their burdens, remember Jesus Christ sweating under the burden of sin!

Besides this you have that other expression: "If it be possible, let this cup pass from Me." Why, the martyrs have gone cheerfully to their deaths, whose deaths have been as cruel as the death of Jesus Christ, and more cruel for the outward part of it. But here the great Champion, from whom all the martyrs who ever were had their strength, when He comes to die says, "If it be possible, let this cup pass from Me." Certainly, He saw that which the martyrs never saw. He suffered in His soul.

4. Christ suffered these things from His Father; that makes the wonder greater, and so His sufferings greater. He did not suffer only from wicked men and devils. Men, indeed, are like themselves, malicious; the devils are like themselves, cruel. Aye, but Christ might have looked up to His Father and said, "But, O blessed Father, Thou hast said from heaven that I am Thy well-beloved Son" (Matthew 3:17). Christ would have accounted it no great matter to have suffered from men or devils, as long as His Father had shined upon Him. Oh, no, but here is the wonder, and the greatest thing for angels and men to admire: God the Father inflicts these sufferings with His own hand upon Christ; the chief sufferings of Jesus Christ were inflicted by the very hand of God the Father Himself. For a king to come and take his own child, to scourge him and put him to death with his own hand, we would say, "Never was such a thing heard of!" Yet thus it was in the work of our redemption. God the Father took Christ with His own hands and put Him to death. "For He made His soul an offering for sin." It was He who bruised Him. If you read Isaiah 53:10, you find that it was the Father who did it. And that was typified in Abraham's coming with his knife to sacrifice Isaac his son. Was not the story of Abraham and Isaac a wonderful thing? Isaac must be sacrificed, and Abraham was to sacrifice Isaac, his only son, with his own hands. What a strange story that is. But that was but the type; here is the antitype. Here God the Father takes His Isaac, His only Son Christ, and sacri-

fices Him Himself. Surely this was some great thing to be done, that God the Father should do it thus Himself.

5. Not only did God come Himself upon His Son and inflict these evils, but He did not spare Him at all.

OBJECTION. "If God Himself must be the Executioner, and come and lay His hand upon His own Son, He will lay His hand gently upon His own Son."

ANSWER. Nay, when Jesus Christ the Son of God came to take our sins upon Him, the Father did not spare Him one whit, but let out the fullness of justice upon Him. In Romans 8:32 it is said that God did not spare His own Son. Certainly, if God would have spared anyone, we would think that it should have been His Son. Oh, behold the justice of God the Father, that when His own Son took sin upon Him, and that by imputation, He must pay the uttermost farthing to justice, yea, though He prayed with strong cryings and tears (Hebrews 5:7)! Though it is true that the Father carried Him through, yet here God would not spare Him, notwithstanding any of His cries. He must suffer to the uttermost, and pay the uttermost farthing that divine justice required to satisfy for man's sins.

Many poor creatures think that, having to deal with God who is a merciful God, though they have the guilt of great sins upon them, yet if they cry out to God for mercy, God will spare them. Why, are you dearer to God than Jesus Christ was? Your sins are your own. His was by imputation; yet when He cried, He was not to be spared. What thoughts must the angels in heaven have had when they saw Him, whom they knew to be the eternal Son of God, under the hand of the Father, and the Father to not so much as spare Him in anything? Certainly, if we do not know these things, or believe them, if we think to put

God off lightly, if we think that a few cries to God at last will be enough to cause God to spare us and pass by all our sins, learn to know God in Christ. A thousand of your vain thoughts about God, and thoughts of pacifying God for your sin, would vanish away and come to nothing if we did but know God aright in Jesus Christ.

6. There is a further wonder in this humiliation of Christ. God did not spare Him; aye, but when God dealt thus with His Son, did He leave Him? For one to suffer much, yea, and though it is much from God, yet so long as they may have the presence of God with them, if God does not leave them, it is not so much. But in all these sufferings, God the Father left Him. This is what is expressed by that wonderful speech of Christ upon the cross: "My God, My God, why hast Thou forsaken Me?" (Matthew 27:46). Never was a speech spoken in this world that had matter of so much admiration as that speech of Jesus Christ, who was the eternal Son of God, in the midst of His sufferings, that He should thus cry out. We many times may apprehend that God has forsaken us, when there is no such thing; but certainly Christ was never deceived in His apprehensions. What He apprehended was true.

But what this forsaking of God was is a very hard thing; it is a great mystery, too deep for us to dive into. But that there was a forsaking, and that Christ was not deceived, but that what He apprehended was real, must be granted; or otherwise we must grant that Christ was deceived, which would be blasphemy for us to say.

7. The wonder in Christ's humiliation was that Christ foresaw all this, and yet willingly undertook it to save mankind. See the heart of Christ in His sufferings towards His elect ones, that

rather than He would see them to be plunged into the bottomless gulf of eternal misery, He put Himself to keep them out. He did it willingly. When He first undertook this great work with His Father, He knew what He would suffer. "A body hast Thou prepared Me; it is written in the volume of Thy book I should do Thy will. And lo I come. I delight to do Thy will" (Hebrews 10:5, 7). What was that will? It was to suffer all these things that I have named unto you.

My scope is now to present as briefly as may be as much of Christ as I can unto you, so that you may have some help to more clearly apprehend Christ, and how to make Him the object of your faith.

8. So the wonder of Christ appears in this, that there should be such a way to save men as this is, that the Son of God should be thus humbled. This we find clearly in Scripture set out for us. But that God would have such a way to save sinners, and no other, is as great a wonder as anything. It is certainly the astonishment of the angels, and the admiration of the saints to all eternity. That the Lord should look upon base man, and that He should have thoughts to save him, was nothing; but when God saw that if he was to be saved that he must be saved after this way, that God should, as it were, trouble heaven and earth to save a poor, wretched, sinful creature; and though God saw that it would cost Him so dearly to save a soul, yet that He should go on with His work to save him, here is the wonder.

But this is the way of salvation, and this is that which is infinitely above reason—not only above sense, but above reason. Which of the heathens could have imagined that there would have been such a way to save man as this? Why, how will you be saved? "I will cry to God for mercy, and break off my sin. I will be sorry with all my heart." Why, if this were the way, there would be no wonder in it. But know, O you sinner, whoever you are, that if ever you are saved you must be saved by a wonderful way. And the truth is, considering that this is the way of saving sinners, we may stand and wonder that any are saved! When you hear of but few who go to heaven, and that most people in the world perish; and when you come to hear the way of saving man and what it cost, and the great difficulty of it, you may then stand and wonder that any should be saved. Oh, whenever you think of salvation, think wisely; it is a wonderful work of God to save a sinner, and the most wonderful work that ever God did. Why? Because the way of saving a sinner is so strange. And truly, my brethren, God begins to work savingly upon the heart of a sinner when the sinner begins to stand and wonder at the way of saving; and till that time it cannot be conceived that God has begun to work savingly upon your hearts.

I appeal to your consciences, you who have gone on in a secure, dead-hearted way, when were ever your hearts taken up in admiring the way of God's saving sinners? Why, if it has done so, that is a good evidence that God is beginning to show Himself unto you in a saving way. But if you go on and have but low thoughts about the way of salvation, if your hearts do not sanctify God's name in admiring the wonderful way of salvation, know that the gospel is yet hidden to you. Certainly you do not yet understand the counsels of God about the way of salvation when your hearts are not taken up with admiring the glory of God in it.

I will but leave this note of trial with you as to whether Christ is revealed to you. Have your souls wondered at Him, my brethren? There are divers things that men wonder at in the world, and their hearts are taken with them, and all because they do not understand Christ, the great Wonder of the world.

We read in Revelation 17 that when Antichrist had gotten a great deal of power, the world wondered at him. Verse 6: "When I saw her, I wondered with great admiration." Antichrist, having a great deal of power, makes men to wonder much at him. Now in verse 8, "The beast which thou sawest was and is not, and shall ascend out of the bottomless pit, and go into perdition, and they that dwell on the earth shall wonder (whose names were not written in the book of life from the foundation of the world) when they behold the beast that was and is not." And yet, those whose names are not written in the book of life, that was written from the foundation of the world, shall wonder at Antichrist, at his great power, and at the way of his falling too. So Revelation 13:2–3: "And the dragon gave him his power, and his seat, and great authority." When the dragon had given his power to the beast, when the civil state and power had given its power unto Antichrist, unto their church-state, so that they had the civil sword in their own hands, and were able by that civil power to force all to come in to their dictates, then the text says that they all wondered at it. But who are they? Chapter 17:8: "Those whose names were not written in the book of life."

So carnal hearts now may be taken with wonder at the pomp and glory of the world, and after the power of Antichrist, because Antichrist prevails in the world; but they are those whose names are not written in the book of life. Those whose names are written in the book of life will never stand wondering at the excellency of Antichrist because of his outward glory. No, those whose names are written in the book of life have learned to wonder at Jesus Christ, not at Antichrist. Let Jesus Christ be never so mean, humbled, low, and persecuted in His members, in His ordinances, yet they see that excellency in Jesus Christ that makes them wonder—and it is such a wonder as darkens all the wonders in the world besides.

Christ Is Wonderful in the Glory of the Father, Part 2

"And His name shall be called Wonderful."

ISAIAH 9:6

The point we are upon is that Jesus Christ is the great wonder of the world. As His name is wonderful, so He is wonderful.

9. There is yet more wonder in it if we consider that God the Father was well-pleased with all this. It pleased Him, for so you may find in Isaiah 53:10: "It pleased Him to bruise Him." It pleased the Father. God the Father took such delight in His Son, and saw Him brought into such a low condition, not only to be in the form of a servant, but in the form and similitude of an evil servant; to be beaten, and so beaten by Himself, and

all this to please Him. Certainly there was some great matter in it, that God the Father should be well-pleased with making His own Son to be a curse for man's sin; and yet we find in Scripture that it was a thing that well pleased God. Certainly, were it not for some great and wonderful design that God had to bring about, God the Father could not have been well-pleased with such a thing as the death of His own Son, and putting Him to death, and that to an accursed death—yet He was well-pleased. Certainly there was a wonderful design that God had to bring about by such a way.

10. The humiliation of Christ is wonderful in regard of the efficacy of His humiliation, that by His death, all the wrath and the justice of God should be, as it were, swallowed up in reference to all the elect. That the wrath and justice of God should be swallowed in a few days suffering of Jesus Christ (of this man, Jesus Christ), that God should account it as much as if all the elect had been under His wrath to all eternity, the efficacy of Christ's suffering is a wonderful efficacy, for it is an infinite efficacy; it is infinitely satisfactory.

11. Christ's sufferings take away the venom and evil that is in the saints' sufferings. Yea, not only are Christ's sufferings satisfactory to God's justice, but they take away the sting and venom of all the sufferings of the saints to the end of the world. The efficacy of Christ's humiliation is in reference to God the Father, and it is in reference to the saints. I say that it is in reference unto the Father in that it satisfies all His justice and wrath. And it is in reference unto the elect ones in that it is that which takes away the sting and the venom of all their humiliations and sufferings to the end of the world.

Though God has so appointed that His saints, whom He sets His heart upon to do good to forever, should here in this world suffer many hard things and be under grievous

afflictions, yet there is such a way taken that Jesus Christ's sufferings should take away all the sting, the venom, the evil of
their sufferings. And so Christ was wonderful in His sufferings
in that regard. There were never sufferings, nor such a death
in the world, that should take away the sting of all sufferings,
and death too, for so many thousands of people—and yet this
did it.

12. Christ suffered as a common Person. Christ is wonderful in His sufferings because He suffered as a common person.
He did not suffer as a particular man, but we are to look upon
Jesus Christ, in all the works of His humiliation, as a common
person. And so all the elect, from the beginning of the world
to the end, are looked upon by God the Father as suffering in
Him, as dying in Him, as being made a curse in Him. As the
first Adam was a common person, and God looked upon all
mankind as dead in him, in Adam, so the second Adam was
a common person, and in His death all the elect are looked
upon as dying, and so as satisfying God's wrath for their sins in
their own person, but virtually in Him as in a head. And in this
Christ was wonderful in His humiliation. Indeed, we do not
understand Christ's humiliation rightly unless we understand
it thus.

We sometimes speak of the great sufferings of Christ, and
so far we understand perhaps that this was for us, that He died
for us; but we do not understand that we died in Him, and that
He was a common Person, and that all the elect were looked
upon as in Him, as suffering in Him, and satisfying God's wrath
in Him. Thus we are to exercise our faith upon Christ's humiliation; and, indeed, this is the mystery of the humiliation of
Jesus Christ.

13. By suffering Christ enters into glory. Christ was wonderful in His humiliation in that by such a way He enters into His

glory. That when God intended the greatest height of glory to a creature that ever was or ever should be, that yet He would have such a way to lead unto it as that Christ should first be brought into such a low condition, to be a worm, and no man, to be accused, to be made a scorn of men, to be indeed in the lowest estate that is almost possible to conceive a creature here to be in; and yet that God should intend this to be the way to the highest degree of glory that is possible for a creature to attain unto—here was the wonderful counsel of God, the wonderful work of God. Now you know that so it was in Christ, for the Scripture says, "Ought He not to suffer these things, and so to enter into His glory?" God manifested in Him what way He would have to bring us into glory, that is, by the way of suffering, by the way of afflictions, by the way of trouble, to pave the way to glory by such kind of pavement as this, was the wonderful work of God.

14. In Christ's suffering appears God's hatred of sin. Here was the most wonderful argument of God's hatred to sin that possibly can be imagined, and the most wonderful pattern and example of self-denial that ever was in the world. Christ was wonderful in that in Him was held out the most wonderful argument of God's hatred of sin. If God had said, "I will set My infinite wisdom to work to find an argument to manifest My hatred for sin," even infinite wisdom could not have found a greater manifestation of His hatred of sin.

Christ in suffering, in His humiliation, was, I say, the pattern of the greatest self-denial that ever was or ever can be. God holds forth His own Son to be the pattern of self-denial to all the world; the Lord sees how we are altogether for ourselves, how hard it is for us to deny ourselves. "Well," says God, "I will not only require that you shall deny yourselves for Me as your duty, and bound as creatures to do it for your Creator, but I will send into the world such a pattern of self-denial that it is impossible for men or angels to imagine a more wonderful pattern of self-denial, My Son, who is equal with Myself, to come in the form of a servant. Although He has a right to all things, He shall empty and deny Himself to the enemies of all kind of misery."

Christ suffered for us. This is what makes up all the wonder, that all this should be done for us, for such poor worms, for such vile base creatures as we are. Why might not men and angels have thought thus: "Why, Lord, had it not been better for ten thousand thousand, and hundreds of thousands, and millions of such creatures to have perished to all eternity rather than that Thy Son should be brought so low, to suffer so as He did?"

"No," God would say, "I will manifest a great wonder in the world in that all this shall be done and suffered for poor worms (men), in whose eternal destruction I might have glorified Myself forever. Though it is true, I could as well have honoured Myself in their ruin and destruction, as I did in the eternal destruction of the angels who sinned against Me; yet I will show forth a wonderful work, that men and angels shall wonder at to all eternity, that such and such things shall be done and suffered to save them who are so unworthy and so vile." Thus Christ is wonderful in His humiliation. These things have been but briefly presented to you so that I might give you a general view of the mystery of godliness there is in the humiliation of Jesus Christ.

Christ Is Wonderful in His Conquest

But it follows that Christ is likewise wonderful in His conquest. He is the most glorious and wonderful Conqueror who ever was in the world.

QUESTION. What did He conquer? What did He triumph over?

ANSWER. He has conquered even divine justice itself, if I may so speak. The law, God's wrath and justice, came fighting, as it were, against Jesus Christ, and Christ encountered them. Yea, He encountered the devil, hell, and death. All these are enemies that Jesus Christ fought with. And certainly, had anyone but seen Christ go into the wars to do battle with these combatants, he could not but have stood amazed at it. "Oh, what will become of this Champion who has entered into such a combat as this is!"

But stay just a little, and you shall see Him leading captivity captive; you shall see Him triumphing over all; you shall see Him conquering and saying, "I have the keys of hell. I who was dead am risen, and have the keys of hell and death." You shall see Him triumphing over wrath and justice, the law, and the devils; you shall all see Him fetching all that He came for out of the hand of the devil. Yea, here is the wonder of the conquest: never was there a man who conquered death but Jesus Christ alone, who had power over death. All other conquerors may conquer and kill men, but they cannot conquer death itself. Now Jesus Christ's conquest was over death itself. He had the very keys of death, and what follows is hell.

That which makes the wonder of His conquest is that He conquers death by dying. What man conquers his enemy by being slain himself? Jesus Christ did so. He conquered all His enemies who came against Him. He conquers them by dying. Colossians 2 speaks of Christ's coming to die upon the cross: "And having spoiled principalities and powers, He made a slew of them openly, triumphing over them in it." When Christ was upon the cross, one would think that He Himself had been triumphed over; for He was brought very low indeed when He was brought there to hang between two malefactors, as if He had been the greatest Malefactor of all. Now one would have thought that devils, wicked men, death, and all had triumphed over Him. But mark that the text says that He there spoiled principalities and powers, and made a show of them openly, triumphing over them in it. We can imagine something of Christ's triumph now in heaven, sitting at the right hand of the Father; that when He ascended into heaven He triumphed. But to imagine Christ triumphing on His cross, that when His enemies were scorning and condemning Him that then He spoiled principalities and powers, and upon the cross triumphed over them, this is a great mystery of godliness. And herein is the wonder of Christ's conquest, of Christ's triumph.

And then the wonder of the triumph of Christ consists in that He has not only vanquished all the enemies of His people, but He has vanquished them by His own power. Conquerors have use of the strength of others, but Christ had enough strength of His own without any addition. And He not only quelled the adversary, but He turned all into good for His people. It is one thing for a conqueror to so overcome an enemy that he shall not be able to do any more harm, but it is another thing to subdue the enemy so far as to make them all to be servants to he who conquers—that is a greater conquest.

Man, by a strong army, may conquer by so killing his enemies as never to hear of them again; but if he can subdue and bring them all to be useful and serviceable to him and his people, this conquest is a great deal more glorious. Now such is the conquest of Christ that He has not only quelled their power, but has brought all to be serviceable to His people. The law is serviceable to them, and now God's justice is for good to them; the very wrath of God is now for their good, and the devil, death, hell, and wicked men are all made useful unto Jesus Christ, and so unto His people.

Last, Christ is wonderful in His conquest in that He conquered likewise as a common person, as a head; and in Him God has made all His saints conquerors. Yea, the Scripture says that they are more than conquerors through Jesus Christ; in Him they are looked upon as having overcome all those things. You may be weakest in yourself and able to do only the least, you may be afraid of every expression of God's wrath, the terror of the law, the threats of wicked men, the temptations of the devil, and of the very thoughts of death or hell, yet I say, if you are a believer, you have conquered all these already. They are not only conquered by your hand, but you have conquered them all, that is, virtually, in your Head. You are made a conqueror over sin, death, and hell in Christ your Head, and so in some measure in yourself. That is, Christ has put such a principle into your heart as will conquer all your enemies who come against you in due time. This is the glory of Christ's conquest, and He is wonderful in it.

More particularly, following the conquest of Christ, there are Christ's resurrection, His ascension, His sitting at the right hand of the Father, and His coming to judgment. In all these we have a wonderful Redeemer. I will very briefly present all these before you, but in a few words intend to show you a little of the mystery of godliness in every one of these so that I might, in a very little narrow compass, present the chief glory of Jesus Christ unto you (I mean the headings of it). Though I am aware that I cannot tell you the thousandth thousandth part of the glory of Christ.

Christ Is Wonderful in His Exaltation

Christ was wonderful in His resurrection. There was never such a resurrection, nor never shall be, as Christ's was. That Christ rose from the dead, I suppose you all know; but learn the mystery of godliness in this, and the wonderful work of God in it. In Romans 1:4 it is said that Christ was mightily declared to be the Son of God in His resurrection from the dead.

QUESTION. You will say, "Why, others rise too. Both godly and wicked men shall rise. How is Christ wonderfully and mightily declared to be the Son of God by the resurrection from the dead?"
ANSWER. Why, thus: Christ undertook to satisfy for man's sins, to pay the debt that man owed God for his sin. God the Father came upon Him, sued out the bond, cast Him into prison, into the jail. Now when Jesus Christ arose from the dead, there was a declaration to all the world that He had satisfied the debt fully to God the Father, that He had paid fully what divine justice required for the sins of man. This was a mighty declaration of Jesus Christ to be the Son of God. Had He not been the Son of God, He could never have risen again, having died upon such terms as He did. Christ died to satisfy God's wrath, and undertook all this. "Lord, I am content to come under the bonds of death till Thine infinite justice shall say that it is satisfied, that it has enough satisfaction."

If all the angels in heaven and all the men on the earth had undertaken such a work, and had said, "Lord, let us all die, and abide under the power of death, until Thine infinite justice shall say that it is enough," they would have abode to all eternity under it; they could never have come out of prison, but would have lain there forever. But now Christ undertook this work, and was content to be under the power of death till God fully discharged Him as being satisfied. God says at length, "I am satisfied. Let the prison doors be opened, and let Him go." So when Christ came out of the grave, He was declared before men and angels mightily in a wonderful manner to be the Son of God. And it is upon this that the Scripture says in Psalm 2, "Thou art My Son; this day have I begotten Thee," which is applied by the apostle in Acts 13, and some other Scriptures, unto Christ's resurrection. This is interpreted by some as if to be that Christ had only been begotten that very day; but Christ was the begotten Son of the Father from all eternity.

Christ coming under the charge of man's sin, and under the power of death, all the while He was in that low estate of humiliation, He did not appear like the Son of God before the world; but when He comes and gets the power over all, and is acquitted and rises again, now He appears like Himself indeed, "the only begotten Son of the Father." He is now mightily declared to be the Son of God. And in this the resurrection of Jesus Christ was wonderful for the wonderful power and efficacy that there is in it. Christ being acquitted, all the elect were acquitted in Him; all were acquitted in Him virtually, though there is another acquitting personally when they believe. At the very time of Christ's resurrection, all the elect were acquitted as in a Head, yet, I say, there is another acquitting from God in one's own person, and that is upon believing. From hence is that notable Scripture we have in 1 Peter 3:21: "The like figure whereunto, even baptism doth now save us (not the putting way of the filth of the flesh, but the answer of a good conscience towards God) by the resurrection of Jesus Christ."

QUESTION. What answer is this that the apostle speaks of? And how is this answer by the resurrection of Jesus Christ?

ANSWER. The answer that the apostle here speaks of is an answer to all demands that God's justice, that the law, and that the devils can make for any punishment that a sinner has deserved. If God's justice should say to a sinner, "You have sinned, and therefore you must die; you must be punished, you must satisfy justice"; if the devil should come and demand that the threats of God should be fulfilled because here is a sinner; if your own conscience should, in the name of God, demand that you should answer for your sin, a good conscience, "by the resurrection of Jesus Christ," is able to make answer to all these demands. One who has a good conscience can make answer through Christ's resurrection, and say, "Why, are these things demanded of me? Christ has satisfied for all. He has satisfied for my sin, paid my debt, and is risen again. Has not God the Father acquitted Him in raising Him from the dead? And there-fore in Him all is satisfied, and this is the answer I make to all the bills that are put against me."

If there are bills put in against man in any court, they come and make answer. Whatever bill can be put against a believer, if the law of God, or any temptation should put in any bill, a believer says, "Here is my answer: all is satisfied in Christ."

Now this is by the resurrection of Jesus Christ. If Christ had died, and yet had not risen again, you could not have answered that all is done. All might have been doing, but you could not have answered that all is done. But by the resurrection of Jesus Christ, you can make answer to any demand.

And observe that this is the answer of a good conscience. Men and women who talk so much of faith, and yet have evil consciences, cannot make this answer by the resurrection of Christ. Those who tell you we are to believe, and that God looks at nothing else but believing, it is true, if they understand it aright, in the point of justification; that is the thing that is necessary for justifying a person. But there is something more that is required of a justified person; and therefore no person can make this answer, "by the resurrection of Jesus Christ", but such a one as has a good conscience. "The answer of a good conscience by the resurrection of Jesus Christ." If you have a corrupt and vile, wicked conscience, your conscience flies in your face for sins that you live in. Know that you can never make answer (to those demands that shall be made against you) by the resurrection of Jesus Christ with any comfort till your conscience comes to be purified by faith. That is the wonder of Christ's resurrection, that He is mightily declared to be the Son of God.

In His resurrection there is a resurrection of all the saints, all the elect ones; for the Scripture says that He was the first fruit from the dead, that is, that as the first fruits sanctified all the rest, and all were consecrated in the first fruits being offered to God, so all the elect ones in Christ's resurrection rose again virtually in Him; and it was a pledge of their resurrection, the resurrection of their souls spiritually to life here and their resurrection to eternal life—and so we are to exercise our faith on Christ's resurrection. This is the mystery of godliness in Christ's resurrection, and hence we have that well-known passage in 1 Timothy 3:16: "Without controversy, great is the mystery of godliness. God was manifested in the flesh, justified in the Spirit."

QUESTION. You say that there is a wonderful mystery in godliness. Why is that a mystery?
ANSWER. God was manifested in the flesh; the Son of God came and took our nature upon Him. That was wonderful, but this is as great a wonder as the other. "Justified in the Spirit" is the same as being justified upon His resurrection; by the power

of the Spirit He was quickened and life was put into Him, and so He rose again, and thereby was declared before all the world to be justified, to stand acquitted from all the charge of our sins that was upon Him. And so compare "justified in the Spirit" with what we have in 1 Peter 3:18, "Put to death in the flesh, but quickened by the Spirit," that is, by the power of His Godhead He was quickened, upon His resurrection. Now one apostle says "quickened" and another says "justified" to show that when He was quickened, that is, when He rose again by the power of His Deity, then He, and all the elect ones, stood just in the presence of God, acquitted of all their sins. This is the mystery of godliness.

There is abundance in every one of these, but it is not my purpose to handle the resurrection of Christ, or His ascension, but merely to give you a little glimpse of the mystery of godliness that there is therein so that you may understand Him aright, so as you may be able to exercise your faith upon Him, not only dying and humbled, but conquering and rising.

Christ Is Wonderful in His Ascension

And for the ascension of Christ into heaven, the manner of it was wonderful. There came a cloud that carried Him up, and the disciples stood gazing. This was a wonder to be gazed at, the ascension of Jesus Christ, body and soul, into the heavens in that glorious way, but especially if we consider that Christ ascended likewise as our Head. He ascended into heaven as the High Priest went into the Holy of Holies. And it is said that we are "set together in heavenly places together with Christ." So you have it in Ephesians 2:6: "And hath raised us up together, and made us sit together in heavenly places in Christ Jesus." For

Christ went as in our names to take possession of heaven; this is the mystery of godliness in Christ's ascension. He went up to heaven, but He went in the name of the elect to take possession. As a man who has bought house and lands may have one appointed by him to go in his name to take possession of the house and land, Jesus Christ, in the name of all the elect from the beginning of the world to the end, went up unto heaven to take possession there, and to prepare mansions for them against their coming. So wonderful was Christ's ascension.

Christ's Sitting at the Right Hand of the Father

In heaven Christ sits at the right hand of the Father, thereby declaring that God the Father was well-pleased with all that He has done because He set Him at His right hand. After Christ had made an end of all His work, He is said to sit down. Hebrews 10:12: "This man, after He had offered one sacrifice for sins forever, sat down on the right hand of God." He had done His work, and God the Father approved of Him, and so honoured Him in setting Him at His right hand, and there gives unto Him all power to rule together with Himself in His kingly office. There He makes intercession continually for His elect, and has that weight of glory put upon Him that is possible for human nature to have put upon Him— that is the meaning of sitting at the right hand of God. These four things are meant by it;

First, when He came to heaven, God the Father, that He might acknowledge that His Son had fully done the work that He was sent into the world for, honours Him by setting Him at His right hand.

Second, He gives unto Him all authority and power to reign together with Himself (Matthew 28:18).

Third, there He is as the High Priest to make intercession for His saints, to be their Advocate continually at the right hand of the Father, to make intercession for them (Hebrews 7:25).

And, fourth, this is to signify that Christ has the highest degree of glory that it is possible for human nature to be capable of. Therefore you must not understand the right hand of God in a corporeal way, as if God had a right hand or a left one, but sitting so in those four respects as I have named. And all these make Christ a wonderful Redeemer: He who shall come up to God the Father in heaven, and who has fully pleased God with what He did upon the earth, and there setting Him upon His own throne, to reign with Him, and there to be forever to make intercession for the saints, and to have the height of all glory to be bestowed upon Him. Certainly this is a wonderful Redeemer.

Christ Is Wonderful in His Coming to Judgment

Then Christ shall come in a wonderful manner to judge the world again; then He shall come to be admired indeed. So you have it in 2 Thessalonians 1:10: "When He shall come to be glorified in His saints, and to be admired in all them that believe." Those who believe in Christ see Him to be wonderful. Now they admire at Him; but when He shall come again in glory at the great day, then He shall appear so wonderful that they shall all stand admiring, and say, "Well, we indeed heard that our blessed Savior was the wonder of the world, and we saw so much as made us admire at His glory; but we never thought that we had such a glorious Savior as now we see we have."

Jesus Christ is wonderful and glorious now, but when He shall come with His thousand thousands of angels; when there shall be such a wonderful change in the world; when the elements melt with fervent heat, the heavens depart like a scroll, and the heavens and earth shake; when all the princes and monarchs in the world, and all the children of men appear before Him—oh, then He shall be wonderful in His attendance, and then in His own person.

He is then wonderful in the manner of His proceedings, in bringing forth all the books of God's forbearance, the books of man's conscience and the book of the Word to proceed with men and angels for their eternal estate—in this Christ will appear then to be wonderful. Thus Christ is wonderful in His humiliation and in His exaltation. But a word or two more.

Christ Is Wonderful in His Working towards His Saints, and in the High Esteem That the Saints Have of Him

"Great and marvelous are Thy works, O Lord God Almighty. Who would not fear Thee, O Thou King of saints!" The great things that Christ does in the world towards His churches are wonderful, and in the great esteem His saints have of Him. They account all things as dung and dross for the excellency of the knowledge of Jesus Christ.

And Christ shall be wonderful eternally hereafter in the highest heavens; and there He will be the matter of the wonder of all the angels and saints. He will be the matter of the admiration, and the praises that God will have for all eternity; it shall be from what the angels and saints see in Jesus Christ. Therefore surely He will be wonderful in heaven.

And then He will be wonderful when the understandings of the saints shall be elevated to the highest pitch that they are capable of. Sometimes we wonder at things because of our ignorance. Ignorant people will wonder at almost anything. With regard to the works of arts and sciences, they wonder because they know but little; but what the most understanding man in the world wonders at, certainly it has some great excellency in it. Christ shall not be the wonder of the saints only while they are here in this world, but when they shall be in heaven, and have their understandings enlightened and enlarged to the height that possibly they can be enlarged to. And yet even then Christ shall be their wonder, and they shall wonder at Christ abundantly more than they do now. Certainly that has real excellency in it indeed, and great excellency, that the more understanding a man is, the more he shall admire at it.

Perhaps poor people may wonder at some men for their parts, yet if they had any great understanding themselves, they would see such a man's parts had little in them. But if a man had such parts that the more any man came to understand him, the higher in degree their understandings were, the more they should wonder, certainly this man had a great deal of excellency in him indeed. So it is in Christ: when the saints shall be elevated to the height, they shall so much the more admire Him.

Further, in heaven Christ shall be wondered at forever; many things are wondered at for the present, aye, but the wonder quickly ceases. We use to say of strange things that they were of nine days' wonder; but Jesus Christ is not only a wonder when the soul first comes to embrace Jesus Christ. It is true, when poor sinners, at their first embracing Jesus Christ, for the very novelty of those things they see in Him, they admire them. They never understood such things before; but the truth is, if that grace is true, you shall not only wonder when you come to Christ at first at the excellency in Him, but the longer you continue as a believer, the more you will wonder. And when you come to heaven, after thousand millions of millions of years, you will wonder as much at Him as you did the first moment.

Those men who have made profession of religion, and seemed to come to Christ, wonder at their first hearing of the gospel. They are like the stony ground that received the Word with joy. Oh, how wonderfully they are affected at the first hearing of the glorious things of the gospel! But mark it, the wonder quickly ceases, and their joy ceases within a little while. They do not now see so great an excellency to admire, neither have they so great a joy. But where there is true faith, the soul not only wonders at Christ at his first coming to Him, but still more and more to all eternity.

And now, my brethren, I think that all the wonders in the world should lie by a while upon this wonder of Christ's being presented to you. We read in Daniel 8 of one who came in a vision and said, "Gabriel, make this man to understand the vision." So shall I call to a Gabriel? No, to Jesus Christ, to Immanuel, He who is the great wonder. O blessed, blessed Redeemer; make these souls understand these things; make them to understand something of this wonder.

We have many wonders of our own, and we tell this and that news; but, oh, that Christ would show Himself to your souls so that you may understand something of this wonder, that your hearts may forever be taken off from wondering at anything in this world. "I have seen," said David, "an end of all perfection, but Thy law is very broad." So we may say, and the heart would say that was brought to Christ, "O Lord, I have seen an end of all the great things in the world, but Jesus Christ is very great and glorious indeed; it is He who has darkened all the glory that there is in the world. But I may say of all these things what is said of Daniel in chapter 12:10: "None of the wicked shall understand, but the wise shall understand these things" that are spoken of Christ. The wicked will not understand; those whom God has not given unto Jesus Christ will not understand, but will be content to part with Christ for anything. Oh, the detestable wickedness there is in the heart of man, that after what has been revealed to you about Christ, so much of His glory held forth for the wonder of the world, that after this yet you should prize your base lusts before all that good and the glory that there is in Jesus Christ. Certainly that man or woman must have the angels in heaven, and all the saints, to acknowledge the righteous judgment of God in the condemnation of them who have lived under the gospel, and have heard what a wonderful Savior has come into the world, if such a one should yet go away and prize a base, filthy lust before all the good and glory that there is in Jesus Christ; take heed of this: certainly, if it is so, if any of you are found at the great day still going on in the ways of known sins, this will be your charge: "You lived in such a place wherein you heard that My Son was the great wonder of the world, and glorious things were shown to you to allure you to believe in Him. Yet He was nothing in your eyes, but your own vile lusts were more glorious in your eyes." Oh, just and righteous is the condemnation of this creature forever! Certainly the sin of unbelief, the sin of rejecting Jesus Christ, must be a dreadful sin, because Jesus Christ is so great a wonder as you have heard.

SERMON 6

$\mathscr{A}$pplication

"And His name shall be called Wonderful."

ISAIAH 9:6

Now we come to the application of all, which is the work of this exercise.

USE 1. Certainly Jesus Christ is little known in the world, if this is He, this great wonder of the world. Oh, how little is Christ known! Christ is but a mere notion and imagination to most people in the world. You heard the very sound of this name, and how Christ came into the world to save sinners; but I appeal to your consciences, when were your hearts taken with the admiration of the glory of God shining in the face of Jesus Christ? Has Christ been made the greatest wonder in the world to you? Some of you have seen many wondrous works of God; some of you, perhaps, in the seas, or abroad in other countries, or if not there, yet you have seen the heavens and the earth, at which you many times wonder. But when did God dart light into your spirits to cause you to see so much of Jesus Christ, whom He has made to be the great wonder of all His works? Certainly, that soul does not know God or Christ savingly who does not know Him as the wonder of the world. It is impossible that such a poor creature as man is should come to understand such great mysteries of godliness as are in Christ in any measure without admiring the glory of that great work, and without saying with acclamation, "Oh, the height, depth, breadth, and length of the glory of God, His wisdom, mercy, truth, and power!"

There may be many notes of trial of faith, but I do not know any one more familiar than this is (at least negatively, it must needs be a true note), that is, that there cannot be faith without it, namely, if the heart has not been taken up with the wonder of Christ so that all the wonders in the world have been darkened in the soul in comparison to Jesus Christ.

USE 2. If Christ is so great a wonder, then how vile a thing it is for the hearts of men to prefer any base, filthy lusts before Jesus Christ! When God has manifested Him in that wonderful way unto the children of men, and shown so much of His glory in Him, yet that their hearts should be taken off from Him, and every base lust to be preferred before Him, oh, how just must the condemnation of such be forever! We may take up that complaint from Psalm 106:7: "Our fathers understood not Thy wonders." As our fathers did not understand, so few there are who understand the wonders of the Lord in Jesus Christ; and, therefore, everything is preferred before Him. With what infinite indignation must God look upon that wretched soul that shall prefer every base lust before Jesus Christ?

I remember Chrysostom, speaking of that passage that says that our vile bodies shall be made like unto the glorious body of Christ, saying, "Were all the world turned into tears, yet they would not be sufficient to lament the misery of the soul that forsakes Jesus Christ." His heart was so taken with the excellency of Jesus Christ that he thought it impossible to lament the misery of the creature that would forsake Him. And so Paul, having his heart filled with the glorious mystery of Christ, broke forth with this dreadful curse, "He that loveth not the Lord Jesus Christ, let him be anathema, maranatha." It is as if Paul should say (having his spirit filled with the glory of Christ), "What, shall God manifest so much of His glory in His Son, and shall base wretched vile creatures prefer their lusts before Him, and have their hearts taken up with other vain things, and not love the Lord Jesus Christ? Let that soul be cursed with a bitter curse." Such a soul indeed deserves to be cursed with a bitter and an eternal curse, who shall hear so much of Jesus Christ, and how God has revealed Himself in that wonderful way in His Son, and yet be unwilling to forsake a base lust for all the good there is in Jesus Christ; let that soul be cursed with a bitter curse. That soul deserves, above all creatures, to have the most bitter curse to be upon it to all eternity.

Certainly the more glory there is in Christ, the more dreadful the condemnation of wicked men will be. "This is the condemnation," that such glorious light has come into the world, and men chose darkness rather than light. How many hear of Christ, and mind little, but only have a noise; they hear some strange things of Christ and let them pass by, and think there is little reality in what they hear; but the only real comfort is in satisfying of the flesh in the lusts of it.

In Acts 13:41 we have an excellent Scripture for the reproof of such as hear the gospel and do not mind it. Beware, therefore, lest that come upon you which is spoken of in the prophets: "Behold, ye despisers, and wonder, and perish; for I work a work in your days, a work which ye shall in no wise believe, though a man declare it unto you." This is spoken concerning Christ, as appears in the verse before: "And by Him all that believe are justified from all things, by which ye could not be justified by the law of Moses." Now then it follows: "Beware, therefore, lest that come upon you, which is spoken of in the prophets, 'Behold, ye despisers, and wonder, and perish.' " It is as if he should say, "You hear the gospel about the glorious way that God has to reconcile sinners to Himself, to justify sinners; but in the meantime your hearts close with your own conceits and your own ways, with the law of Moses, and think by your own good meanings and your own good works that you shall do well enough and shall stand before God. But, says the apostle, "Beware lest that come upon you which is spoken of in the prophets, 'Behold, ye despisers, and wonder.' "

Perhaps when you hear such things declared unto you, you account it strange doctrine, and you stand and wonder what the meaning of those things should be. But as you wonder, so you despise; you condemn it as a strange thing that you were not wont to hear heretofore, and as a thing you cannot understand the reason of. This is the usual guise of carnal hearts: when they hear any doctrine, though there is never so much of God in it, and of the mystery of the gospel that is revealed in it, yet if they do not understand the reason of it, if it appeals to them as a new thing, they wonder indeed; but they despise it, condemn it, slight it, and pass over it, as they did Paul's doctrine. "What will this babbler say? He brings us news of a strange God, and the like." These are things that people are not acquainted withal, and so they cast them off and despise them. But mark what the text says: "Take heed; beware lest this come upon you, that you shall behold and wonder, and despise and perish too; for I work a work in your days, a work which you shall in no wise believe, though a man declare it unto you."

There shall be the great counsels of God revealed in your days and in your congregations; there shall be revealed those counsels of God whereby God intends to save many souls; and here and there God will make known these things to save poor souls. But you in the meantime, being conceited of your own understandings or your own civil righteousness, that you are not so bad as others, and that you are in a good case and condition all this while, you hear, wonder, and despise, but you shall perish, and shall never come to believe those great things that God in your days shall reveal for the salvation of the souls of others. This is a most dreadful curse that is upon the hearts of many men and women who hear the great things of the gospel. It is said in Acts 2 that some spoke the wonderful things of God, and yet there were some who did but mock. This is the condition of some, that their spirits secretly despise and condemn those things that they should adore; such things as upon their hearing they should even fall down upon their faces and adore God in beholding them. And yet, I say, slighting them and resting on their own ways and conceits, here is the curse of God upon their hearts: though they hear them, yet they shall not believe them. "I work a work in your days, a work that you shall in no wise believe, though a man declares it unto you," says the Holy Ghost. This Scripture is very much fulfilled in congregations where the gospel comes to be preached.

USE 3. If Jesus Christ is so great a wonder, certainly then the misery of mankind is very great. If there is such a need of so wonderful a Redeemer, oh, the dreadful breach that sin has made between God and man that required such a wonderful work of God to make it up! God would have you have a right understanding of this, and have serious thoughts about it. God would not have sinful, wretched man think that the breach between God and him is a light matter, a little thing. No, when the Lord has sent His Son into the world, and has declared Him to be this wonderful; when the Lord shows what a wonderfully glorious work of His there is in His Son for saving mankind, He thereby declares unto you and would have you know that the breach that your sin has made between God and your own souls is a wonderful breach.

Certainly, were the misery of man no other but such as the power of angels, as the power of any mere creature could help out of, Jesus Christ would never have come into the world; there would never have been such a wonderful work of God to redeem man. But now, when you hear that the way of God to redeem man is so wonderful, you have cause to lay your hands upon your hearts and say, "Oh, the depth of misery that my soul has fallen into! Oh, the desperate disease of my soul, that must have such a wonderful cure! Oh, that ever the great and infinite God should work so wonderfully for the salvation of such a poor, wretched creature as sinful man is!"

My brethren, we do not sanctify the name of God in the great thing that God would be sanctified in unless we have right apprehensions of the dreadful breach our sin has made between the Lord and our own souls, so that we might have right apprehensions of this wonderful work that God has done for the salvation of mankind. This is the reason why God so many times brings sinful creatures into such great straits, into the very gulf of despair oftentimes, before He reveals the saving knowledge of Jesus Christ unto them. It is, I say, because the Lord would have His name sanctified in this wonderful work of redemption by Jesus Christ so that the sinner might be prepared to stand and admire the wonderful glory of God in Jesus Christ.

There is nothing in the world that God looks so much for as this, to be sanctified in these wonderful things that He has done for mankind in Christ. And if we have but slight thoughts of the breach that our sin has made, certainly we cannot but have slight thoughts likewise of the work that God has done to deliver us from our sin. You think that your sin is a light matter, but know that when you have sinned against God there must be the most wonderful work of God to reconcile you to Himself that ever God did from all eternity, or will do to all eternity. This is the greatest wonder, His sending Jesus Christ into the world. Know therefore the depth of your misery by this: if God should have devised, as it were, from all eternity how to have manifested the wonderful misery of mankind, no greater could be found than this wonderful work of His in the redemption of man.

USE 4. Is Jesus Christ the great wonder of the world? Hence then all believers have exceeding cause of rejoicing in hearing what Christ is, what a wonderful Savior they have: "Let the children of Zion rejoice in their King."

Rejoice that God has so honored you that He has wrought so wonderfully for your salvation. Certainly, as your redemption is, so are you; that is, there is some reflection of the glory of your Redeemer upon you. How God has honored you before His angels! And how honorable you shall be hereafter when it shall appear to all the world that the infinite God so gloriously worked for the saving of your soul? God looks upon all the kings of the earth as worms. "Yea, all the nations of the earth as the drop of the bucket, and the dust of the balance, as nothing, less than nothing." You see how meanly God values all the nations of the earth. But when He speaks of His Son, who is your Redeemer, then He says, "His name shall be called Wonderful." He is wonderful in the eyes of God the Father. You who have such a wonderful Redeemer as this is, certainly your condition must be a comfortable one.

The main comfort that believers may have from this glory of Christ, as has been opened to you, is that hereby they may see Jesus Christ as a full object for their souls to rest upon, whatever their condition is. You have an all-sufficient Savior; you have an object that you may venture your soul, your eternal estate upon, for He is a wonderful Redeemer. Conceive your misery to the uttermost that you possibly can; suppose that you saw the guilt of all your sins before you, and apprehended your soul as being bound over to eternal death for your sin; suppose that you saw the justice of God coming out against you to require satisfaction for your sin; the curse of the law likewise brings you under it, and you see the bottomless pit ready and open for you, and the horrible, vile iniquities that you have been guilty of presenting themselves unto you with all their aggravations; suppose all this, and you stand now before the great God, ready to receive the sentence of your eternal estate. These things may make your heart to shake, and indeed they will where they are seen really. But in the midst of such a sight, if God gives you a sight of your Redeemer, who is so wonderful, here is enough to draw forth faith, yea, to beget faith in the soul. Let this be presented, whatsoever your misery is, yet know that here is a wonderful Redeemer who can not only cure ordinary diseases and deliver in ordinary troubles, but can wonderfully deliver, and no cure can be too hard for Him.

Oh, therefore, you troubled soul, who apprehends the evil of your sin and the dreadful danger that you are in, oh, that you could see this wonderful Redeemer before you! You would see Him to be an object for the most vile, wretched sinner who ever lived upon the face of the earth to rest upon. And because God the Father thinks so wonderfully of His Son, therefore He would not have us only to believe in His Son in ordinary cases, but in extraordinary cases. You who are believers, and hope that you have any part in Christ, know that God expects that you should sanctify His Son as a wonderful Redeemer. Now if you can only believe in Christ in an ordinary way, when your condition is ordinary and your straits not very great, this is not to sanctify Christ as a wonderful Savior.

Let this be said to your heart when temptations are strong, and when your heart is ready to sink in any extremity. It may be that temptation comes and tells you that your condition is extraordinary; it asks you who was ever so left of God as you are. Then lay these truths upon your heart that have been revealed in opening the wonderfulness of Christ, and say this to your soul, "O my soul! You have heretofore believed in God; but have you sanctified the name of Christ as being wonderful? Have you believed in Jesus Christ, as in Him whose name, by God Himself, is called wonderful?" You have, you think, believed in Him as a Savior, as a Redeemer; but have you believed in Him as being this wonderful in His name, in His Person, in His offices, in His endowments, and in all the great things that He has done, in the glory of the Father that shines in Him? Have you sanctified His name in all those particulars wherein Christ has been made known to be wonderful? Certainly, believers do not sanctify this name of Christ unless there is some kind of proportion between their faith and all these glorious things that are revealed of Jesus Christ. It is He who is a full object for your soul to rest upon in all straits whatsoever. When the men of the world are at their wit's end, having their ordinary helps fail them, yet you who are a believer, and knows who and what Jesus Christ is, and the glory of God that appears in Him, need not be at your wit's end; for you have Him whose name is wonderful to be the object of your faith.

The consolation to believers from this title of Christ is in that certainly, if there is such a wonderful Redeemer, whom God

Himself glories so much in, and accounts Him as being so wonderful, then it must follow that God intends wonderful things for the saints. No wise man who has abilities will in a wonderful manner busy himself about a trifle. Certainly, if the Lord thus works for mankind in His Son, if the Lord provides such a wonderful Savior for the children of men, we may fully conclude, that God has wonderful thoughts to do great things for mankind. The thoughts of God for the good of mankind are very great and very glorious; they are some high things, some glorious things that God aims at for mankind. Oh, raise your thoughts up therefore! Let all who are men raise up their thoughts and think, "Surely there is some great happiness for the children of men." God revealed it from heaven when He told us that such a wonderful Redeemer had come to the earth. But, O you believers! Do you in a special manner raise up your hearts and expect glorious things? And though you have little from God for the present, yet conclude that God has wonderful thoughts about you who are the members of Jesus Christ; and know that there must come a time when wonderful things must be bestowed upon you, or otherwise God would lose the honor of all the wonderful things He has done in Christ—and that He will never do. God will at length bring every believer to such a height of glory as before men and angels it shall be declared by the glory of your souls that Jesus Christ was a wonderful Redeemer. Such glory you may have, though I cannot tell the particulars.

If I should attempt to open the happiness of the saints, what it will be in heaven, we would quickly be swallowed up. But one would think that this one thing would be enough to fill the heart of the believer with joy: "I shall have so much happiness from God one day as must declare before men and angels, that Jesus Christ was a wonderful Savior, such glory as God Himself will glory in."

God will on that day say, "Oh, look here! Look upon this poor wretch, who for a while was such a vile, wicked creature, a child of wrath, and of perdition in itself; and look now what a height of glory this soul is raised up to. And now give your testimony whether My Son is not a wonderful Redeemer." This will be the condition of every poor believer who lives; and comfort yourselves in exercising your faith in this.

Whatever I am now for the present, though but a lump of clay and filth, yet I, being a believer and Christ being mine, my condition must be such one day as God the Father will say before men and angels, "Behold the wonderfulness of My Son in what I have done for this soul." And it may be enough to satisfy your soul for the present, that God will show Himself wonderful in your good and in your salvation. So it may be said of every particular believer, "Your estate shall be such one day as if there were none other saved in all the world but yourself." Jesus Christ will manifest Himself wonderful in your salvation; for indeed that is what He aims at, to be wonderful in the salvation of His saints, in bringing them unto glory; and that is the comfort of all believers from this title of Christ's being wonderful.

But now then as your comforts are great from this title, so your duties should be in some way proportionate too. You should therefore honor the Father of Christ as a wonderful Savior. Labor therefore to search into this deep mystery of the gospel.

Oh, what a shame it is that those who profess themselves to be Christians should understand so little of Jesus Christ! God expects that we should study the gospel, search into the gospel, so that we may see more of Christ. And the more we see, the more still we shall wonder; for Christ is an infinite depth, and the more we search into Him, the more we shall see cause to wonder. In Ephesians 1, mark what a prayer Paul makes for the

Ephesians, in verses 17–18. He told them before that he did not cease to give thanks for them, making mention of them in his prayers. But to what end? "That the God of our Lord Jesus Christ, the Father of glory, may give unto you the Spirit of wisdom and revelation in the knowledge of Him."

He not only prays that they might have some knowledge of Him, but that they might have a spirit of wisdom and revelation in the knowledge of Christ, and this from the God of our Lord Jesus Christ, and from the Father of glory.

Mark what titles he gives to God when he prays for them, that they might have the knowledge of Jesus Christ; it must be the God of our Lord Jesus Christ who must do it, the Father of glory.

God never shows Himself to be the Father of glory so much as when He gives the knowledge of Jesus Christ to a soul; then God makes Himself to appear indeed to be the Father of glory.

And the apostle prays further, "The eyes of your understanding being enlightened, that you may know what is the hope of His calling, and what the riches of the glory of His inheritance in the saints, and what is the exceeding greatness of His power to usward who believe." And in Ephesians 3, from verses 14–20, "For this cause I bow my knees unto the Father of our Lord Jesus Christ, of whom the whole family of heaven and earth is named, that He would grant you according to the riches of His glory, to be strengthened with might by His Spirit in the inner man, that Christ may dwell in your hearts by faith, that ye being rooted and grounded in love [all this now is but a preparation to what he would desire further, and that is] that so you may be able to comprehend with all saints, what is the breadth, and length, and depth, and height, and to know the love of Christ, which passeth knowledge, that ye might be filled with all the fullness of God."

This is a most admirable Scripture, and surely the Spirit of Christ filled the heart of Saint Paul. Such kinds of Scriptures as these are mighty strong arguments to evidence the Scripture to be the Word of God, when we read such passages as these, that have a spirit in them beyond the spirit of any man. Certainly, it was beyond the spirit of any man to express himself in such a manner so as to say that he bowed his knees unto the Father of our Lord Jesus Christ, so that they might comprehend with all saints what is the breadth, length, depth, and height, and to know the love of Christ which passes understanding, that they might be filled with all the fullness of God.

What I would especially observe is that Christians should not content themselves with a little knowledge of Christ, but they should labor to comprehend what is the length, breadth, depth, and height; they should labor to dive into the mysteries of the gospel. It is said of Moses, when he saw that wonderful work in the wilderness, he said, "I will now turn aside and see this great sight." You have it recorded in Acts 7:30: "There appeared to him in the wilderness of Mount Sinai an angel of the Lord in a flame of fire in a bush. When Moses saw it, he wondered at the sight, and as he drew near to behold it...." He had a sight of it at a distance, and yet so much as he wondered at it; and then he drew near and the Lord spoke to him.

So it should be with us: we have some sight of Christ, but is it not at a distance? We hear a minister speaking of Christ to us (the great wonder of the world); and it may be that upon this hearing we are ready to think that there is something in Christ beyond what we have apprehended heretofore. Aye, but I beseech you, brethren, do not let it pass away so. Those things that have been spoken concerning Christ, God will require an account of. And know that it is a dangerous thing to have the glory of Jesus Christ pass by any soul and do it no good. If we had been preaching to you of moral virtues, or any deep discourse about any point, save about Jesus Christ, there would not have been so much danger of letting it pass without profit. But when God sets before you the excellency of His Son, know that there is a great deal of danger if you hear such things without profit.

Therefore you need to say upon hearing such things, as Moses said, that you will draw near; that you will go and pray over these again, and beseech the Lord that He would reveal these things into you. Pray with David, "O Lord, open my eyes that I may see wonderful things from Thy law." By law there is meant those things that were revealed in the Word of God; and surely upon our hearing what God has revealed in His Word, we have cause to pray with more earnestness, "Lord, open our eyes that we may see wonderful things in Thy gospel." But mark it, when Moses drew near, then God spoke to him and revealed Himself further to him. If Moses had stood wondering at this sight and had gone no farther, it may be that he would not have had God reveal Himself so clearly to him; but when he drew near, then God spoke to him.

So if your hearts are taken with what you hear of this wonderful Savior, and then you draw near and take pains in your closets by meditation and prayer to see what is the meaning of this wonder; if you say, "Why, Lord, do I hear of such things and not understand them? They are things that nearly concern me; and shall I not understand them?" If you labor to draw near, God will speak and reveal more of His mind to you.

But more of this text in the Ephesians, we must labor to comprehend the heights and depths, and to know the love of Christ which passes knowledge.

OBJECTION. You will say, "These things are too wonderful for us to know."

ANSWER. Nay, the apostle prays that they "may know that which passeth knowledge." Though the fullness of the glory of it passes all knowledge, yet still there may be so much of the knowledge of these things as may help you to sanctify God's name and make your hearts spiritual; for the text says, "That ye may know the love of God which passeth knowledge, that ye might be filled with all the fullness of God." It is a very strange idea for the creature to be filled with God, and if we did not have it in Scripture, I would not have dared to have used such an expression. But here it is, "to be filled with all the fullness of God." This phrase is a great deal higher; but how does this come to pass? By comprehending the height, depth, length, and breadth; that is, by understanding Jesus Christ, and the glory of God in Him. By this means the soul comes to be filled with all the fullness of God.

What is the reason that Christians are so empty in their spirits, in their conversations, but because they know so little of the mystery of the gospel? If you understood the mystery of the gospel, how the Lord makes Himself known in the face of Jesus Christ, this would fill your heart with all the fullness of God. Those Christians are the Christians filled with excellency indeed who comprehend the height, depth, length, and breadth of this wonderful work of God in Christ. Nothing sanctifies the heart so much as the knowledge of Christ in a right way.

Seneca has an expression concerning the heavens: "Oh, the heavens are a wonderful spectacle, and a spectacle fit for a reasonable creature to be employed about! Though we should get little benefit by knowing the motions of the heavens, the sun, moon, and stars, yet the beauty and excellency that is there, and the wonderful work of God in the heavens, cannot but take a rational creature. Now if the wonderful work of God in the heavens is such as must take a rational creature, then, oh, what is the wonderful work of God in Jesus Christ! Therefore let us make it the chief of our study to study the Lord Jesus."

Luther had an expression to the same purpose: "Oh, I am vehemently, extremely displeased with myself. I hate myself because I cannot get that great benefit, that great work that there is in man's redemption, because I cannot get it to be transfused into my very bones and marrow. I would fain get it in there."

Paul, in Galatians 1:15–16, said that he was separated from his mother's womb and called by grace, and had Christ revealed in him. Oh, blessed is the soul whom the Lord has separated for Himself so that Jesus Christ might be revealed in him; that is a blessed soul. You know how Paul accounted the knowledge of Christ. He called it the excellent knowledge, and the excellency of knowledge, and accounted all things as dung and dross in comparison. And David said in Psalm 119:27, "Make me to understand the way of Thy precepts, so shall I talk of Thy wondrous works." When you come together, you can be talking of this and the other news, but were your hearts filled with the knowledge of Jesus Christ, you could not but talk of the wonderful things that God has done for your souls in Jesus Christ.

And as we are to labor to search that we may know more, so we are to give God the praise of this wonder that He has done. Psalm 107:8: "Oh, that men would praise the Lord for the wonderful things that He hath done for the children of men." It is meant there, I confess, of the wonderful works of God's providence, but surely, if God is to be praised and magnified for His wonderful works of providence, much more for the wonderful works that He has done for the soul in Jesus Christ. And so in Psalm 86:9–10, you have an expression to the same purpose: "All nations whom Thou hast made shall come and worship before Thee, O Lord, and shall glorify Thy name, for Thou art great and doest wondrous things." Oh, that this Scripture were fulfilled, that all nations might come and worship the Lord, and glorify God because He is great and does wonderful things. The wonderful things of God in His works of creation and providence are not so much regarded as the wonderful things He has done in Christ; and therefore the Lord expects that the saints should glorify Him more for that than for anything else. The truth is, God does not respect any of the glory that He has from His creatures unless He has it because of the wonders that He has done in His Son.

We should study Christ, and praise and bless God, and have our hearts enlarged for Jesus Christ. This is the duty of believers to whom God has revealed Christ as wonderful, that in their conversations they should hold out the wonderful glory of Jesus Christ. You should so walk before men as to manifest to all the world that your Savior is a wonderful Savior.

And you should manifest it by the wonderful change that takes place in you. The soul that has a part in Christ, whose name is wonderful, honors Christ if he manifests that since he came to know Jesus Christ, a wonderful change is made in him. What a change is made in this youth, child, young man, neighbor, or friend! Not long ago, what an ignorant person he was! But since he went to hear the Word, oh, the understanding in a little time that such a one has received in the mysteries of the gospel! Such a one was not able to go into God's presence to express himself in prayer any otherwise but by reading a book; but now, oh, what a spirit of prayer God has given to such a poor wretch, who was so ignorant just the other day! Now, oh, how he can pour out his soul before the Lord! Such a one who not long ago was a profane and loose liver, and sensual and base in his life and conversation, now, oh, how holy, how heavenly, how spiritual he is. Now he would not commit the least known sin, if he might gain a thousand worlds for it! Such a one who was false in his service before, now how trusty he has become! Now we may trust our life and all that we have with him now. Such a one who heretofore was a swearer, oh, how he reverences the name of God! Such a one who was a froward, passionate-spirited man or woman, now how meek and gentle they are! What a mighty change there is in the spirit of such a servant, wife, husband, or neighbor! And such a one who was altogether for himself, proud and haughty, now, oh, how humble and submissive he is! Now he can deny himself of anything.

We read that when Christ commanded the winds and the waves, the text says that "all people wondered at Him." So when the winds of your passions are up, if you can bid them to be still, all will wonder at it. Oh, how does so great a change come? Such a one who was impatient before in any suffering, now, whatever he suffers, how like a lamb he is, and does not open his mouth! Now, in the midst of afflictions, pains, and troubles, he can lie rejoicing and praising God. And such a one, though he has never such strong temptations to draw him on the other side, yet now he can resist the strongest temptations. Before, if a companion did but hold up his finger, he would go with them; but now, I say, he can resist strong temptations. And, oh, how he accounts it his glory and happiness to suffer for Jesus Christ!

This manifests Christ to be a wonderful Savior. It was the speech of a heathen, seeing the Christians suffer with such great patience, "Of a truth, the God of the Christians is a great God, who enables them to do such great things." So you must so walk in your life that you must manifest that Jesus Christ is a wonderful Savior.

And be ashamed to complain of any difficulty in any duties that you are set about. You are set about such a duty, and you complain that it is hard, difficult, and tedious. Is it for your Savior that you do it? You should be willing to go through fire and water. And in this one thing the wonderfulness of the change of a soul appears as much as in anything. Those things that before were accounted as burdens, now the soul accounts them as privileges and the joy of its heart; others cannot do so. The gospel makes such a change, and in this change of your heart and life Jesus Christ is held forth in the world to be a wonderful Savior. But if you can do no more than those who are strangers to Jesus Christ, what honor does Christ have in your life and conversation?

If Christ is a wonderful Savior, then everyone who hears of Christ should think it a dreadful thing to miss Jesus Christ. Oh, then, let all souls to whom Christ is made known pursue after Him! O you wretched soul, who has not yet understood the way of God towards mankind, now labor to know it! If the Lord has wonderful thoughts for saving mankind, then let your thoughts be these: "And after all this, shall my soul perish eternally? Shall I be cast away, notwithstanding that God has wrought such a glorious and wonderful way for the salvation of souls? Must I perish at last for all this?"

Your heart should make towards God, and be encouraged because the way of salvation is so wonderful. Why, may not your soul come in likewise and be saved? There is not the worst of you all but there is help in this wonderful Savior to help and redeem you. Had you hearts now to come in and to fall down before the Lord when you get alone in your closets, and say, "Lord, I have heard that a wonderful Savior has come into the world, and has done wonderfully for the redemption of mankind. Oh, that He might be wonderful in my salvation also, that I may be among the number of those who shall for all eternity be admiring Thy glory in Jesus Christ."

Many of you rejoice that God has wrought wonderfully to

preserve you sometimes out of dangers; aye, but what are all the wonderful works of God towards you unless you have your part in Him whose name is called Wonderful?

USE 5. Last of all, let us long for that time when Jesus Christ shall appear in all His glory. He appears now to the souls of His saints as very wonderful, just as He is set out in the Word; but there is a time when Christ shall come and appear in all His glory in another manner than we are able to set Him out. After the blowing of the seventh trumpet that you read of in the book of the Revelation, "then is the mystery finished." And what is the finishing of it? In chapter 11, then is the voice heard, saying, "The kingdoms of this world are become the kingdoms of our Lord, and of His Christ, and He shall reign forever and ever." Then shall the Lord Jesus Christ come and appear in all His wonderful works to the children of men, and to be admired in His saints. Then shall John 14:20–21 be fulfilled. Mark what Christ promises there to His disciples: "At that day, ye shall know that I am in My Father, and you in Me, and I in you. He that hath My commandments and keepeth them, he it is that loveth Me; and he that loveth Me, shall be loved of My Father, and I will love him, and will manifest Myself to him."

At that day you shall know it. It seems that His disciples understood but a little of this mystery before; but, Christ says, "There is a day that you shall know that I am in My Father, and you in Me, and I in you." And be of good comfort, all believers; there is a time coming when you will see Christ more wonderful than now you do. You now see Christ to be wonderful, and your hearts are taken in some measure, taken off from all the creatures, to admire Jesus Christ. In Acts 3:11–12, when the people wondered at the cure that the apostles wrought upon the lame man, mark verse 12: "When Peter saw it, he answered unto the people, 'Ye men of Israel, why marvel ye at this? Or why look ye so earnestly on us, as though by our own power or holiness we had made this man to walk? The God of Abraham, and of Isaac, and of Jacob, the God of our fathers hath glorified His Son Jesus.' " It is if they should say, "Why do you wonder at us? Know that the God of Abraham, of Isaac, and of Jacob has glorified His Son Jesus. It is He whom you are to wonder at."

The saints have their hearts taken off from creatures, from men, and from instruments; and they look upon Him whom the God of Abraham, Isaac, and Jacob has glorified, even Jesus Christ—and He is the matter of their wonder. But do you wonder at Jesus Christ now? Know that Christ will come ere long in another manner to be admired by His saints in all His glory. Christ was wonderful when He came with sin, and when He comes without sin He shall be more wonderful. He shall come in all His glory with His holy angels to make good all that He has promised, and to bring with Him all whom He has purchased; and then we shall see Him as He is.

Now we see Jesus Christ but through a glass, and yet our hearts are taken with Him. We wonder at Him now, but, oh, how we shall wonder when we come to see Him as He is, when we shall behold His face in glory. We now see the Lord Christ in His ordinances but as in a picture. When there are treaties made between one prince and another about a possible wedding match for their children, the first sight that they have of one another is but by a picture; and if they are delighted with merely seeing the picture of one another, much more will they be delighted and enamored with the person when they come to see them in person.

So it is with the saints: here all that the saints can see of Jesus Christ, that makes them to wonder at Him, and to account Him to be the chiefest of ten thousand, is all by seeing Him in a picture, as it were. Jesus Christ is in heaven, and He sends us His picture in His ordinances. So Paul says in Galatians 3, concerning the ministry of the Word, that Jesus Christ had been evidently set forth as crucified among them. Now, are your hearts taken with the sight of Christ, when you see Him as it were in a picture? Know, as Christ said to Nathanael, "Because I said unto thee, 'I saw thee under the fig tree, believest thou? Thou shalt see greater things than these.' " So you shall ere long see Jesus Christ as He is. "We are now the sons of God, but it appears not what we shall be; for when He shall appear, we shall be like Him, for we shall see Him as He is."

And you shall not only see Him, but you shall so see Him that He shall never go out of your sight. You have but a little glimpse of Him now for the present, and your soul rejoices in that. But the time is coming when you shall see Him, and your eyes shall feed upon Him forever. The Lord Christ shall go up and down the heavens as the wonder of the angels; and all the saints shall be following, wondering at Him to all eternity. The luster of the Deity shall be shining through the humanity of Christ, and men and angels shall stand gazing and wondering at the glory of Jesus Christ for all eternity. "Oh, let us comfort one another with these sayings," and in the expectation of the glorious appearing of Jesus Christ. And those who shall long for the glorious appearing of Jesus Christ, upon seeing Him here, have good evidence that they belong to Jesus Christ, and shall be partakers of the wonderful things that Jesus Christ has wrought and purchased with His own blood.

And thus I have opened to you and applied this glorious wonder of Jesus Christ. "His name shall be called Wonderful." He is wonderful in the Word. Oh, that He may be wonderful in your hearts and in your lives!

THE EXCELLENCY
OF THE SOUL

The Soul Is Worth
More than All the World

*"For what is a man profited if he shall gain
the whole world and lose his own soul? Or what shall
a man give in exchange for his soul?"*

MATTHEW 16:26

I have endeavored to show something to you about the
excellency of the name of God, and likewise the excellency of Jesus Christ, and what He is, so that you might
have right apprehensions of God and Christ. Now I shall desire
to show you somewhat about the excellency of your own souls.
Our Savior, going Himself to suffer, tells His disciples what they
must expect in the following of him: "If any man will come after
Me, let him deny himself, and take up the cross and follow Me"
(verse 24). These are the terms, says Christ, upon which you
must follow Me: you must be willing to deny yourselves and to
take up your cross, to suffer hard things if you would follow

Me. Christ would have His disciples know the worst at first, and not please themselves in a fool's practice, thinking that by following Him they would get great matters to themselves in the world. "No," He says, "expect no such matter; but deny yourselves and take up My cross."

OBJECTION. But this seems to be hard; it may be that our cross may mean the loss of all, the loss of our lives, and must we take up that?
ANSWER. Yes, says Christ in the verse before my text. Do not be solicitous about what your cross is likely to be, only be willing to take it up. And the truth is, the more willing you are to take it up, the better it will be for you; and you will get nothing by seeking to shift for yourselves. "For whosoever will save his life shall lose it, and whosoever will lose his life for My sake shall find it" (verse 25). It may be that when you meet with sufferings in the world, you will think to shift this way or that way, but you will get nothing. "If you would save your lives by forsaking the truth, it is the only way to lose your lives. But if you are willing to lose your lives for My truth, you shall save them; or what if by forsaking Me and My truth, when you meet with suffering, you should save your lives and your estates, and live bravely in the world. Do you think that you gain anything by this? You are infinitely mistaken. If you cast up the account, you will find that you have gotten nothing at all. "For what is a man profited if he shall gain the whole world, and lose his own soul?" And thus you see how the words come in.

These words that I have read unto you are worthy of exceedingly serious consideration. And indeed, they should be as thunder in every man's ears. Some Scripture that a minister may preach on may concern some particular person in a congregation more than others. But here is a text that concerns everyone who has a soul, man or woman, high or low, old or young. What shall it profit anyone to gain the whole world, and to lose their own soul? I have read of one who gave counsel to John, King of Portugal, that he should repeat this text to himself, and spend one quarter of an hour in the meditation of it: "What shall it profit a man if he gain the whole world, and lose his own soul?" And he would make the words of this text to be the close of his prayer continually: "What shall it profit a man to gain the whole world, and lose his own soul?" This was wholesome counsel; and certainly the right meditation and understanding of this text would be of admirable use to every soul. You have in the words these two things plainly hinted:

First, there is in every man a soul, a spiritual substance, besides what is visible and sensible.

Second, this soul of man is more worth than all the world. It has such an excellency that if a man gains all the world and loses that, when he has cast up his account, he may put his gains in his eye and he shall find himself to be a miserable creature.

We might make more divisions or subdivisions of the words, but I will content myself only with those two things, and speak chiefly to the latter. Now to make way for that, I will speak a little of the former: "What is a man profited if he shall gain the whole world, and lose his soul?"

Every man has a soul, a rational spiritual substance beyond what is visible or sensible. Job 32:8: "But there is a spirit in man, and the inspiration of the Almighty giveth him understanding." There is a spirit in man besides the bodily substance that you see; there is a spirit in man, such a spirit as is capable of the inspiration of the Almighty to give understanding. And in Genesis 2:7 it is said that "God formed man of the dust of the earth, and breathed into his nostrils the breath of life." Here is another manner of man's creation than that of other creatures. God said of other creatures, "Let the earth bring forth creeping things, and it was so." But when He came to man, He formed man's body out of the dust of the earth. As for his spirit, He breathed into his nostrils the breath of fife. I have read of a people who would not be persuaded that there was any difference between beasts and them. And truly there is something to do to persuade carnal hearts of any great difference between a beast and them in relation to God, or to another life. But certainly there is a spirit in man; there is something beyond that body of yours that is visible, which infinitely concerns you to look to.

First, we see that there are actions in men that are beyond that which concerns the body at all. And therefore, surely, there is a spirit in man besides what the body is; the highest actions of men are such as do not concern the body. For example, the knowledge of the heavens, the knowledge of angels, or of spirits—what has the body to do with such things? The knowledge of the mysteries of the gospel, and conversing with them, are abstracted notions from all kind of bodily substances. Add to these the knowledge of God and Christ, yea, the very knowledge of mathematic notions; many notions that are in arts and sciences are abstract from all bodily things. Certainly then there is a spirit in man beyond that bodily substance that appears common with brute beasts.

Second, yet there is a power in man to curb his body, to deny himself of that which is most suitable to the body. Paul said in 1 Corinthians 9:27, "I keep under my body, and bring it into subjection." Surely there is something in man that is above the body, that has so much command of the body as it appears the spirit of man has to beat down the body. "If thou best a man given to thine appetite, when thou sittest at the table of a great man, put a knife to thy throat" (Proverbs 23:1–2). A man is able to curb his appetite; though the body has never so strong a desire to such and such things, the soul of man is able to curb his body and deny it. "If thy right hand offend thee, cut it off, or thy right eye offend thee, pluck it out" (Matthew 18:8–9). There is a power in man to deny the body that which it desires never so much. A beast cannot do so; it cannot deny that which is suitable to its sense in every way unless there is some stronger sensitive thing to take him off. But man is able to deny his sense when there is no sensitive object before him to take him off. By that dominion that the soul of man has over his body, he is able to curb his body and to deny his body. Therefore surely there is a spirit in man.

Third, that which the Scripture makes the chief actions of man to consist in, which have any reference to God, are such things as are done by something beyond the body. Whatsoever a man does, if it is only the body that is exercised, and sense, it is not acceptable to God. "Bodily exercise profiteth little" (1 Timothy 4:8), says the Scripture; and 1 Corinthians 13:3: "What if I give my body to be burnt?" A man may give his body to be burned; there all the senses may concur in it, and yet if there is not a spirit in man to act upon any higher ends and grounds than anything that his body can reach unto, it is worth nothing; it is not regarded.

Fourth, there is a spirit in man beyond this bodily substance; for when this bodily substance is decaying and moldering away, there are many thoughts in a man about an eternal estate—and these are more fresh and lively sometimes when the body is moldering away than ever there were before. There are no creatures but angels and men who take any cognizance of an eternal estate, who take any thoughts about what is to come hereafter. We say that nature does nothing in vain; surely God would not have put such kinds of workings in man about another condi-

tion after this body shall molder away unless there is something
that concerns some other part of man besides that bodily substance of his.

Fifth, there is certainly a spirit in man beyond his bodily
substance: for we know that there are real pains and torments
upon a man's spirit, such as the burdens of conscience in the
reflex act that a man's conscience has upon himself summon-
ing him to appear before the great God. Though a man's body
is in never such health, and has all outward accommodations
about him—music, good cheer, friends, estate—yet there is
that horror and torment in his spirit, sometimes through the
consciousness of the guilt of sin, that he is not able to bear.
Nay, were there not something beyond this bodily substance,
certainly this could never be. Verily, then, there is a spirit in
man; and hence therefore you see that there is something that
concerns you all beyond your present outward, and bodily
condition. Let no man think that he has provided well for himself when he has provided money, house, lands, good cheer,
clothes, and such kind of things. Do not think that you are
happy in that: for these are things that concern your outward
man. There is still another substance in you that you are to look
after, you who takes little notice of such things as these are.

Neither ought you to think that you have provided well
for your children when you have provided an estate, an inheritance, something to leave them. Know that there is another
substance in your children besides that outward bodily substance you look upon. Do you see a fine feature, comely parts,
comely countenance, and your children finely clothed? Aye,
but know that there is a spirit in that child besides that bodily
substance that you are to look after. Certainly, man is very far
fallen from God in that none scarce takes notice of his own
spirit. We do not only naturally live without God in the world,

so as to know little of that infinite divine Spirit that is the first Being of all things; but we live without the knowledge of our own spirits, of our own souls. Truly, few men know their own souls. A man's eye sees things that are outside him, but he does not see his own eye; and so by the soul we come to understand many things outside us, but yet how little do we understand of our own souls? Well might the psalmist therefore complain and say in Psalm 49:20, "Man that is in honor, and understandeth not, is like the beasts that perish." God indeed made man at first in honor, but now he has become like the very beasts. He minds little or nothing more than the very beasts themselves; he blesses himself if he has enough for the body for a while, as if nothing else concerned him.

I appeal to your consciences in this thing, whether the uttermost sphere of your thoughts have been any further than merely within the compass of bodily matters. If you should come to a beast and talk to it about trades and titles of honor, about the arts and sciences, and such kind of things, what is all this to a beast? Give a beast hay or corn, and such kind of things that are suitable to it, and it minds those more than it does any notions that you are able to tell it.

And truly it is thus with sensual men, even as the atheist who says in his heart that there is no God. So there is a kind of atheism in their hearts to say that they have no souls, that there is no difference between them and the brute beasts. Hence it is that they favor spiritual things so little. Tell carnal men of the excellency of the name of God, tell them of Jesus Christ, how wonderful He is, of the wonderful mysteries of the gospel, and of the things of eternal life, and they are dry things to such a one. He does not savor them. Tell him of money, meat, drink, sports, clothes, and such kinds of things, and they are suitable unto him; there is some savor in them. But as for the great things of the kingdom of God and of eternal life, there is no favor at all in them. Thus far has man fallen from God, and lives, for the most part, as if he were capable of no higher good than merely to eat and drink, and live for a while here like a beast. Thus does the devil gull and deceive most of us.

Now my brethren, this is a work that I have undertaken, and it as much concerns the ministers of God to show unto you what you are yourselves, what God has made you, as to show you what God is and what Christ is so that you may come to understand yourselves. You can never come to know your reference unto God until you come to know what God has made you. This is therefore my scope in this Scripture, to show unto you what God has made you, and that you have souls within you, and souls of exceedingly great worth (I will not say "infinite," for none is infinite but God Himself), but more worth than all the world, than all the creatures that God has made except the angels in heaven. The souls of the children of men are most excellent creatures. If a man or woman seriously considered that they have souls in them beyond their bodies, it would raise them up a little.

But this next point that is the main and principal one.

DOCTRINE 1: The soul of man is the most excellent part.

Did men but know the worth of their souls, it could not but raise them very high above those poor empty vanities that they have minded all this while. Therefore, there is in man not only a soul, but that soul has more worth than all the world so that if it should be lost, that man who gained the whole world would be a great loser in his bargain.

Know, therefore, that there is not the poorest man or woman living, nay not the poorest child who lies begging for a crust of bread at your door, but this child has a soul in it that is worth more than heaven and earth. This poor, ragged, tattered child who lies in rags, I say, crying at your threshold and begging for a piece of bread, has a soul in it that has greater excellency than the sun, moon, and stars, than all the heavens, than the sea, than the earth; put all the creatures in the world together that are under angels, the spirit of this poor child has more excellency in it than all these things.

Natural life has more excellency in it than any creature that has no life. I remember Augustine said of a fly that, because it has life, it has more excellency in it than the sun itself, because though the sun is a glorious creature, yet it has no life in it. Life in the meanest creature has a greater excellency than anything else that has no life.

But the soul has the highest natural life that is, and is capable of the highest happiness that any creature is capable of, and therefore is more excellent than all the world, but that we shall come to in its order.

The excellency of the soul may be discovered, first, in the relationship it has to God. God challenges a peculiar relationship to the spirits of men; and therefore in Hebrews 12:9 God is called the Father of spirits: "Shall we not much rather be in subjection to the Father of spirits and live?" It is as if God did not so much look after and regard your bodies, the outward man, but He is the Father of spirits. And in Zechariah 12:1, there is likewise an expression to the same purpose, that "God did form the spirit of man within him." God accounts it a special part of His glory that He makes the spirits of men. He is the Father of spirits. But I shall not now enter into that controversy of the generation of the soul. Thus far these Scriptures, with others, evidence that God has a more special hand in producing this spiritual substance than He has in other creatures.

Second, the soul is under God's command only. No creature can have power over the soul of a man; he may force his body, but his soul cannot be forced by men or angels.

Yea, third, and it is under the power of no creature to inflict evil upon it. "Fear not them that can kill the body, and can do no more" (Matthew 10:28; Luke 12:4–5); that is all they can do: they can but kill the body. Do not fear them, "but fear Him, who after He hath killed the body, hath power to cast the soul into hell, yea, I say unto you, fear Him," says Christ. So it appears by the text that no creature can hurt the soul. The devils themselves cannot do it; they can propound objects before the soul, but unless the soul consents they cannot force it. Only God has power over the soul. Therefore Christ says, "Fear Him," that is, fear God who has this power. All other creatures, this is all they can do; they are able only to kill the body.

But, fourth, the excellency of the soul of man, in reference unto God, appears especially in the large capacity that it has to receive the image of God, its ability to work according as God Himself works, to enjoy communion with God, and to receive the communication of those choice excellencies that God has to communicate. These things show the excellency of the soul, the capacity the soul has of divine good.

1. The soul is capable of having the image of God stamped upon it. Whatsoever the body has, it is but in way of reflection from the soul. We know that princes who are great and rich, unless necessity compels them, do not usually stamp their image upon leather, brass, or copper, but upon the choicest metals, upon gold and silver. So when God would have a creature upon which He would stamp His image, He does not choose a mean creature, the brute beasts, or any senseless creature, but He chooses the most excellent of His creatures, angels, and the spirits of men, who are one as gold and the other as silver. The

great God stamps His image upon these two, and only upon these two. These are the two principal metals, gold and silver, angels and men's spirits, upon which God stamped His image in their first creation.

2. Not only does the soul have the image of God upon them, but it is able to work as God Himself works. No other creature is able to do so but angels and men's spirits. And this is the principal thing that shows the excellency of the soul: it is able to understand the first Being, God Himself, and to make God to be the last end of all things. What is God's work, wherein the very happiness, if I may so say, of God Himself consists but in understanding Himself as the first Being, and working unto Himself as the last end, and the enjoyment of Himself? That is God's own happiness. Now of such excellency is the soul of man (however by sin it is depraved) that it is capable of understanding an infinite, eternal first Being; it is capable of working towards this first Being as the last good of all, which is the same way and kind of working as God Himself works.

3. The soul is capable of enjoying communion with God Himself. What is God's happiness but to enjoy Himself as the only good? Now the soul of man is capable of the enjoyment of God, of having communion with the infinite first Being of all things; and so he is capable of living the same life that God Himself lives. For the Scripture says that the heathens were estranged from the life of God (Ephesians 4:18; Colossians 1:21); so it appears, then, that believers are not estranged from the life of God, but live the life of God in the enjoyment of communion with Himself. For indeed there could be no communion unless there was living the same kind of life. For example, a man and a beast cannot have communion together. Why? Because they do not live the same life with one another; their lives are of different kinds. So, were it not that the soul

was capable of the same life that God lives, it could not be capable of communion with God.

4. And further, the soul is of such a nature that it is capable of the communication of the choicest excellencies that ever God did or will communicate unto any. Certainly there are very glorious excellencies in God, in the infinite Fountain of all good, in the infinite first Being of all things. And this God, being an infinite good, takes infinite delight in the communication of His goodness. Now, I say, the souls of men are of such a large extent as they are in some way capable of the enjoyment of any good that God has to communicate, that He has revealed in His Word. Yea, and the truth is, when we hear of God's communicating Himself to His Son, who has a human soul as well as a body, we cannot but conceive that a human soul is of that large extent as it is capable of the highest and excellent good that God has to communicate to any creature. We cannot but think that the soul of Jesus Christ has as much of God's goodness communicated to it as ever creature had or can have.

Now the soul of Jesus Christ is of the same nature with our souls as His body. He took the same kind of flesh as we have, only there was no sin; and so His soul was the same kind of soul that we have, only it was not sinful as ours are. Now, if the soul of Jesus Christ is capable of the highest good that God the infinite Good has to communicate to any creature, then the souls of men and women are also capable. How is it that you have looked after your souls no further, but only to be serviceable to your bodies, to get meat and drink, and be, as it were salt, as the philosopher says of the Epicurean, that the soul serves him no end but to keep his body from stinking. Yet know, whatever you are, though now a sinful, wretched, vile creature, and deprived of the chief excellency that your soul is capable of, yet that soul that you have is capable of the highest good thing that an infinite God has to communicate. Oh, that God, by your owning this, would a little but raise your spirits to think that you have been deluded and deceived all this while. This is the excellency now of your souls, in reference unto God.

5. There is in the next place a further reference that your souls have to God, and that is the contiguity, if I may so speak, with God Himself; that is, of all things that are here in this world, the soul of man is that which is next unto God Himself.

QUESTION. Next to God? What do you mean when you say that the soul of man is contiguous unto God?

ANSWER. I mean that God has made all creatures for Himself, but He has made them all for Himself to come to Him by man. He has made all these inferior things in the world for man, and man for Himself; and so God comes to attain the end of all things in this world by man, so that man is next unto God. God would have the glory of all the creatures in the world. But how? By man. God says, "All these things that I have made, I will have them be in subjection to man; for so they were in their first creation. And as I shall appear in all other of My works, so shall this creature honor Me, fear Me, admire Me, and magnify Me, upon taking notice of and receiving in that good that there is in any creature. All the goodness there is in the creature comes to Me. But how shall I have the glory of it all? Why, I will make a creature that shall be, as it were, between Me and other creatures, that shall partake of the nature of other creatures, but so as he shall have a certain kind of divine beam of My excellency, and shall be able to take notice of Me and to receive in My goodness. What he receives of the sweetness of the creature, he shall receive it as My sweetness and My goodness. It comes from Me; and so he shall reflect it upon My face again."

Man's soul is like a glass: a glass takes the beams of the sun that shine upon it and casts them toward the sun again, as upon a wall. The beams of the sun come into the glass, and then the glass can reflect them this way or that way. So the glory of God shines in the world, and man's soul is as the glass. When it was in its first purity, it was as a clear, crystal glass, and received all the beams of God's glory. All the glory of God that shined in all His creatures was received into man's soul, as the beams of the sun into a glass; and now man is able to reflect the glory of these beams upon the face of God again, and to return all again to God. For as all things that are good come from Him, so all good should return again to Him. But how does the Lord come to enjoy His goodness that He lets out from Himself? How does He come to have it return back again to Himself? Why, the way of His returning is by the angels in heaven and the spirits of men. These are the two excellent creatures that God makes use of to fetch in all the glory that He has from all His creatures, that they in an active way should reflect it all upon the face of God again. Certainly the soul of man is of an excellent nature then that is contiguous with God Himself, next to Him. It is no matter whether a man is rich or poor, learned or unlearned, yet he has a soul that is capable of this.

Yet further, as for the excellency of the soul, it is excellent in relationship to God, and so in relationship to the angels. It is of the same kind of nature that they are of; they are spirits, and so is the soul of man. Yea, it has the very same name with God Himself. God is a Spirit, and so is the soul of man; it is of the very same nature with the angels, and so is able to converse with them as well as with God Himself. But as for the way and manner of conversing with those spirits, little is revealed in the Word, and therefore we can say little of it.

Further, the excellency of man's soul will appear in its excellent endowments. Look upon the soul of man in his fallen estate, and what admirable endowments some men have, as in the excellent knowledge that some men have of arts and sciences, or the knowledge of the heavens. It is a very glorious thing that they are able to ascend up in their understanding, to know all the motions of the heavens, and to be able to tell you to a minute of an hour what kind of motions there will be, as appears plainly by eclipses. Man knows arts of navigation, so that he can compass the world up and down that way. If it were but in these sensible things that we see so much art in, as in these mighty buildings, which shows that a man out of a deal of rubbish can raise and erect such a building as this is, this shows the excellency of man's soul; and if there is so much excellency in it naturally that it can do such things, then what can it be raised unto and enabled unto by a divine power? What can it do when it is enlarged by grace, and made partaker of the divine nature?

Further, the excellency of the soul appears in its immortality of it. "Fear not them that can kill the body, and can do no more" (Luke 12:4–5). Certainly, if the soul were mortal, as the body is, then the man who kills the body kills the soul too; and therefore we may fear a man not only because he can kill the body, but because he can kill the soul. But Christ says, "Fear not them that can kill the body, and can do no more." The soul is as an eagle that gets out of the cage, and so it flies away. Stephen said, when he was to die, "Lord Jesus, receive my spirit" (Acts 7:59). Why, if so be that his spirit had died with his body, he would not have needed to have said, "Lord Jesus, receive my spirit." And so Paul said, "I am in a strait, and know not what to do, whether to live or die" (Philippians 1:23). But he thought it was better for him to be dissolved; it was not to be destroyed, it is but a dissolution. He rather desired a dissolution that he might be with Christ, which is best of all. Certainly, it was this that made the strait: "If I die, I shall be with Christ immediately; and if I live, I shall enjoy some communion with Him, and likewise do a great deal of service for Him." If Paul had thought that his soul and body should have died both together, certainly he would have desired to have lived rather than to die; for when he lived his soul enjoyed communion with Jesus Christ, and he did an abundance of service for Him. Now is it possible to think that a man who did as much service for Christ as ever any man did, and who enjoyed so much sweet communion with Jesus Christ, that such a man should be willing to die? Certainly not, except that he knew that upon the dissolution of his body his soul would enjoy further communion with Jesus Christ than it could do here. The soul is an immortal substance; it runs parallel with eternity. Of such an excellent nature is the soul of man.

Further, the excellency of the soul appears in that it is the measure of all other kinds of excellency. For example, however far anything may be subservient for the good of the soul, so far that thing has an excellency in it; and if it is not subservient for the good of the soul, it has no worth and excellency in it. Suppose a man has a great estate in the world, many friends and many places. Now there is some excellency, you will say, in these things. But are these subservient for the good of your soul, that your soul can enjoy communion with God so much the better? Then these things are good to you. But if these things hinder the work of your soul, and do not help it forward in the service that it is most capable of and made for, then there is no excellency in these things. Indeed, I know no one better sign that a man understands the true worth of his soul than this: what does he account to be the measure of the excellency of all the things of this world? You would fain have an estate, and outward things in abundance, as other men have. Why, you say, they are the good creatures of God! I grant it, they are so; but wherein do you think the excellency of these creatures most consists? Certainly, if you come to know the true worth of your soul, you will say, "God gives me these outward things, and blessed be His name, by a larger portion of these things am I enabled to do larger service for God. My soul is freed from encumbrances in the world, and they help forward the work that my soul is specially concerned in, the service of God. And therefore I account it a greater good to enjoy these things than to be without them." Now if you come to reason in this manner, it is a sign that God has shown you what the true worth and excellency of your soul is.

But that I might draw to a conclusion, this is what, above all things, will demonstrate the worth and excellency of the soul, the great price that was paid for it. That Jesus Christ should be willing to lay down His life to purchase the pardon of the sin of your soul, to deliver your soul from eternal misery, shows the great worth of the soul. "We are not redeemed by silver and gold" (1 Peter 1:18), said the Apostle Peter, by any of these "corruptible things, but by the precious blood of Jesus Christ" (verse 19). According to the price that is paid for one, you may know the worth of such a one. Suppose there were divers men who were taken captives. One is but an ordinary mariner, you will say, and perhaps forty pounds will redeem such a one. But suppose the other is a gentleman, a knight, or a nobleman; there must go out five hundred, or two or three thousand pounds for their redemption. According to the excellency of the man, so must be the price of his ransom. So, my brethren, when we consider the price of men's souls, that were taken captive by sin, what was paid for them, it was a price that was more worth than ten thousand thousand worlds. Certainly, the soul is of an excellent nature. Indeed, it cannot be imagined that Jesus Christ would have taken man's nature upon Him and died an accursed death to have saved the whole world from being dissolved. Suppose it had lain upon this, that heaven and earth must have been dissolved unless Jesus Christ would take man's nature upon Him; certainly Jesus Christ would have allowed heaven and earth to go to nothing rather than to have done as He did. But when Jesus Christ saw that these immortal souls by their sin were brought into such a condition that they must perish to all eternity unless He came and took their nature upon Him, laid down His life, and died an accursed death, He said, "Rather than such precious souls which My Father has made capable of enjoying so much good from Him, and bringing glory to Him; rather than these should perish, I am content to come and die, and to suffer the wrath of My Father." Surely the price that was paid for souls holds forth the great worth of them. In the death of Christ we may read in large characters the worth of a soul.

And, my brethren, even the body itself, because it is as the case of the soul, is a very excellent thing. Of all the corporeal things that ever God made, the body of man is the most excellent thing. Therefore David, in Psalm 139:14, speaking of his body, says, "I am fearfully and wonderfully made; marvelous are Thy works, and that my soul knoweth right well." And then verse 15: "My substance was not hid from Thee when I was made in secret, and curiously wrought in the lowest part of the earth." When he says "curiously wrought," the word in the Hebrew signifies embroidered. The body of man is embroidery. In Genesis 2 it is said that God formed man; and here in Psalm 139 that God embroidered him. And, therefore, Gallen, who was an atheist a long time, when he came to see the anatomy of a man's body, cried out, "Now I adore the God of nature." The Lord has wrought the body so craftfully because it is the case of the soul, and that, being such an excellent creature, must have a suitable case. If you have a fine watch, you will not put it into an ill-favored, dirty, leather case, but will have a fine silver case for it. Now because the Lord made an exquisite piece, the soul of man, which was the masterpiece of God's creation next to the angels, therefore He put it into a very exquisite case. This shows the excellency of those spirits that are within us. However they may now be defiled with sin, yet thus they were made at first. When we are speaking to men about their own excellency, one would think that then they should attend.

I have spoken of God and Christ's excellency, and they may seem to be things above you. But now I am speaking of your own excellency, what you are, and what you are capable of. Oh, remember this, you poor people and others, for (as we shall show afterwards) you have souls as excellent as the greatest men in the world. And there is nothing to the contrary, but you may have that spiritual substance of yours filled with so much good as is infinitely more worth than ten thousand thousand worlds, if you have hearts to look after it.

I shall add one thing more that shows the excellency of the soul in the relationship that it has to God: the soul is satisfied only with God Himself; nothing can fill the soul of man to satisfy it but God Himself. For the true object of man's understanding, it is not this truth or the other truth, but truth in general, and the highest truth, and that is God. And the object of this soul is not this or that good, but good in general, the highest and the chief good, and that is God. Let all the creatures in the world present themselves before the soul of man to be his portion, and man's soul would say, "These are not the things that can satisfy me." Augustine said, "Lord, Thou hast made us for Thyself, and our heart is unquiet till it comes unto Thyself." And this is the excellency of man's soul, it is above all creatures. It is a virtue in the soul of man to have a holy kind of pride, to think all creatures in the world to be too little to be its portion of it. And God takes this well. He well likes it that we should know our own souls so far that we should have this kind of pride of spirit, as we may so call it, or rather a right elevation of spirit, to look upon all creatures in the world as too low and too mean to be the portion of the immortal soul.

Many other things have been delivered about the excellency of man's soul, so that you might know something of your worth, that you are too good to be slaves to the devil. And it is good for you to know your own worth in this thing so that your hearts may be elevated above those bare things that you sought to have your happiness in. All those who have ever had true wisdom have accounted souls to be very precious. I remember Zozomen, the ecclesiastical historian, said that the martyrs suffered torment in their bodies as if they were other folks' bodies, and not their own; they did not look upon them as any part of themselves, but on their souls as themselves. And so you find in Scripture that it is the soul of man that is a man's self. For this compare my text in Matthew with Luke 9, where you have the same speech of our Savior setting out the excellency of a man's soul. In the one it is, "What will it profit a man if he gain the whole world, and lose his own soul?" In the other it is, "If he lose himself." This is all one, losing a man's soul and losing himself; for a man's self is his soul. The body is but the case; it is but the outside—and so indeed some of the heathens accounted their bodies. Anaxarchus, when he was beaten in a mortar to death by the tyrants, called to them, "Beat, beat as long as you will; you beat but the outward part of Anaxarchus; it is but the vessel in which he is."

The devil himself has a high esteem of souls. The devil does not care, if he may gain men's souls, what they have for their bodies; the devil does not envy any wicked man to prosper in this world, to have a healthful, lusty body, and to have stature, strength, and beauty. But if he sees that there are any means for the good of their souls, he envies that. If the devil can but have their souls, he does not care what they have otherwise. But we must come to the application of this first point in my text, of the excellency of man's soul.

The Application of the First Point

"For what is a man profited if he shall gain the whole world and lose his own soul? Or what shall a man give in exchange for his soul?"

MATTHEW 16:26

USE 1. Surely then we ought to look upon every child of man with some reverent respect and honor; there is not the poorest child who lies crying at your doors for a crust, but has a soul in it worth more than heaven and earth. The consideration of this should make us look upon the meanest child or servant, the poorest body, with an honorable esteem and respect; however the glory of their souls is darkened for the present, they still have in them such souls as are capable of a kind of infinite good, more than all the other works that ever God made except the angels. Do not look upon your servants who are under you with scorn and contempt; do not use them doggedly, as if they were brute beasts. Remember, though you are a master, a mistress, or a governor, you are a governor of one who has an immortal soul, worth more than all the world. "A good man," says the Scripture, "is merciful to his beast." And surely then a good man will be merciful to one who has an immortal soul, and it may be an immortal soul better than his governor. How many have more respect for dogs, for brute beasts, than they have for servants, children, and poor people who have immortal souls? I have read of the Turks, that though they are noted for being most cruel people to men, as you heard of their cruelty to those in the gallies, yet they are very pitiful to brute beasts; and therefore they will give alms and stipends out of charity to maintain brute beasts with. There is a story of a youth who was abusing a bird that had a long bill, and was likely to have been stoned to death in the street; they so hated cruelty to those kind of creatures, though they are cruel to men. Many have this Turkish disposition, who are dogged and cruel to those of their own kind, to those who have immortal souls together with themselves, though pitiful even to brute beasts. This is the first use: look upon all who have these souls with an honorable respect, considering they have that which is of so much worth.

USE 2. If man's soul is of so much worth, how can we look upon many people without having our hearts raised in the meditation of the dreadfulness of God's justice upon men for sin? God has made man an excellent creature, and given to every one a soul worth more than the world; but when we look upon some people who have lost the beauty of their souls, and now have no other use of their souls but to all their days be employed in scraping kennels and raking in the dust heaps in your streets, in attending upon horses and swine, and this is all that they have to do in their lives—oh, what a low condition has man fallen into, who has no other use of such a rational immortal substance that God has given him but merely to make him serviceable all his days to tend swine, beasts, horses, scrape kennels, and such kind of things as these are!

OBJECTION. But it is lawful for men to be employed in these things. Poor people must be employed.
ANSWER. That is true. It is lawful to be employed in such things; but when men and women have such poor and mean employment, and have no higher thoughts but merely to get bread by such employments, and their souls are busied all their days about nothing else but those things, this shows the woeful fall of man, and manifests a dreadful fruit of God's justice upon the children of men for their sin. Certainly man, who was made in honor, has become like the beast that perishes in this regard. And when we see the condition of men to be so low, so base and vile as they are, so beneath the excellency of a rational and immortal soul, oh, let us raise our thoughts to the meditation of God's divine justice! It is a fearful fruit of the justice of God upon man for sin. What, is this the creature who has an immortal soul made by God, worth more than ten thousand worlds, who lies scraping from morning to night in a kennel, and has no other thoughts for any higher excellency but only if it can get a lump of bread to live by, there is all they have to do, as if they were born for no other end? Oh, is this the creature who has such an excellent soul? Surely sin has made a great breach between God and man, and has brought mankind into a very low and mean condition. And yet worse than these are those who have no other use for their souls than to be drudges to the devil and slaves unto their lusts. Of this I shall speak to more afterwards; I only mention it now to give a hint to the meditation of God's justice upon man for his sin.

USE 3. If the soul of a man is of so great an excellency, then certainly it must be an honorable work to be busied about souls, an honorable employment for God to set one man or more to look to, and tend the souls of others. Oh, what a difference there is in the employment between working in wool and iron all day long, or scraping in the dust heaps (as before) and in an employment of attending upon souls, to be used by God as the instrument of converting these souls, and bringing them to their former excellency in which they were made, yea, and to raise them to a higher excellency than ever they had in the first creation! If we prize men's employments by the subject of their employment, then certainly this is the most glorious employment that any creature in the world can be capable of. What is the reason you account being a goldsmith a better trade than a blacksmith but because of the subject that the one works about rather than the other. One works upon iron and the other upon silver and gold; therefore one is a more honorable trade than the other. Now, if the subject upon which they work makes one to be more honorable than the other, what trade in the world can be so honorable as the work of the ministry? Ministers work about immortal souls, in bringing them to God, to live to God, and to enjoy communion with Him. Why do we account a physician a more honorable profession than a horse leech? One looks to the bodies of beasts and the other to the bodies of men. If there is such a difference between the body of a beast and the body of a man, that he who is employed about the one is accounted honorable and he who is employed about the other is accounted low, then certainly the employment of the ministry must be honorable, for it is about souls.

The magistrate looks unto your peace, the lawyer to your estates, the physician to your bodies, and the minister to your souls; though outward respects may be given more (and should be) to the magistrate, yet certainly the employment about immortal souls must be the most honorable in the world. It is the honor of the angels (Psalm 91) to take care of the bodies of the saints. If it is the glory of angels to take care of God's people, what glory does God put upon the ministers of the gospel to look to souls? And truly, in this thing God has put more glory upon men than upon angels; for God has not made it to be His set ordinance that angels should convert souls, but He has made it so that men should be used to convert souls by preaching the Word. And let all the angels in heaven show an employment so honorable as this one!

You would account it a great honor to have the body of a prince to watch over. Surely there is no immortal soul but is more precious than all the princes in the world; and if the Lord should give unto you the care of all the creatures except the souls of men, it would not be such an honorable work as to give you the care of any one immortal soul. This the apostle says in 1 Corinthians 4:1: "Let a man esteem us as the dispensers of the mysteries of Christ." "Let them esteem us." It is true, ministers of the gospel should be willing to lie under the feet of any to do good to their souls; but because we know that it is a great hindrance to the work of their ministry when brutish carnal spirits have low and mean esteem of their work, therefore we find that the apostle would ever be setting up the honor of this work. "Let a man esteem of us as the dispensers of the mysteries of Christ." And 1 Thessalonians 5:12–13: "We beseech you, brethren, to know them which labor among you, and are over you in the Lord, and admonish you, and to esteem of them very highly in love for their work's sake." And Hebrews 13:17: "Obey them that have the rule over you, and submit yourselves; for they watch for your souls as they that must give account, that they may do it with joy and not with grief, for that is unprofitable for you." Oh, it is a sad thing if one whom God sends to watch for the souls of people shall be forced to return his account to God with sorrow of heart, and say, "Lord, Thou who knowest all things, knowest what desires I have had, and what endeavors to do good to the souls of this people, how it has been my study and my prayer, to find out what might be most profitable for their souls, how willing I was to venture my life in seeking to do good to their souls. But, O Lord, I have spent care, study, and strength, and even almost my life in vain; little good do I find done to the souls of this people. Lord, they reject Thy Word and condemn it; they do not mind it. There are other things that their hearts are upon, to follow the lusts of their flesh, as if to be they had no immortal souls to look to." I say, if any faithful minister of God shall go to God and take his moan thus unto God with grief and trouble of heart, it will be very ill for you; it will be a fearful moan in the ears of God against a people when any minister shall justly make this to God against them. Therefore the apostle says here, "Obey them that have the rule over you, and submit yourselves: for they watch for your souls, as they that must give account, that they may do it with joy and not with grief." Consider, so far as any have charge of souls, it is a heavy burden that is upon them, a heavy weight. Surely, whatsoever should take charge of so many thousand souls as belongs to this congregation would have weight and burden enough upon his shoulders, you should pity them who have this charge over you.

I remember Chrysostom, in his writings upon this very Scripture, said that he wondered how any of these who are here said to watch over men's souls could be saved, because the charge is so great that is upon them. And I have read of one who, being called to the work of the ministry, would by any means avoid it and professed that he would not for all the world have the charge of a soul one day upon him. Certainly it is a great work, and requires very much seriousness and diligence to have a soul committed to someone. If a man had a precious pearl committed to his charge that would be worth ten thousand pounds, that he must look to it and keep it, he would hardly be able to sleep quietly after he had so great a charge committed to him. And truly, if men are careful who only have beasts committed to them (as Jacob said concerning his uncle Laban's cattle that he looked to them so as that he endured the frost in the night and the heat of the day), much diligence and care then should they have who have the charge of souls.

USE 4. If souls have such excellency, then certainly those who have most soul-excellency are the most excellent people. We may judge here who they are who are the most excellent upon the earth. "The righteous is more excellent than his neighbor." Perhaps his neighbor is richer than he, or has a more comely body than he; but yet the righteous is more excellent. Why? Because all excellency must be judged by that which is most proper to the creature, and that which is the chief part of the creature. If you would judge the goodness of a knife, you will not judge whether it is good or not by the shaft, but you will judge it by the metal of the knife; you judge by that wherein the chief of the knife is. So if you will judge the excellency of a man or woman, you must judge his excellency by the excellency of that which is most proper to him.

Now, for sense, for the body, the brute beasts have sense; they have flesh and blood as well as we, only we differ in these rational immortal souls that God has given to us. Therefore, those whose souls are filled with divine excellency are to be most honored; they are indeed the lords and ladies of the world. Therefore the Scripture speaks of those whose outsides were mean enough, in the latter end of Hebrews 11, who wandered in sheepskins and goatskins, yet were such as the world was not worthy of them.

Indeed, a man of understanding is of an excellent spirit. We read of the ark of the covenant that the outside was of badger skins; it had a poor and mean outside, but within were the cherubims, and gold was within. And so many have very mean outsides, but within there is a great deal of excellency; and others who have brave outsides, and are well-clad without, yet if you look within them what vile souls have they! "The heart of the wicked is little worth," says the Scripture. Perhaps his land and his house may be worth something, but his heart is worth little. Many a man who has perhaps a hand full of sores yet may have a fine, embroidered glove upon it; and a dunghill may be strewn with herbs. In the wintertime filthy dunghills, you know, are covered with white snow; on a fair, frosty day they look as glittering as the snow that is upon a fine meadow, but are still nothing but filth. So it is with many a man who has a fine outside. It may be covered over with a great many outward excellencies, but within the spirit is nothing but carrion, nothing but abominable stuff that is filthy and loathsome in the eyes of God. A sore leg may have a fine stocking or boot upon it, and so a sore, putrefied soul may have a brave outside upon it. But that God who is a Spirit, who looks unto the spirit, and those men who know what spiritual excellency means, if they see a man or woman have a filthy, defiled, corrupt soul they cannot but esteem them accordingly. Whatsoever the body, or the outside is, those are the most excellent in God's esteem, and in the esteem of the holy angels and the saints, who have the most excellent souls, for that is the best part of man.

USE 5. If the soul of man is so excellent, let us bless God for our souls; bless God, I say, who has given unto you these immortal souls that are of so great a worth. Oh, what cause have every one of you to bless God that He did not make you a toad, a dog, or a snake; that He did not make you any vile brute creature, but that when you were before Him in the common lump out of which God made His creatures that He should rather choose you to be one who would have an immortal soul so precious, rather than to be a brute creature?

Bless God, I say for this, for by this means, first, you are looked upon by the angels themselves, with honor, and with respect, till such time as the angels certainly know your reprobation, and that you are sent down to hell. Though you are wicked for the present and your souls are defiled, yet the angels know nothing but that these souls, though now much fallen from God, may be such as may live with them to enjoy eternal communion with God together with them—and therefore they look upon you with honor.

The providence of God is more towards you than towards any other creature in the world. Does God take care of oxen, asks the Scripture? True, the providence of God is over all His works; there is not the least worm that stirs without His providence. Aye, but does God take care of oxen? It as if the Holy Ghost there should say that the providence of God over other creatures is nothing in comparison to what it is over the spirits of men, over those who have immortal souls. When God looks upon the creature to whom He has given an immortal soul, "Why," says God, "My Providence shall in a special manner be over this soul." And certainly the thoughts of God have been from all eternity working towards those who have immortal souls in a more special manner than towards any of His other creatures. However you think of God, yet it is certain that God has had His thoughts towards you one way or other from all eternity, and intends to fetch out a great deal of honor to His name from you one way or other; and therefore His providence is towards you. God observes you, and marks what way you take. His eye is upon you, for He intends to bring some great glory out of you. God will not lose His creature fully. You may lose your own souls, but God will not lose the glory that He might have from you; but He will have glory from you one way or other.

And if God has given you immortal souls, you have cause to bless Him because whatsoever you are now, yet you are such as are capable of all the good that ever Jesus Christ has purchased; and therefore it is a happy thing for one to have an immortal soul, because they are not out of capacity of receiving that good that the Lord Christ has purchased for His people. The brute beasts are capable of no higher good than to eat, drink, and live here a while, and have their senses to be pleased, and then there is an end of them. But know, whatsoever you are, you are capable of all the good that ever Christ has purchased; and therefore your condition is a great deal better in that respect than the condition of all other creatures in the world. You have a soul within you, so God has made you for eternity one way or another; and He intends to have you live for all eternity in one condition or another. It is a happiness to be made such a creature that God should have thoughts about from all eternity.

It may be that you will say, "It would be better if it were otherwise with us."

I confess that such is the condition of some, through their living and dying in sin, that it would be ten thousand times better if they had been dogs, or toads, and serpents, aye, but that is but through their wickedness. But it cannot be said of the wildest man alive, for there is none of you but for all angels or men know may live eternally to the praise of God's grace in Christ. You have such natures as are capable of it. Now it is true, if you should die in your sins then it might be said at that instance when you die that it had been better that you had been toads or serpents, or anything in the world. But would not this be a sad thing for a man who has such an excellent nature to live and die so that they may wish hereafter that they had been toads or dogs? How many are there who are willing, so they may live like a beast, to die like a beast? Aye, but that you cannot bring yourself to die like a beast, you must be infinitely worse or infinitely better than the brute beasts. But bless God that you have a nature capable of so much good whatsoever you are in other respects, though God has made a great difference between you and others who are of the same kind in your outward estate.

God has made a great deal of difference between poor and rich, between a poor beggar who lives in so mean a condition, and between a nobleman, a prince, or an emperor. Aye, but this difference is made in the outward estate and body; there is no such difference made in their souls. You have a precious soul within you that is naturally as good as ever any emperor had in the world. So philosophers say of the souls of men that men's souls are equal, and one is not better than another by nature; what they are better by is afterwards, by education, or by common gifts of the graces of God—but by nature all men are equal. And, therefore, that wherein man's excellency is, is in his soul. You are as high as any emperor it the world, and, therefore, the Scripture would have no difference made between the souls of men.

In Exodus 30 you find that God would not have difference made between the souls of men. It is said in verse 14: "Everyone that passeth among you, that are numbered from twenty years old and above, shall give an offering unto the Lord." God will have an offering from every one of them. Now mark what He says in verse 15: "The rich shall not give more, and the poor shall not give less than half a shekel when they give an offering unto the Lord to make an atonement for their souls." There must be the same atonement made for souls, the same for both the rich and the poor. And as I said the last day in opening the excellency of the soul, it appears by the price that was paid for it. So here they are equal in this: the poor man's soul must have as great a price paid to save it as the richest man in the world. And therefore bless God for your soul in that He has made you equal with the kings and princes of the world in that your soul is your more noble and excellent part.

Bless God for soul mercies above all mercies. If the soul is excellent, then bless God who has granted you soul mercies. Though He has denied you bodily mercies, it is no great matter. If God should take away your eyesight, yet if He opens the eyes of your understanding, the eyes of your soul, you are happy. Suppose that you are lame in your body; yet if you can walk in the ways of God's commandments, and run there, you are a happy creature. It may be that you lack food, aye, but if God feeds your soul with spiritual manna, feeds you every day with food from heaven and takes care for the feeding of your soul, you are not as miserable as you thought yourself to be. You may have tattered clothes, aye, but if God has provided the righteousness of His Son to be a garment to clothe your soul every time you appear before Him, you are a happy creature in that. Therefore, when your heart is ready to murmur that God has denied you bodily mercies that He has granted to others, think, "Aye, but has not God recompensed me in soul mercies?"

I make no question but there are many souls who bless God that they have lived to this time, though they have suffered hard things for their bodies; many who have lost, and been plundered of all, yet bless God that they have lived to the time wherein there was so much plenty of the food of souls. Oh, those truths of God that have been revealed unto us since those times! But had those who had the power before had the power still maintained, we would never have had such truths made known unto us; they account all recompensed in soul mercies. Ephesians 1:3: "Blessed be the God and Father of our Lord Jesus Christ, who hath blessed us with all spiritual blessings in heavenly places in Christ." Mark what the apostle says there, for his heart is filled with this: "Blessed be the God, and the Father of our Lord Jesus Christ." For what? That He has given us good trading and good incomes, that He has given us food and raiment? We are to bless God for this, aye, but the apostle's heart was above this. Therefore he says, "Blessed be the God and Father of our Lord Jesus Christ, who hath blessed us with all spiritual blessings in heavenly things in Christ." These are the blessings indeed that we have cause to bless Him for—spiritual blessings, soul mercies. As for bodily mercies, we know that the heathens and reprobates have had as great a share in them as anyone in the world. But blessed be God, for though we are denied these outward bodily favors, yet we have the spiritual blessings. "Oh, thanks be to God, and the Father of our Lord Jesus Christ, who hath blessed us with spiritual blessings in heavenly places in Christ." And this now would be a good argument that you know the worth of your souls: if you can be blessing God for spiritual blessings in Jesus Christ above all blessings, and account yourselves rich enough if you have the riches of spiritual blessings.

Oh, if the soul of man is so precious, what a great pity it is that God should not have the honor of men's souls, of such a noble and excellent creature! It is a great pity that there should be any creature under the sun that God should not have the honor of; that God should not have honor from every pile of grass, from every bit of bread that is eaten, from every stone in the street. But that God should give to mankind such an excellent spirit, a soul more precious than all the world, and yet that God should not have the glory of this, oh, this is an evil thing under the sun indeed! This must strike at the heart of God; for the truth is that God has His glory from all other creatures by the soul of man. As for other creatures, He has His glory but passively from them; but with regard to man's soul, He expects to have His glory actively from that, that man by his soul should come to know this God, the infinite first Being of all things. Man should fear Him, worship Him, serve Him, have communion with Him, and praise Him. And therefore David says in Psalm 103: "My soul, praise thou the Lord, and all that is within me praise His holy Name." And he concludes: "My soul, praise thou the Lord." And so it is in Psalm 104.

Now, upon the consideration of what has been said of the excellency of our souls, we should lay a charge upon them to honor and serve God. What a sad charge will this be to many a man at the great day, when God shall say, "Had you been made a dog, I would never have had so much dishonor as I have had. I would have had more honor if I had made you a dog; there I would have had my honor passively, and no dishonor from you. But now, that being made an immortal soul, as it was capable of honoring Me, so of sinning against Me." The more excellent a thing is, the more capable of evil it is as well as of good. No creatures but angels and men are able to sin against God. Oh, it is a pity that God should not have the honor of your immortal soul! God had more honor from Nebuchadnezzar, when he was driven out among the beasts, than when he sat upon the throne as a king.

And that would have taken another lifetime to have labored

to persuade you to take heed of dishonoring these souls of yours. God has put a great deal of glory and excellency upon them; do not dishonor them. And many ways could have been said how men put dishonor upon their souls in conclusion. Oh, that you would but learn to love your own souls!

To love them? That is a strange exhortation, you will say, to exhort men to love their souls.

Oh, that you would but do it! In Psalm 22:20 David calls his soul his darling. The souls of men should be indeed their darlings, not their bodies. It was a speech of a courtier to his friend, "I love you as my own soul."

"Oh," he said in reply, "then you do not love me at all. If you had said that you had loved me as your body, then I would have thought that you loved me; but I see no love you have to your soul." It was the prayer of the Apostle John, in the epistle that he wrote to his host Gaius, I suppose you that know Scripture and are not unacquainted with it, in his third epistle, "Beloved, I will above all things that thou mayest prosper, and be in health, even as thy soul prospereth."

I shall close all I intend for the present with that Scripture. It seems that Gaius was a holy man, but a man of a weakly and sick body; and therefore John, writing to him, prayed thus: "Above all things, I desire that thy body may but prosper even as thy soul prospereth." It is as if he should say, "O Gaius, you have an excellent, gracious soul, endued with admirable graces of the Spirit of God; your soul is full of God, though your body is weakly. Oh, that you had but as good a body as you have a soul!" It seems that Gaius had a great deal more care of his soul than of his body.

But, my brethren, consider this, would not this be a curse to most men, for one to pray thus for them, "O Lord, give them such bodies as they have souls?" It would be as much as to say,

"Lord, let that body be blasted; let it be filled with diseases; let it be filled with rottenness; let it consume away; let it be a noisome and loathsome body, for his soul is so." The souls of most men are filled with diseases; they are noisome and loathsome in the eyes of God. It is a happy thing, my brethren, to have better souls than bodies; that was the happiness of Gaius, and so it would be your happiness if you could say so.

You have great care of the bodies of your children, aye, but have you a greater care of their souls? If you have, it would be an excellent sign that God has made you to understand what true excellency means. It is a great question among divines, and among philosophers too, about the propagation of the soul, how it comes in, whether by the parents or immediate creation. Truly there is one argument that it is not likely to come in by the parents, because we see that there are scarcely any parents who have any care for the souls of their children; but they are altogether caring that their bodies may be fine, and that they may be brave. And as they look at their children, so they look at themselves. They love their bodies to the uttermost, to make provision for the flesh, but no further. How it would affect you if, when any of your children go abroad, or your husband or wife, if you should hear that they have fallen and broken their legs or arms? But when you go abroad and fall into sin, and get a wound to your souls—as every sin gives a deadly wound, yea, such a wound as only the blood of Jesus Christ is able to cure it—nothing is made of all this, as if we were nothing but lumps of flesh. Oh, have a care for your souls; labor to love them, and make them to be your darling. You need to have a care for them, for as they are precious, so they are tender. As it is with watches and finely crafted instruments, those that are most delicate are the easiest hurt; the very air will put them out of temper. And so it is with the souls of men, because they are such excellent things.

They are things of a very curious nature, and a little thing will hurt them. As a little thing will hurt the eye, for that is a more excellent member than your finger or leg, so the soul is a more excellent part; and therefore it is that which is most in danger to be hurt and mischiefed, yea, and to perish. And if your soul perishes, your body will follow after. What will become of that if your soul is lost and perishes? But the only way to love your bodies well and aright is to love your souls.

USE 6. If God has given unto us such precious souls, oh, then let not us dishonor our souls.

QUESTION. Dishonor them? Why, how may a man dishonor his soul?
ANSWER. First, a man dishonors his soul when he lives idly and makes no use at all of it, any more than if he had but the soul of a brute. Psalm 24:4 speaks of him who had not lifted up his soul unto vanity. The old Latin, Arius Montaeus rendered it, "He that hath received his soul in vain." And indeed, most people do receive their souls from God in vain, or to no purpose; they make no more use of them than the philosopher said of the swine that had his soul only as salt to keep the flesh from stinking. This is all the use many men make of their souls, only to keep their bodies from smelling, and from corruption.

Second, we dishonor our souls when we employ them about low and mean things that are unworthy of them, and make those to be the chief things that we employ them about. It is the misery of man so to do; and it is the sin of man so to do. How many men who have such precious, immortal souls as these are, know no higher good to employ them about than to be, it may be, all day or night shuffling a pair of cards, casting dice, or at gaming tables? This is the highest good that they know how to employ their souls about. What a poor, mean, low thing this is! What a dishonor to such a soul this is!

If any of you have servants who are of good breeding, good parentage, who are of excellent parts, who have lived long with you, who have skill in your trade, if you should set them to do nothing but pick straws, they would account it a great dishonor put upon them. Truly, what do you do with these precious immortal souls of yours that are worth so much, even more than the world, but employ them in such poor things, even to pick straws, as it were? If a man had pearls, and every one of them was worth a kingdom, and if he knew no other use to make of them than to stop holes in mud walls, one would think it to be great folly in him, so a great dishonor put upon those pearls that are of so much worth. Why, every one of your souls are worth more than all the pearls and kingdoms in the world; and for you to do nothing else but spend the strength of your souls about gathering of a little dirt together here in this world is a great dishonor to your souls.

We have a story of Domitian, who was a great emperor, and yet he had such a low and mean spirit that he spent the greatest part of his time catching flies. This is recorded of him as an argument of the lowness and meanness of his spirit, unworthy a man of so great a dignity. Oh, our souls that God has made so high and put such glory upon, what are they busied about in most people? I remember Gregory Nazianzen telling of some, and among others of Origen, to be of the opinion that the souls of men were made altogether at the first creation, and lived as glorious spirits till they sinned against God, and all those that sinned against God were thrust into the bodies of men as into a prison, and those that did not sin live still with God in glory. Jerome, in his 32 Epistle, speaks of that opinion as prevailing. Plato, though a heathen, speaks of the souls of men, and thought that they were made altogether before their bodies, if not from eternity. These men thought the souls of men to be so precious that they could not come into the bodies of men but for their faults, as a punishment to them, because they saw how meanly men's souls lived while they were in their bodies; and therefore they thought it impossible for such a precious soul as a man had to come to live so meanly, were it not for God's anger punishing the soul for some sin or other. Oh, do not dishonor them by employing them about unworthy and low things.

Third, do not dishonor them by defiling them by casting filth and dirt upon them. Would not a prince account himself dishonored to have the filth and dirt of the street to be cast into his face? Certainly, when you defile your soul by sin, you do as vile an act as casting dirt in the face of a prince. There is no prince's body upon earth so excellent as the soul of the poorest and meanest man, no filth in the world so vile as the filth of sin; and by your sin you cast this filth upon your soul, and so smear and defile it. You love to have clean and handsome bodies, and are loath to come into company all smeared and besooted. But how often do you go into the presence of God most abominable and loathsome! Oh, do not put that dishonor upon your souls!

Fourth, do not dishonor your souls by making them drudges to your bodies, by making them to be caterers to provide for the body, and to satisfy the lusts of the flesh. "I have seen," said Solomon, "servants upon horses, and princes walking as servants upon earth" (Ecclesiastes 10:7). This was an evil, Solomon thought; but to see our base, vile bodies set up, and our souls to be brought under as servants and slaves to this body, oh, how vile it is! If you should see a great prince to be made a slave to some houseboy, you would account it a great leaving of his condition, a dishonor put upon him; but while you make your soul to be a slave to your body, it is a great deal worse. Seneca, though he was but a heathen, yet had this notable saying: "I am greater, and born to greater things, than that I should be a drudge to my body, and the slave of my body." A heathen thought himself too great, and born to greater things, than that ever he should bring that soul of his to be a drudge and slave to his body. And indeed, if we knew our souls, we would think so too, and we would never make them drudges to our bodies, merely to satisfy the lusts of the flesh. And yet how many men and women are loath to die only upon this ground, because then they shall have no more satisfaction to the lusts of the flesh? Oh, what dishonor is put upon this precious and excellent soul in this! But it is much more dishonor when you make it a drudge and slave to the devil. It is an evil to have our souls to be slaves to our bodies, but a greater evil to be a slave and drudge to the devil, that the devil should have command of them, and carry them up and down as he pleases. It is reported that Theodosius and another emperor used to call themselves the vassals of Christ. But for those precious souls to be vassals to the devil, this is too great a dishonor that is put upon them.

Fifth, you dishonor your souls by begrudging the time and cost that is spent upon them. How many men and women think the time is lost that is spent upon their souls more immediately! They must indeed sometime pray, and sometime hear the Word, but the time, and all the charge they are at for their souls they look upon almost as lost, and so begrudge it, and so would fain be about something for their bodies. Speak to them about praying in their families, and they have a business to tend to. And what is all their business for but only for their bodies? Indeed, we should rather turn our plea the other way and be loath to spare time for our outward estate rather than for those immortal souls of ours. It is a wonder how anyone who knows the worth of his soul can find in his heart—but upon mere necessity, and out of duty—to spare time for his outward condition. The soul is dishonored when the time and cost that is bestowed about it is grudged, as if it were merely lost and cast away.

Sixth, we dishonor our souls when we do not lay up provision for them against an evil day. This is a dishonor put upon them.

Seventh, you dishonor your souls when you think to satisfy them with anything but God Himself. If you should have any of your quality friends come to your house, and if you should set a bowl of swill before them and think to satisfy their hunger that way, they would think a great dishonor had been done to them. Now if you think to satisfy your souls with anything here but God Himself, you do, as it were, bring bones to set before a prince. It was a speech unworthy of a man which we read of in the gospel concerning rich Dives, "Soul, soul, take thine ease; thou hast goods laid up for many years. Soul, soul, eat, drink, and take thine ease." Why, what did that have to do with eating and drinking? How unworthy was this, I say, of one who had an immortal soul thus to speak. Oh, this is a great dishonor that is put upon the soul!

Now learn in a right way to put honor upon your souls, to love them, to make them your darlings, and to manifest your love to your souls.

1. You can do this by having your thoughts often upon them. We manifest our love to a friend by having our thoughts run upon him. Oh, let your thoughts run much upon your souls: "I am thus and thus in regard of my outward estate; in regard of my body, through God's mercy, I have all my limbs and senses, and comfortable provision for it. Oh, but my soul, how is it with you?" Be often conferring with your souls, as you

know one friend loves to confer with another. Can you say that you love such a friend who is your next neighbor, and never spend any time in conference together, scarcely ever speak one with another? Certainly so it is with the souls of men: they think but little of the terms that their souls are in with God, of what conditions their souls are in, whether good or bad. And the day is yet to come wherein many a man has spent one half hour in confession with his soul, to know how terms stand between his soul and Almighty God. Oh, love your souls by thinking on them, and thinking often of what should become of them.

2. Love your souls by making them empresses of your bodies, by keeping your bodies under them. Those whom the Scripture sets out unto us who have had the most precious souls have ever more beat down their bodies and kept them low. Paul was one of the most precious, spirited men who ever lived upon the face of the earth, yet he said, "I beat down my body. I beat it black and blue lest, after I have preached to others, I myself become a reprobate." He did not think his happiness to consist in pampering his body, no, but he beat it down; and therein he showed his love for his soul in that he made his soul to be empress, as it were.

It is the speech of a learned man upon these words in our text, "Subdue the earth (that is, your body and all earthly things) to your spiritual part, your soul." If one should tell you how hardly the ancient martyrs, those worthy instruments of God who were precious men in their time, used their bodies, you would hardly believe it. But this is certain, there were never any who knew the true worth of their souls but they made them the empresses of their bodies. Ambrose said of Valentinian, "No man was ever such a servant to his master as Valentinian's body was to his soul." Bring your bodies down, and therein you will show the greatest love unto your souls.

3. Labor to put comeliness and beauty upon your souls as much as you can, and therein you will show love and respect for them. Adorn them with those graces that may make them amiable and lovely in the eyes of God Himself. 1 Peter 5:5: "Be clothed with humility." Those who understand the Greek language know it to be a word that signifies a dress that gentle-women used to have upon their heads with ribands, such as they used to wear in those days; and so they thought themselves very comely, and the apostle alludes to those kind of dresses. Oh, humility is the finest dress for a woman in the world, and so for men too! The finest clothes that you can put upon you are the clothes of humility; and so any grace of God's Spirit is the clothing of the soul. Oh, therefore, show your love for your souls by laboring to deck and adorn them with such clothing as this is.

4. Show your love for your souls by providing for them while God affords the means; labor to understand the want of your souls, and be willing to be at any charge and cost for their good. If your head aches, or if you have any little pain in any of your members, how you are willing to be at a great deal of charge so that you may have ease for your bodies? Now look out for your souls. The one is a sign that you love your bodies well, and the other will be a sign that you love your souls as well.

5. Show love for your souls in the excellency of things that are suitable to them, in conversing with God and Jesus Christ, with the mysteries of the gospel, and with heavenly things.

6. Show your love for them in laboring to attain the end that they were made for, the uttermost happiness that they are capable of. Then indeed you show true love for your souls when your care is to bring them to attain the end that God made them for. Certainly, when God made a creature of so much excellency, He intended a glorious end for it. And let

this now be your great care, and manifest your love for your souls by laboring to attain the end that God made them for. But this shall suffice for the first point, of the preciousness and excellency of our souls.

SERMON 3

The Loss of the Soul
Is a Dreadful Loss

We come now to the second doctrinal point, and that is the main point indeed in the text.

DOCTRINE 2: The loss of this soul is a most dreadful loss.

"Skin for skin, yea, all that a man hath will he give for his life." Even the devil himself could say so. The loss of bodily life we account a great evil; and therefore the Scripture calls death by the name of "the king of terror." Is it so great an evil to lose a bodily life, to have the soul and body be separated? Is the face of a bodily death so ghastly? Oh, how great an evil, and how ghastly is the face of eternal death, and the loss of the immortal soul! This point, my brethren, is a point of exceedingly great concern to understand. We shall therefore:

First, inquire what we mean by the loss of the soul, or when the soul may be said to be lost.

Second, inquire wherein the dreadfulness of the loss of the soul consists.

Third, I shall discover to you some aggravations of the evil of the loss of the soul.

Fourth, we shall apply all.

QUESTION. What does Christ mean when He says, "What profiteth it a man if he gain the whole world, and lose his soul?"

ANSWER. First, know that we are not said to lose our souls because they shall be annihilated and cease to be; the ceasing of the soul to be is not the loss of the soul; the ceasing indeed of our bodily lives is the loss of our lives, but it is not so with the soul, for the soul of no man or woman shall be lost so.

Yea, and this would not be the greatest loss for the soul to cease to be. There are two degrees of evil that are beyond the evil of ceasing to be: to be miserable, to be in pain and torture, is worse than not to be; and to be sinful is worse than to be in pain. Therefore, ceasing to be is not the greatest evil. So what is the loss of the soul then?

First, the loss of the soul is in the privation of it, in all the good and excellency that the soul is capable of, the privation of the true good that the soul was made for.

Second, it consists in its departing and wandering from God. As a sheep is said to be a lost sheep that wanders up and down in the wilderness, so that is a lost soul that wanders away from God, the Fountain of all good.

Third, it consists in subjecting it to that misery and evil that is contrary to what good it is capable of.

And then fourth, it consists in the succorless and helpless condition that it is brought into. We speak of being "lost to all these things." When a man has lost his estate, we account such a man as a lost man; and when a man is brought into a great deal of misery, who heretofore was in a great deal of happiness, we account such a man to be a lost man. But especially, when a man is succorless and helpless, when he has no way to help and relieve himself, then he is a lost man indeed. And according to the degrees of these four things, then a soul may be said to be lost. And here for the present every man and woman's soul in the world by nature is a lost soul.

First, every man and woman, as they come into the world, is deprived of the glory and excellency that God endowed the souls of men with in their first creation. We are all deprived of the glory of God, Scripture says.

Second, all souls now naturally wander away from God; they continually depart and wander from the infinite, glorious first Being of all things. You who are an old man or woman, who have lived many years, and God has not revealed Himself in working the true work of conversion in you, to change your estate, know that your soul has been departing and wandering from the Lord all the days of your life to this very moment. You are like a lost sheep, wandering up and down in the wilderness, and in danger of being destroyed every minute of every hour by some wild beast or another. Though your soul has not been made a prey to the devil so as to destroy you utterly, yet you have been in danger all the while that you have been wandering from the Lord to be preyed upon by the devil, and utterly to have been cast away.

Yea, and third, there is a great deal of misery upon your soul if you know that, contrary to the light that He has set up in your understanding, there is blindness in you; there is error in you. Contrary to that holiness that was at first in thy heart and soul, there is nothing but sin and wickedness. All the spawns and seeds of all kind of sin are in your heart. There is a great deal of that evil that is contrary to what your soul was made with at first; there is enmity in your soul against God Himself.

Yea, and fourth, your soul is in a succorless, helpless, shiftless condition in respect of what you are able to do, or what all the creatures in heaven or earth are able to do for you. Let all the angels in heaven and all the men in the world join together to seek to do good to your soul, they are not able to deliver your soul from that evil that it is now in, and that it is in further danger of. This is the reason for the phrase that you have in Luke 19:10: "The Son of man is come to seek and to save that which was lost." We are all lost sheep going astray, and Jesus Christ came to seek and to save lost souls, souls deprived of the glory of God, souls wandering away from God, souls filled with evil, souls succorless and helpless in regard of any power in any creature in heaven and earth to save them. Christ beheld how such precious souls were every one of them lost, and He came to save them. He was pleased to come from heaven to seek and to save souls thus lost.

Now though souls are for the present in a lost condition, yet there is a further loss of the soul than this; for if the soul is neglected here, it will be lost forever. There are many who are lost for the present; and yet afterwards Christ finds them, and there is joy in heaven at His finding them. But there is a loss that shall be eternal, and that loss is more dreadful than the former, yet the soul has the degree of it, but not the perfection of the former.

Now the loss of the soul in hell consists in these three particulars:

1. The full and perfect eternal rejection of the soul from God, and from all good in Him, together with the fullness of all kind of evil that the soul is capable of—this is the condition of a lost soul that perishes.

2. It consists in making this soul to be perfectly sensible of the loss of that good, and of all the evil it is possessed with, mak-

ing it perfectly sensible of it. Here men and women are in lost conditions, but they do not know it; they are not sensible of it. But God will bring the soul into such a condition that it shall be made perfectly sensible of the loss of all the good that it might have had, and of all the evil that is upon it.

3. It shall be in such a condition, so succorless, so helpless, that it is not only beyond the power of angels, and all men to help it, but so succorless, so lost, that God's mercy, and all the good there is in Christ, shall never save it, and as God has set and ordered things, can never save it.

Now then these things being opened to you, you will understand what this text means. When you read this text you think there may be truth in it, and in general you will assent unto it; but if you come to understand but these things, then indeed you cannot but all subscribe to it and acknowledge it. Oh, it is indeed a dreadful thing, the loss of the soul! But because it is a point of so great importance, I will not satisfy myself merely in telling you these things, but will endeavor to open unto you what the evil of this loss is so that if, it might be, by presenting this before the souls of men, they may see more the danger that they are in, and how the devil has gulled and deceived them all this while. It may make many souls to be at a standstill if they come to know what this loss indeed means.

I shall endeavor to open this in the three last particulars that I named:

I shall speak to the rejection of the soul from God so as to be deprived of all the good there is in God, and that it is capable of. For the understanding of the evil of this, we must inquire what is that good that the souls of men are capable of, or else we cannot come to understand what an evil thing it is to lose it.

As for the good that the soul is capable of, I will but only name some headings unto you, for in a treatise that some of you have in your hands, of Moses looking to the recompense of reward [*Moses' Choice*], there are the principal headings of the good and excellency that the soul is capable of, and shall be blessed in heaven eternally with. Apprehending the loss of these things will discover much of the evil of the loss of the soul. I will but in a very brief way present unto you the glory of God upon the soul, the image of God, the life of God, and the divine nature that the soul is capable of.

Now for the soul never to live the life of God; not to have His image, nor any of the glory of God upon it, is a fearful evil to those who know the excellency of these things; of the blessed vision of God in heaven, to see Him who is the infinite first Being of all things, to see Him as He is, to see Him who has all excellency in Him, and to see all the good there is in God as the good of the soul. The soul is capable of understanding the mind of God, to have all the glorious counsels of God about His works and ways that He has had from all eternity to be revealed unto, so far as concerns it, and as in any way may make it happy. To live to see what the ways of God have been from all eternity, and what they shall be to all eternity, and that for the good of this soul, so that it may be forever in His presence, and to stand and look upon His face and see Him as its Portion, oh, this must be a glorious thing! Certainly, if the presence of God put such a glory upon the heavens, it must put an abundance of glory upon the soul that shall stand immediately always in His presence. To have eternal communion with God, that is, to have the embraces of God, embracing the soul and delighting Himself in it above all other His works but the angels and His Son; delighting Himself in the soul and embracing it, communicating and letting out Himself in all His luster and glory when He shall have enlarged the soul to be able to the uttermost to receive that glory that He has to communicate; and for Him to converse with the souls of men to all eternity in a familiar way, as one friend with another; for the soul to be letting itself out again to God (for that is communion, God's letting Himself out to the soul, and the soul letting itself out back again to God); now, I say, it is the greatest delight God has in Himself, His Son, and Spirit, and angels, letting Himself out to the souls of men (those who shall be saved).

On the other side, it must be an infinite delight to the soul to always be letting itself out to God. What delight do men take in eating and drinking? Now if there is such delight in the palate meeting with a piece of meat in the mouth because of the suitableness between one object and another, oh, what delight must there be when this immortal, precious soul, being enlarged to the uttermost with all excellency, shall meet with an infinite God, the infinite first Being of all things, as the most suitable object, and to be letting itself out to God, and God letting Himself out to it again.

Again, the good that the soul is capable of with God is to have a union with God, for the soul to be made one with God, to be united so as to be made one with Him. "He that is joined to the Lord is one Spirit," said the apostle. And Christ said in John 17, "Father, I will that those that Thou hast given Me may be one with Me, as Thou and I are one." Spiritual things most unite one to another; there may be a thousand beams of the sun united, and almost into one point, because it is of a more spiritual nature. So when the soul shall be made one Spirit with God, it being a spirit, and God likewise a Spirit, there will be an exact union one with another. And so the more spiritual things are, the more they communicate one to another. In nature, the more corporeal a thing is, the less it communicates itself. The earth does not communicate itself with any nature; the water communicates itself more than that, and the air more than that, and the fire more than that. The sun is less corporeal than any of these elements that we have here, and therefore it communicates itself more than the element does. Now God being a Spirit, and the souls of men being spiritual, oh, what a communion will there be of each to the other!

The soul is capable of fruition of God. Union, communion, and fruition? What is that, you will say? That is to have God not only to be united to it, but to have a kind of possession of Him, to have the use of all that there is in God that can make me happy, to have the full use of it when I will. Man enjoys a thing when he can have the use of such a thing whenever he will. The souls of the saints shall enjoy God, that is, they shall have the use of all the glory and good there is in God that can make them happy whenever they will, and shall have as much use of God as they will. Surely they must be happy who shall thus enjoy God. If a man had the fruition of the world, so that he could have the use of all the good things in the world whenever he would, you would think him to be happy. But this is the happiness of the souls of the saints: they shall have such a fruition of God that they shall have all the use of God that they will, and when they will.

Fruition has in it a reflect act. Though a man has a great deal of riches given to him, yet if he does not know this, or if he knows it and yet does not have the comfort of it, he does not enjoy it. Such a man, though he is born to a great deal, yet if he has not the reflect act to know that he has it, he does not enjoy it. So we enjoy but little of God now because God, though He is the portion of a gracious heart, yet the heart does not know this fully. But when knowledge shall be perfect, then the soul shall perfectly know what good there is in God, and how far my soul may be and is happy in the enjoyment of this God. I shall know how to make use of God to the fullest, and shall have continually the comfort of all that good there is in God.

The presence and communion with Jesus Christ that the soul shall have, besides that of God the Father, shall be in being with Him where He is. It is a blessed thing here "to follow the Lamb whithersoever He goes," but to always be with Him, to always have fruition of Him, and to have communion likewise with all the saints and angels, and all the blessed spirits, is a blessed thing indeed. I remember reading that Cato, when he was about to die, said, "O blessed day, for now I shall go to the souls of wise men and philosophers." And so, upon that ground, he accounted the day of his death a blessed day because he would go to have communion with the souls of philosophers and wise men. But how blessed is it then for our souls to have communion eternally with angels and blessed spirits? "You are come to an innumerable company of angels, and the spirits of just men made perfect" (Hebrews 12:22–23). When a soul is converted, it comes to have some kind of communion with an innumerable company of angels, and with the spirits of just men made perfect. It has the assurance of it here, and shall have the enjoyment fully and perfectly hereafter.

The continual exercise that the soul shall be busied in will be to forever be blessing, magnifying, praising, and worshipping God, receiving in from God and letting itself out to God. The eternal Sabbath that it shall keep, and then the eternal rest that the soul shall have when it comes to God, comes there to its center; there it has perfect peace and rest, and can never have trouble further.

Yea, and it shall live in God; not only God live in it, but it shall live in God. Though the similitude comes short of it, as the fish swim in the sea, so the soul shall be swimming in the infinite ocean of the excellency of the great God. It is said that John was "in the Spirit on the Lord's day" (Revelation 1:10). So the soul shall live in God. "Our life is hid with Christ in God" (Colossians 3:3). But our life shall be plain and apparent, not hidden, but apparent before angels, and all the rest of the blessed; and so our lives shall be after another manner than now they are.

Now to open every one of these things would be very large, so that it suffices now only to present them to you to show in a short view the good of the soul in the full enjoyment of God, and what it shall have from Him, so that you may see what the loss of the soul means. Now if these things are true and real, oh, what a dreadful thing it is for a man to lose his soul, for a man to come to lose all this good that others who have souls like him shall come to enjoy, and that he might have enjoyed as well as others! If there were no more in the loss of the soul than to be cast away from the good that it is capable of, it might show unto us this loss to be very dreadful.

It was a speech of Augustine's long ago, speaking of that place where Dives desired Lazarus to come with one drop of water to cool his tormented tongue, that if there should be but one drop of heavenly felicity let into hell, it would quench all the fires of hell immediately. Chrysostom had such an expression, that he would rather suffer thousands of years in pain and torment in hell than he would lose the good that he might have in the enjoyment of God. He accounted the loss of God to be the greater evil. And it would be a good sign of a soul that understood its own excellency, and what good it were capable of, to fear as much the loss of God, and what good it might have in God, and to account that as great an evil to it as pain, horror, and torment.

Why, when we come to express the wrath of God to you,

and the evil that sin deserves, we speak of hellfire, and so does the Scriptures. If we would set out the great evil of punishment (when we speak to men and women who are led by sense), we tell them of their bodies being thousands of years in scalding lead, and kept alive there; and this would startle and amaze them. But certainly the evil of the soul's rejection from God, and being cast off from the good that there is in God, is as great, if not a greater evil. And it would be a good sign that God is going to show what our souls are to us, and the true excellency of them, if we begin to be affected with the loss of God Himself, and the good we might have in God—not only afraid of hell because of fire and torment there, but afraid of having our souls lost because we are afraid of being deprived of such infinite good as otherwise we might come to enjoy with God. A gracious heart has more thought about losing the good that there is in God than of the pain that he should feel in hell.

Let me set it out a little in this resemblance, of the eye being deprived of light. An eye that has beheld the glory of the heavens and of the creatures, though it should never have any pain, but only such an ill humor as to take away all light from it, why, what hurt is here done to the eye? It is only the absence of a good thing; the eye feels no pain. But what man in the world would not rather be willing to have his eyes to see, and not to be blind all his life time, than to have the enjoyment of thousands of gold and silver? Now if the bare absence of the sight of a man's eyes is so great an evil, and he would rather endure almost any pain rather than have his eyes deprived of the light, then certainly the absence of God must be a most dreadful evil to the soul. When the sun shines in its luster, how beautiful it is. And how pleasant is that compared to when it is midnight, when it is dismally dark? Why, what is done? It is only the absence of one thing, the sun that shines gloriously upon us; and at midnight the sun is gone. So what a mighty change and alteration would there be in the soul if it should be deprived of the presence of the Lord? If the Lord, who is infinite in glory, is present with the soul, and shines upon it to all eternity, how glorious will it be! But if God withdraws Himself fully and everlastingly from the soul, what a dismal night of darkness will there be! And therefore it is a most dreadful thing for the soul of a man to be lost in regard of this first particular, in regard of the privation of that good that it is capable of.

The Eternal Loss of the Soul

*"For what is a man profited if he shall gain
the whole world and lose his own soul? Or what shall
a man give in exchange for his soul?"*

MATTHEW 16:26

The eternal loss of the soul consists in this: when the soul in hell is so possessed with sin as to be contrary unto God eternally. The soul cast away from God is possessed of all the evil of sin so as to hate God, to abhor Him, and to blaspheme Him. That is one particular of the condition of a lost soul.

As every soul here by nature is deprived of all that goodness in which it was created, and as it wanders from and is at enmity against God, so, when the soul is lost eternally it is perfectly against God, and hates and blasphemes God forever. You who are a wicked man, you will sin; but when God has cast you away

240

from Him eternally, then you shall have your belly full of sin; you then shall be fully given up unto sin. Revelation 16:11: "And they blasphemed the God of heaven because of their pains and sorrows." That is spoken of the beast, of antichrist; but if men here blaspheme God because of their pains, what shall they do who are damned in hell, they who shall have the vials of God's wrath poured out upon them?

QUESTION. How does it appear that for the wicked to be given up to sin is such an evil unto them, whereas here it is their delight to commit sin?

ANSWER. Though they love sin, and though sin is their delight here, yet hereafter, when they are cast off from God forever, then they shall not find that delight in sin as now they do. To give you an example, put a fish into a pot of water, and the fish swims, plays, and delights therein because it is the proper element of the fish to be in the water. But if you put fire under that pot of water wherein the fish plays and takes delight, then that which before was the delight and element of the fish thereby becomes its pain and torture. So though sin in this life is delightful unto wicked men, because it is their proper element to be in sin in this life, yet afterwards sin shall be their pain because then the wrath of God shall be mixed with it, which will make it pain and torture.

Again, the loss of the soul consists in this, when the soul is fully possessed of all the evils that are contrary to all the good it is capable of. Thus shall it be with the lost soul eternally.

As the saints shall be enlarged and made more capable of good (which they shall enjoy to all eternity) so those who are wicked and lost souls, which souls shall be opposite to God, shall be enlarged in their capacities, and be possessed and made capable of all contrary evils.

First, they shall be cast under the eternal curse of God. They shall be eternally under the curse of the Almighty.

Second, they shall have all the faculties of the soul be filled with the wrath of God; they shall have the understanding to be filled with what may increase torment in it. As for the conscience, they shall have the worm gnawing, that never dies; and they shall have their thoughts employed and running upon those things that will be so hideous unto them, and shall have the will continually crossed by God Himself; they shall have the heart sinking under the wrath of the infinite God in despair forever. Brethren, the soul of man is a very large vessel; and because we know but little of the large extent of our souls, therefore it is that we are so little sensible of the loss of them, or of the pain and torment they are capable of or liable unto. But as the soul is larger than the body to take in comfort, so is it larger than the body likewise to take in pain, misery, and wrath. We should be sensible of such an expression as this, to have all the members of the body to be filled with fire, so as to be on a hot, fiery, burning coal, and that to all eternity. This you would think could not but be an extreme misery. But the soul's capacity is far larger than the body's. And to have the soul filled in its every faculty with the wrath of God is far greater pain than to have the body in such a condition, which is the condition of a lost soul.

Further, it consists in having the power of God stretched forth to bring evil and wrath upon it, and that to the uttermost. Romans 9:22: "What if God, willing to show His wrath, and to make His power known, endured with much longsuffering the vessels of wrath fitted unto destruction?"

The infinite power of God is put forth in enlarging their natures, so that they may be more capable of evil.

The infinite power of God is put forth to uphold their

natures, so that they be not sunk down with those dreadful evils that God has to put upon them.

The infinite power of God lets out upon the soul whatever it can bear to make it miserable, so as not to be annihilated therewith, which it shall bear forever. And further, a lost soul is to be continually under the stroke of God's justice. When it has lain under its pains for thousands of thousands of years, divine justice says, "I am not yet satisfied."

Now this that is required is so that the soul should lie under the wrath of God until such time that God may have as much honor by punishing it as He has had dishonor by its sinning against Him. And that must be forever because God can never have as much honor by punishing it as He has had dishonor by its sinning against Him. And as the soul should have had eternal communion with God and Christ, it, being lost, must have communion instead thereof with the devil and the damned spirits in hell. And if this is the condition of a lost soul in hell, as it is, then what shall a man gain in gaining the world if he loses his soul?

But further, to make this misery appear to be misery indeed, there is required a perfect sense of all these evils; for a man or woman may be in a lost condition, as many are now, but they do not understand it, and therefore are not sensible of it.

But the soul that is lost eternally, the Lord shall so far enlighten its understanding as may make it sensible of all its evil. Certainly many this day are in such a condition, and if they understood the lost condition they are in it would make them tremble. But when the soul is eternally lost, it shall then perfectly understand what its lost condition is; and then the thoughts of its mind shall be so busied about its misery that it shall not be able to ease itself one moment, but its thoughts shall be busied about its condition, so far as may make it miserable. And the Lord is

GOSPEL REVELATION

able to make a creature as sensible of misery as He pleases; for it is the propriety of God to make a creature as sensible of all the evil that is upon him as He pleases; and if so, then when all these evils come upon the creature, and the Lord intends to make the creature fully sensible of it, then certainly it must be miserable indeed.

Further, then, this loss of the soul consists in that it must have nothing to support it when the burden of the wrath of the infinite God shall be thus upon it. Also, there shall be no mixture of any good to bring relief or ease, nor any intermission of time; it must not be one moment of time out of this condition of misery, but must be in it continually to all eternity.

Further, its misery consists in this, because God will keep all the faculties of the lost soul in their utmost activity, whereas now it is not so with us; for if misery and pain are upon us here, after a while our activity and sensibleness of it are partly gone. But the Lord will make such souls as are eternally lost as perfectly sensible of this misery every moment as ever they were the very first moment they went into that misery.

Last, in regard of the irrecoverableness of the lostness of the soul once it is lost, the soul, when it has departed from the body, then all the power of God can never help nor recover it; but then the stream of God's wrath shall carry it with that mighty force so that it shall not be able to all eternity to have the least actings of itself towards its deliverance forever.

There shall be no Mediator between God and the lost soul, none to mediate for it. Now, had not we a Mediator between God and us, we would all be certainly lost. But for the soul that is once lost eternally, Jesus Christ will never tender up any work of mediation for such a soul; that soul is certainly gone and lost irrecoverably. And the gates of mercy will forever be shut against such a soul.

For to further open and set forth the dreadfulness of the loss of the soul, there are divers aggravations wherein the misery of it will further appear:

1. If the soul is thus lost, then the body is and will be lost also. It will bring the body into the very same lost condition of misery that it is in itself, so far as it is capable of misery. And that will be so upon these two grounds:

First, because the body, all the time a man lived in this world, was the only or most immediate instrument that the soul had to work and to sin by. And certainly God must have that body and curse it that belonged to the soul, because it was the only instrument of the soul to sin by.

Second, the body must be miserable also because when such a lost soul shall be united unto the body, the very extremity of the soul must bring misery upon the body also. For example, when Christ had the apprehensions of His Father's wrath and displeasure in His soul, how did it work upon His body even so as to cause clots of blood to fall from Him? Now, what caused this pain in His body but the terrors of God in His soul? And if it was so with Jesus Christ, who only had sin imputed unto Him, then certainly the body of a damned creature must be in very great and dreadful torment, to which this soul is united. A holy man cried out, "Thy arrows stick fast in me, and Thy hand presseth me sore; there is no soundness in my flesh because of Thine anger. Neither is there any rest in my bones because of my sin" (Psalm 38:2–3). If the anger of God caused this misery to David's body for his sin, what misery will that be when all the faculties of the soul shall be filled with the wrath of God to their utmost capacity? Oh, I say, what dreadful evil and pain will there be unto the body united to such a soul!

2. When the soul comes to be in this lost condition, then it

must come to be in the most dreadful and most miserable condition that ever any creature is in except the devils themselves.
The Scripture tells us that it is an evil thing to have "riches kept
for a man's hurt." But then what an evil is it, and will it be, for
a man to have an immortal soul for his hurt? This is the condition of a lost soul.

3. The soul will have none to pity it in that miserable lost
condition it is in. If a man in this world should lose his estate,
or any great loss, he would have many to pity him. If a man loses
by fire, then he may obtain a gathering whereby his loss may be
partly made up or be relieved. If you lose your children, you
have your friends to pity you and to console you. But the man
who shall have his soul lost shall be in such a condition as he
shall have none to pity him.

True, we are all lost by nature, but in our lost condition we
have God and Christ pitying us, the angels looking upon us with
pity, and the saints pitying us. But hereafter, if lost, none shall
pity the soul in that condition when its loss is eternal. God shall
not pity it; but then the blessed God shall look upon it as an
object of His eternal curse. But no pity shall be had for souls in
their lost condition; neither shall Jesus Christ pity them. True,
Jesus Christ came to seek and to save those who were naturally
lost, but you have done what in you lay to frustrate the ends of
Christ's coming. And as Christ shall not pity you, so mercy itself
shall not pity you, but be so far from pitying you that it shall
plead against you.

Angels shall not pity you, because they shall be taken up in
blessing and praising God for His works, and for His righteous
judgments upon you.

Neither shall the saints pity you. Though it be your father,
out of whose loins you came; though it be your mother, out of
whose womb you came, yet they shall not pity you, though you

are lost, and lost eternally, but shall rejoice at it and bless God for His justice upon you. Therefore the condition of a lost soul is miserable.

4. The loss of the soul will prove unto most who are lost to be an unexpected loss. There are very few who have any apprehensions of the loss of their souls, but they think they may go on in sin and yet do well enough. It may be that you hear a minister speak of the loss of the soul, but you flatter yourself and think that you shall do well enough. But at length, before you are aware, your soul may be lost, and that unexpectedly. Then it must be dreadful because it is so great and unexpected. For example, if a merchant should hear that his stock in the Indies was safe and well there, and afterwards there should come news unexpectedly that all is lost and gone, how it dampens him! And consider that it will dampen you hereafter, though now you flatter yourself, if your soul should be lost eternally. It will be a dreadful loss in regard of the unexpectedness of it.

5. It will prove to be a dreadful loss because the loss of every soul that shall be lost will prove to be a willful loss. This is a great perplexity to a man in this world, when he sees that he is undone, and that merely through his own willfulness. This will be the aggravation of the soul's loss, at the day when it shall plainly appear unto them that it was through their own willfulness.

"Ye will not come to Me" (John 5:40), said Christ, "that ye might have life," and you will not endure to hear of the danger you are in of being lost eternally. Oh, how willful must the lost of those souls be, who will not give ear to hear of the danger their souls are in of being thus lost! How willfully you run on in wicked courses, which God hath given command unto the contrary in His Word! How willfully you cast off the means that God has appointed for your salvation! But know that you perish willfully, if you willfully reject or neglect to improve the means that God has given for the saving of your souls. I say, that man or woman who shall willfully cast off those truths of God that would save them willfully perishes.

OBJECTION. But I do not sin willfully, but am overtaken with sin.
ANSWER. A man sins willfully when all that is in God's Word that has been given to persuade him not to sin does not prevail but outward, carnal motives do. He sins willfully and, if he perishes, he will be found to perish willfully.

OBJECTION. I am ignorant, and if I knew better I would do better.
ANSWER. Yet it is willful, because you are willfully ignorant; and therefore your loss is willful.

6. The loss of the soul is aggravated because the eternal loss of the soul will be a great loss for a little matter. For a man to venture the loss of his soul to gain a kingdom, he would think it something; yet the text tells us he would be a great loser. But if he is so great a loser to gain a kingdom for his soul, then how great an evil will it be for a man or woman to lose their souls for trifles! You do not get the world for your souls, but perhaps you venture the loss of your souls to get sixpence, or twopence. It may be that, upon the fear of the displeasure or anger of your master or mistress, you will venture the loss of your souls in telling a lie to excuse you. It may be that to satisfy a base lust for one quarter of an hour, you will venture the eternal loss of a precious soul, which is worth more than ten thousand worlds.

Did you never go into the place where condemned persons were, and ask them what they are there for? Why, it may be some of them will say that is was but for a small matter; it may be the undue gaining of two or three shillings, and now their life must go for it. So many lose their souls for trifles, for nothing, for a base lust, which is worse than nothing. The consideration of this will make it the more dreadful.

7. The loss of the soul will be very dreadful because many will lose their souls who are very nigh to saving their souls. The nearer a man or woman comes to saving their souls and yet loses them, the loss of the soul upon that consideration will be more dreadful to them. And it is thus with many who have many good workings in and upon their hearts, so that they are in a very good forwardness unto the everlasting salvation of their souls. And yet there comes some lust that drives them back again. The loss of the souls of hypocrites, therefore, will be dreadful to consider: "I was in so fair a way to salvation in the use of means, and content to leave so many evil ways, and yet I had one that I would not leave, and for this have I lost my soul. I was content to take up so many duties, and yet by my heart's embracing one sinful lust I have lost my soul." Herod heard John the Baptist gladly and reformed many things, and yet he had one sin that he would not part with. Those who are nearest the salvation of their souls, and yet lose them at last, this will be a great aggravation of the misery thereof.

8. An eighth aggravation of the loss of the soul is the consideration that they have lost their souls, and that so that they have nothing in lieu of them; they shall not only lose their souls, but they shall even lose the thing for which they ventured the loss of their souls. For example, if a man should have his heart so set upon a trifle as to lose his whole estate for it, and after he has lost his estate he should lose that thing for which he lost his estate too, this would aggravate the loss of his estates much more. Just so, if you lose your souls for the world or for plea-

250   Gospel Revelation

sure, if your souls perish, yet you shall lose both your souls and that thing, be it what it will, for which you ventured and lost your souls.

And you shall have no more pleasure or content than those who ventured the loss of their souls for it.

9. The ninth aggravation of the loss of the soul is the shame that shall be put upon those souls who shall be lost, who perish eternally. This shall take place when your acquaintances, your neighbors who dwelled next to you, who knew you, who dwelled in the family with you, who kept fast days with you, and went to the meetings with you; when they shall be those who shall be with God forever, eternally blessing and praising Him, and shall point you out with their finger before God, angels, and blessed saints, and shall say, "Behold, this is he who was a hypocrite, who sat under the same Word, and who partook of the same means and ordinance as I did, and yet he has lost his soul"; when they shall say, "Lo, this is the man that made not God his stay" (Psalm 52:7). So all they who perish shall stand before men and angels, and be pointed at by them, saying, "Lo, this is the man, and lo, that is the woman, who did not make God their strength, but who so loved their sin that they would not by any means be persuaded to part with it, but would rather venture the loss of their souls to enjoy their sins and fulfill their lust rather than part with their sins to save their souls."

10. The tenth aggravation of the misery of a lost soul will be when they shall see others taken up into the kingdom of heaven who were as unlikely to be saved as themselves, and they themselves shut out and eternally lost. It may be that you who are a carnal master may see your poor servant taken up to God, and you yourself shut out. It may be that the carnal father or mother may see their child saved, and yet they themselves lost. Oh, this will be a sad aggravation of their loss! And thus

you have heard the dreadful loss of the soul, together with the aggravations thereof in these ten particulars.

SERMON 5

The Application

*"For what is a man profited if he shall gain
the whole world and lose his own soul? Or what shall
a man give in exchange for his soul?"*

MATTHEW 16:26

USE 1. Is it so that the loss of the soul eternally is so dreadful a loss, as you have heard it is? Oh, then let everyone here bless God that their souls are not thus lost! It might have been so long ere this time when such a kinsman of yours died, or your fellow servant, or when such a neighbor or acquaintance of yours died. If you had died when they died, your soul might have been eternally lost.

This I can assure you, that naturally you are all lost; and what makes the difference between your soul and the condition of a lost soul, as you have heard, but the mere mercy of God? Oh, therefore bless God for His mercy unto you, that your soul is not as yet a lost soul! Think thus with yourself: "Lord, if these things are true, and so dreadful to hear of, then what would be my misery if it should prove that I should be the person made sensible thereof, experiencing the misery I hear of, to be the miserable condition of a lost soul?"

The Scripture says, concerning the joy and happiness of the saints, that "eye hath not seen, nor ear heard, neither hath it entered into the heart of man" to conceive what the happiness shall be of those who shall be saved (1 Corinthians 2:9). And the like may be said of the misery of the souls who are eternally lost. The Scriptures say that "if our Gospel be hid, it is hid to them that are lost" (2 Corinthians 4:3). I beseech you, therefore, to remember what has been spoken concerning the condition of lost souls, and lay to heart what has been spoken out of the text, lest within a little time you feel what has been spoken to be a truth, and so be forced to cry out, "True it is, I heard such a day out of such a text what the miserable condition of a soul eternally lost was. But now I find it by experience to be true, and the one half that I now feel, I could not then conceive."

And the reason, my brethren, why I lay the misery of lost souls thus before you is to the end that none of you might be thus lost. It is a blessed thing for you to hear these things; for how many are there who have lost their souls who, till they were thus lost, never so much as heard anything about the loss of their souls, which, if they had, who knows what might have been done by them for the saving of their souls? Beloved, such a subject as this cannot be spoken unto you without trembling; for certainly this subject will be much adding to the prevention of the loss, or else it will mightily aggravate the loss of your souls, if ever they are eternally lost. Therefore, all I have at present to counsel you is to lay these things to your hearts seriously, as also to bless God for your souls, that as yet they are not in this dreadful, eternally lost condition.

USE 2. If the loss of our souls is as dreadful as you have heard, bless God that your souls are not gone and thus lost, as has been opened unto you. It may be that you have lost your husband, your wife, your child, your friend, or a great part of your estate; but blessed be God that your soul is not lost. In a great fire, men usually lose most if not all that they have; and when a man comes to view what he has lost and finds that he has lost this thing that was in such a parlor, and that which was in such a chest; but if at length he finds that such a jewel that he had in the house, or such a bag of gold, in which most of his estate consisted, is not lost, though all the lumber, all the household stuff is lost, that comforts him in all other of his losses. So it should be here: whatever we lose, we are to be comforted in this, that our souls are not gone and lost. It is a notable Scripture in 1 Peter 4:19: "Wherefore let them that suffer according to the will of God commit the keeping of their souls to Him in well doing, as unto a faithful Creator." It is as if the apostle should say, "You are likely to meet with great sufferings; you may likely be deprived of all that you have, of your estates, and of all your comforts, and may come to suffer much—yet commit the keeping of your souls to Him as well doing, as unto a faithful Creator."

OBJECTION. "Why," they might have said, "but what shall become of other things? If storms, and tempests, and sufferings come, what shall become of our estates? What shall become of our livelihoods and of our bodies?"
ANSWER. "Why," says the apostle, "as for them, for your estates, for your bodies, it may be that they perish. You are not so much to look after them, but commit the keeping of your souls unto Him, as unto a faithful Creator." The apostle here exhorts them what to do in times of sufferings, and by what he expresses he implies that they should take no care for outward

estate or body. "It is enough that your souls are well; commit the keeping of your souls to Him, as unto a faithful Creator. We have enough if that is safe."

You know that in time of danger, such as fires and at other times, if a man has any precious thing, he carries that immediately to some special friend and commits the keeping of it to him. An example might be his writings, and such things wherein his estate most consists. So, says the apostle, in the time of public danger, take care to commit the keeping of your souls to Him, as unto a faithful Creator, and you are well enough.

USE 3. If the loss of the soul is so dreadful a loss, let us bless God then for Jesus Christ, without whom all our souls would have been eternally lost. Never has there been a soul in all the world but must have perished unto all eternity had not Jesus Christ come into the world to be the great Savior of souls. All the angels in heaven, and all the men in the world, could never have saved one soul. Christ saw this, and His bowels even yearned towards so many thousands of precious souls; and rather than they should perish, He was content to come and make His own soul to be an offering for sin (Isaiah 53:10). The soul of Christ was made an offering there, and what was that but for the saving of souls? We may therefore, concerning Christ, well say as did the elders in Revelation 5:9, "Thou art worthy...for Thou wast slain, and hast redeemed us to God by Thy blood."

He does not say, "Oh, Thou art worthy, O blessed Savior!" He does not say that, but this, "Thou art worthy to take the book, and to open the seals thereof; for Thou was slain, and hast redeemed us to God." There is infinite worthiness in Christ, and He is worthy of all the honor that we are possibly able to bring to Him, had we ten thousand times more strength than we have to do it.

"For He was slain, and hath redeemed us to God by His blood." If there were a company of poor people upon the sea who were in danger of being lost, their own ship, through stress of weather, fallen to pieces, and they upon a plank, and ready to be swallowed up of every wave; and if there should come a ship and save their lives, how would they be affected with such a mercy as this! Now bless God for His goodness, that such a ship should come by at such a time. We would all have been lost if this ship had not come by just at this time. So when we read the gospel, we read of Jesus Christ, God-man, coming into the world and standing between the wrath of the infinite God and sinful souls, let us then consider how infinitely we are bound to bless God for Jesus Christ; for we were ready, even all of us, to be swallowed up into the bottomless gulf of the wrath of the infinite God. The waves of God's infinite wrath were ready to have covered over all mankind; only the Lord Jesus Christ came and even leaped, as it were, into the very ocean of God's wrath, into the very flames of the wrath and justice of God, to pluck out our souls and to save them. Let us then bless God for Jesus Christ, considering that the loss of souls is such a dreadful loss, and that they are only saved by that great Savior who has come into the world.

USE 4. If the loss of the soul is so dreadful, then it must be a dreadful evil for anyone to have a hand in this loss, or to in any way further it. Take heed that you have no hand at all in so great an evil as this is. Oh, how much better that you had never been born, than to have a hand in so great an evil! We account those to be miserable creatures who have a hand in the loss of kingdoms; but to have a hand in the undoing of one soul is a greater mischief than to be the cause of the undoing of a whole kingdom. If one should be the cause of the ruin of the outward estate of everyone in a whole kingdom, you would say that certainly it would have been better if that man had never been born. Certainly, you who have a hand in the undoing of any soul, you were born to do a greater mischief than such a one; if any friend of yours takes a course whereby he undoes himself, when the evil consequence of his unwise courses appears, you are ready to say, "Blessed be God I had no hand in it." If people will damn their souls eternally, take heed that you have no hand in it. And if any of your children, friends, servants, acquaintances, or neighbors should perish eternally, yet it will be a great mercy if you have no hand in it.

People may have a hand in the loss of other men's souls in many ways. One way is by carelessness of the souls of those committed to their charge; they may come to be lost by your carelessness. By your neglect their souls may perish. And especially it concerns those who take the charge of souls; they need to look to it that those do not cry out against them in hell, that it was through their neglect that they are here now, and must lie here forever. Oh, the cry of a soul against a man is a dreadful thing! Perhaps the souls of some of your children may be in hell, crying out against you for neglecting them, that you did not regard them. You let them profane Sabbaths; you could hear them swear and did not rebuke them, or if you did it was but very slightly. You never instructed them in the ways of God and eternal life; you were the cause of the destruction of their souls by your wicked example. They saw their parents do thus and thus, hate goodness and good men; they saw them scorn at the Word, or neglect and codemn it—and upon that they did so too, and now they are in hell for it, cursing the time that ever they were born of such parents.

There are many souls, no question, in hell, cursing the time that ever they came into such a wicked family wherein they saw so much wickedness, wherein there was no worshipping of God, nor any means to come to know God. And upon that they went on securely in wickedness, and now are sunk down to eternal misery.

You may be the cause of the destruction of other's souls by drawing them to sin. When you actively draw anyone to the commission of any sin, you do what in you lies to cast away that precious, immortal soul. And have never any of you had a hand in this? Have you never been instruments to draw others to some sin or other? If you have, either these whom you have tempted are yet alive or they are dead; if they are alive, know that you are bound in conscience to work now to the uttermost for the good of their souls. You must make it your great work, if it is possible, to do them as much good as ever you did them hurt; for certainly soul satisfaction is required of men as well to bodily satisfaction. If you have wronged a man in his estate in any way, although it was seven or twenty years ago, if God comes to awaken your consciences, it will not serve your turn to return and repent, that is, to be very sorry that you have done it, and ask God for forgiveness; but before you can have peace you must make satisfaction where you have wronged, if God enables you.

Now, does God stand so much upon it, that if someone has but wronged a man in his estate that all the sorrow and repenting in the world will never bring peace of conscience without restitution, where there is the ability? Then certainly if someone has wronged another in his soul, and has endangered the damnation of that soul by drawing him to sin, it is not enough that you see your sin and are sorry for it; it is not enough that you will never seek to draw others any more. No, you are bound, if such are alive, to go to them if you can, and to seek now to do them as much good for their souls as you were a cause of evil.

What if this soul should perish at last by the sin that you

were a cause to draw them to? You need to look about you while
they live so that, if it is possible, you may make satisfaction for
that soul wrong that you have done to them. It may be that
such a one is dead; now then see what a case you are in: there
is someone drawn to a sin by you, and now he is in hell for that
sin that you were the cause of. What a case have you brought
yourself into now? Is it any otherwise likely but that you must
follow? Shall one be in hell for a sin that you were the cause of,
and do you think always to escape? Here is the dreadful estate
that any man brings himself to when he draws others to sin. You
need to look around you, and let your heart be affected with
the sin that has been punished with the eternal damnation of
those souls that you have drawn to that sin.

And not only are you guilty by tempting to sin, but by
encouraging to sin, by dissuading from that which is good.
It may be that some souls have been forward to that which is
good; they have begun to inquire after the ways of God. And
such have gotten into your company and you have sought to
take them off. What, you say, will you be such fools as to believe
everything that is said? And you will be melancholy and mad
and say, "Who are they but a company of simple people who do
thus and so?" And thus you have been a means to hinder the
good work of God in others, and to draw them from the good
way that they were a beginning to set their feet in. And so now
they begin to be out of love with the good ways of God, and you
have been the cause of it.

Now, if their souls perish—and it may be that some of them
are in hell already—truly, if a man's heart were as hard as any
iron or steel in the world, one would think that such a meditation as this would break his heart in pieces: "I know nothing
to the contrary but that some may be in hell because of me."
I might mention many other ways how a man might have his

hand in the loss of the souls of others. In whatever way you have had a hand in the sins of others, or in keeping others from good, in so many ways you may have had a hand in the loss of their souls. But I do not intend to stand upon this point, only consider it; and may the Lord strike the hearts of those who are guilty in this way.

But the main use that I would spend the chief part of the time in is this one:

USE 5. If the loss of a soul is so dreadful, then hence is rebuked the folly and madness of most people who have no care of their souls, but through their own wretchedness and vileness allow their souls to perish eternally. All their care is in pampering their bodies and making much of them, but little minding their souls and their eternal estates. Certainly, when the bodies of those souls shall meet them at the day of judgment, it will be a very dreadful meeting. When your immortal soul shall know what it is to be lost forever, and shall be brought to join again with your body, how do you think it will look upon this cursed carcass? "Oh, this is that carcass, that body of mine, for whose sake I must perish forever! Yea, and we must now be joined together to be fuel for the wrath of the infinite God to burn upon for all eternity!"

Certainly souls are lost and perish. They go down to hell as bees fly to the hive in the time of a storm. There are many ways by which the soul may be lost, though there is but one by which it may be saved.

Ways in Which Men Lose Their Souls

Here let me mention the several ways by which men come to lose their souls:

1. There are some who lose their souls by wandering up and down in darkness all the days of their lives, by wandering in the ways of sin, in the dark, and so are a continual prey unto the devil. Many in many places, the generality of people, go on continually in blindness and darkness, in the vanity of their conversations, knowing nothing of God or of their own souls. And the first time that the eyes of their souls are opened and enlightened is when they are irrecoverably undone. Yea, the first thing that many souls ever understand concerning themselves is this: "I am lost and undone forever." It is so with many. Certainly, they know nothing about their own souls, nor about God, till they come to know this: "I am cast away from God, and have lost my soul forever."

2. Others lose their souls by pawning them away.

QUESTION. Pawning them? What is that?

ANSWER. Why, you know what it is to pawn a thing. When you come and receive from a broker such a thing, you lay something else to pawn for it upon the condition that within such a time you will bring them such a thing that you bargain for. And if you do not bring it by that time, then you lose your pawn. Thus many pawn away their souls. When there is a temptation to any sin, and you have a mind to commit that sin, now upon the commission of this sin you lay your soul to pawn to the devil, only upon the condition that if you repent and believe before God cuts you off, then you shall have your soul again. Upon these terms most people sin, and in case you do not bring repentance and belief in Christ, your soul is gone.

I appeal to you, there is a temptation to sin; you know it is a sin, and there is a great deal of danger in it. But you have a mind to that sin, and you will have it. You will acknowledge this much: "Indeed, if I do not repent then I shall be damned;

but before I die I hope to repent, and so I hope that my soul shall not perish." That is as much as to say, "I will lay my soul in pawn, and if I can bring repentance before I die I will have my soul again. But if I do not, then my soul is gone."

Thus, upon the commission of every sin, you lay your soul to pawn. The devil has it upon such terms as these. Now how many thousands have lost their pawn? They have not brought faith and repentance before they died, and so the devil has kept the pawn, and will keep it forever. And this laying of such a pawn is much more dangerous than the ordinary laying of pawns to brokers.

First, there is no such pawn that possibly can be laid as this, the soul of a man. Men and women who have any wisdom will not lay pawns of those things that are precious to them. It goes to their hearts to think, "What, must I lay this to pawn! I thought I should never have lived to see the day when I would lay such a thing to pawn." Aye, but when you come to lay your soul to pawn, you lay a more precious thing than all the world is.

Second, when you lay a thing to pawn, you prefix your own time to redeem it again, perhaps two, three, four months before you bring that which is bargained for. But when you lay your soul to pawn, you cannot set a time. "What dost thou know, O fool, but that this night thy soul may be taken away from thee?" (Luke 12:20).

Third, when you lay such a thing to pawn, you make a bargain to bring something to redeem it that you have in your own power, or make account that you shall have in your own power to bring. You will not make the bargain to bring such a thing that you are sure you shall not have in your own power. Now when you lay your souls to pawn, you lay them to pawn for that which you do not have in your power; nor can all the creatures in heaven and earth help you in your need, for what you need is faith and repentance. All the angels in heaven, and all the men in the world, cannot help you; it is only in the hands of God, of the infinite, blessed God against whom you sin, and whom you provoke. And yet how many thus pawn their souls? No marvel if men lose their souls because they pawn them so foolishly and wretchedly.

3. Men lose their souls by wounding them. They give them deadly wounds, upon which the souls of most perish.

QUESTION. Wounding their souls? How do they wound their souls?

ANSWER. By that I mean the commission of sins against conscience; to commit a known and willful sin gives a wide gash in the soul, a most fearful wound! Every sin against conscience gives a wound that requires a salve to heal it that is more worth than a thousand worlds. Sins against conscience, against light, and against knowledge are deep wounds unto the souls of men. And it is not usual for such wounds to be healed, for they not only strike at the life of the soul, but they harden the heart of the sinner exceedingly, and keep off the means that might do the soul good. You go abroad into company, and there commit a sin against your conscience. Oh, you have given a gash to that precious soul of yours. You have given it a deep wound, and unless you look to it, and that immediately, your soul may die forever! A man who has received a deep wound presently sends for the surgeon, and if it bleeds well he hopes the cure is more hopeful. So when you have committed sin, if indeed it bleeds, that is, if your soul is immediately sensible of it and is affected with it, and mourns and laments, and so seeks after the surgeon, there may be hope. But men and women wound their own souls by willful sins, sins against their consciences, and yet they are not sensible of them. They do not so much as bleed, but they lie in the very open air, as it were, and are not bound up at all, Ah! There are thousands and thousands who die and perish this way.

4. Some lose their souls by being deceived by them. Satan persuades them that they are in a good condition, that all is well with them, and that they need not fear. What need do they have to trouble themselves? These are but the melancholy thoughts of such and such kinds of people; there is no such great matters required in sorrow for sin, and all it takes is a "Lord, have mercy upon us," and by being in Christ, hoping in God's mercy, and the like. And thus, by such kinds of delusions as these are, many souls are gulled and deceived by the devil, and so perish forever. They are like Jonah, who was asleep, and awakened in the midst of a dreadful tempest. So certainly these souls, when they come to know themselves and to be awakened, will be in the dreadful tempest of God's wrath. Samson heard, "The Philistines are upon thee," when he lay in Delilah's bosom; and so there will be that dreadful noise one day to these souls, "The wrath of God and the curse of the law is upon you, and it must lie upon you." Oh, the dreadful sorrow there will be when the soul shall see that it is deluded and gulled! Many of you are extremely vexed when you are deceived about any little part of your estates; but to be deluded and gulled by your souls, so as they must be lost forever, this will be extreme horror another day.

5. A fifth way of losing our souls is by selling them.

QUESTION. Selling them, what do you mean by that?
ANSWER. It is said of Alexander VI, who was pope, that he sold his soul to the devil for the popedom; there was an express contract between the devil and him that if in such a year he should come to be pope, the devil could have his soul. But there is a

twofold selling of our souls to the devil, besides such a kind of contract as when the devil shall appear in a bodily shape, and so people sell their souls to him.

First, when men seek advantage for themselves by any unlawful means; they seek the gain of the world, or any profits or pleasures, by cheating, cozening, wronging, swearing, or for-swearing. There is such a thing that you would have, and that you may have, if you will be false in your bookkeeping, in your reckonings, or if you forswear yourself for gain. I say that you as truly sell your soul to get that gain as ever any conjurer did who made a contract face to face with the devil.

"I would have such a gain," you may say.

"Why," says the devil, though you do not see him, "then you must lie, you must cheat, you must swear."

"I will do it," says the soul. And thus many times you sell your soul to the devil. You who are merchants, if someone should come and offer you a little for a commodity that is of great value, if you have such a piece of ware in your shops that it is worth forty shillings, and one comes and offers your two pence for it, why, you would rise in disdain against it. "What? Offer me two pence for that which is worth forty shillings?" Oh, when the devil comes to buy your souls your hearts should rise in disdain! "What? Shall I venture the selling of this soul of mine, that is more worth than ten thousand worlds, for such a poor gain as this is?" And yet many of you do.

Second, a man sells his soul when he resolutely gives himself up to all manner of wickedness. Thus it is said of Ahab in 1 Kings 21:20, "Ahab sold himself to work wickedness," that is, Ahab, in a resolute way, was set upon a manner of wickedness that might serve his own turn. When a man shall be set upon this, that whatever way of wickedness may be subservient to the attaining of such and such designs that he has, he will venture upon it, this man sells his soul in this case to the devil. Ahab sold himself to work wickedness.

6. Sixth, men lose their souls by their being poisoned; their souls are poisoned, and so they come to be lost. Now the poison of the soul comes either from wicked company or from wicked errors.

By keeping wicked company, you keep in infectious air; you go from home sometimes and meet with such wicked company, and you get your bain, your poison there. And poison works in divers ways: sometimes it will cause one to swell mightily. How many, when they come from their wicked company, come home with such swelling hearts, in such an outrageous way, swearing and fighting, blaspheming, scorning, and condemning all ways of godliness. Now these have been abroad, and have gotten poison, and so they shall be, and are ready to burst with it.

There are other kinds of poison that will not work till a quarter or half a year later. A man may go into company, and get his poison, and yet it not work upon him till a quarter of a year later. I remember a philosopher seeing two women who were wicked talk together. "Oh!" he said, "Now the viper is taking poison from the asp." And indeed, it seemed to be a proverb in Tertullian's time that the viper borrows poison from the asp. So when wicked company is infusing wicked principles, here the poison is gotten from the asp. Perhaps wicked company comes with their sweet cups, and perhaps you drink down the wine merrily. But, together with the wine, wicked things are infused into your spirit that are poisonous. When you are in wicked company, and hear the ways of God spoken against, and hear the saints of God railed on, and the good Word of God spoken against, when you draw this into your heart, poison goes down in this cup! It is likely to poison your soul, and to be your undoing forever.

There is another kind of venom, and that is wicked errors and heresies, when men drink off the "cup of fornication," as when they are taken with the great errors of popery—this poisons the soul. 2 Thessalonians 2:10 is a most dreadful place for that very error, speaking of antichrist, that he "should come with all deceivableness of unrighteousness in them that perish, because they received not the love of the truth, that they might be saved; and for this cause God shall send them strong delusions, that they should believe a lie, that they all might be damned who believe not the truth, but had pleasure in unrighteousness." This is a most dreadful text against those who drink in the errors of popery.

But you may say that they are learned men, and have a great show of truth, with all their deceivableness of unrighteousness. So how are you deceived by them? Because you do not receive the love of the truth that you might be saved. And for this cause, God shall send you strong delusions to believe a lie, that you might be damned. God sends strong delusions so that men might believe those errors and drink in that cup of fornications, that they might be damned forever.

If it were only that one error drunk down in the grossness of it, that is, that the righteousness that I must tender up to God for satisfaction to divine justice, and for any eternal salvation, must be my own righteousness, my own works, there is enough in just that to poison a soul to eternal perdition. And there are many other ways that may endanger the soul extremely, and very ill consequences may be gathered from good principles. As for that principle of our justification by free grace in Christ, it is only by Christ that we are justified—that principle is exceedingly good. But from thence such dangerous, venomous consequences may be drawn as may extremely endanger and, I have no doubt, envenom and

poison many thousands of souls, upon which they draw consequences for looseness and against humiliation for sin, and
against obedience to the law, as by Moses. All the principles
and errors that are against the strict ways of God, that tend to
any looseness, certainly are envenoming principles. Oh, take
heed of any doctrine, of any conceits, of any opinions that
in any way tend to looseness! They will certainty poison and
envenom your souls, so that your very errors may be enough
to damn you eternally. Many lose their souls by poisoning.

7. Many lose their souls by venturing them; there are many
ventures upon which many come to their souls. There are four
cases wherein a man may lose his soul by venturing it.

First, by rashness: men who are inconsiderate and rash in
their ways will suddenly fall upon things before they examine them. That rashness and suddenness of yours to fall upon
things before you examine them, and to go on in a rash way
the most part of your life as many do, this endangers the loss
of your soul.

Second, others venture the loss of their souls by doing things
that are doubtful, that their consciences misgive them in, and
tell them, "Oh, this is not right. I doubt that I sin against God
in this." And yet they will go on and venture before they satisfy
their doubts. But take heed of doing anything with a doubtful
conscience, for you know what the Scripture says in Romans 14,
"Whatsoever is not of faith is sin." If you doubt, you must not
venture to do a thing till you have examined your doubt and
there see upon what ground your doubt is built. So if you presume to do a thing doubtfully, it may cost you your life.

Third, some venture the loss of their souls by presuming
upon God's patience. "Why, the Lord is a patient God, and
He has spared me so many years. All this while I have been
spared, and have done well enough. Why may I not hope that

God will spare me still, and be patient with me still?" How many wretched, sinful creatures venture upon this? Perhaps they have been brought up in wickedness and profaneness. God has been patient towards them, and yet they can sin again and again and live very merry lives. Now all this time you live upon the mere patience of God, and think that because God has been patient this long, therefore He will be so still. We may indeed venture upon the grace of God in His Son, for sanctification as well as for pardon, but not to venture either upon patience, or anything else, so as to continue in our sins. Though God has been patient this long, you do not know but that upon your next venture the cord of mercy may crack, and you may sink and perish eternally. That may befall you in one day that has not befallen you all your life before now. Take heed, my brethren, of venturing upon patience; for there is not a word of promise to strengthen that to you. Indeed, faith is a kind of venture, but that ventures upon the Word and the promise of God; and it is good venturing upon that. But when you venture upon patience, you have no word to assure you that patience will hold. You have no word to make this good unto you, that though God has been patient so many years, therefore He will be so still.

Fourth, men venture upon their own lives. They are young, and they hope to live many years yet. "I know others who live to be old men, and why may not I live and have my pleasure as well as they?" And thus they venture. But what if the thread of your life should be snapped asunder? What will become of you then? Will you venture your eternal miscarrying upon such a brittle and frail thing as your life is? Oh, it is a desperate venture when men and women will venture thus, that "if God takes away my life now, certainly I must perish forever."

Now I put it unto every soul in this place, let this be the case

now: examine what you think in your consciences your conditions would be if you should hear a voice from heaven saying
unto you presently, "This soul shall have no more time to make
provision for eternity." I am persuaded that in such a place as
this is there cannot but be many who would in their own consciences say, "If God should take away my life now, I fear I would
be lost forever." I doubt, if we could go from one to another,
and lay our ears to the bosoms of men, and could but hear what
the consciences of men say upon this that has now been put to
them, that you would die in the condition in which now you are.
Whatever repentance you have had, be it good or bad, your soul
must depend upon; and if it is not right, your soul must perish.
I fear that upon such a message from heaven, many a man's and
woman's heart would ask them, and their consciences would
tell them, "I am afraid I would be lost forever." Oh, for you to
be content to be in such a condition any one moment, that if
you should die that moment, your soul would be damned, you
are a bold and presumptuous sinner, a most desperate wretch.

8. Many lose their souls by starving them, that is, such as
neglect the Word of God, the food of the soul. The soul should
feed upon the Word of God as the body does upon any food.
These men neglect God's ordinances; they do not care to come
to the Word, either to feed upon it privately or publicly, and
think that there is no need of the Word. But if they can procure
food for their bodies and make a living, and if they can obtain
that which may satisfy the flesh, that is all that they look after.
But as for feeding their souls by the Word, that is little minded
or regarded by thousands. Oh, how many who belong to this
congregation will perish eternally, even that way, by starving!
We pity people whom we see are ready to die of starvation. If we
hear of a prisoner starving, even the poorest body, we account

it an inhuman thing in those who knew of it and did not relieve them. To see a beast die by starving, we account it a cruel thing; and it can scarcely consist with the heart of a man to see so much as a dog perish by way of starving. Now to see immortal souls, thousands of them, die and perish, and drop down to hell as rapidly as may be, and that for want of the food of their souls, merely for starving, should be an object of pity and commiseration.

Because we are sensual, we are only affected with such things as concern the body immediately; but for the soul, how many do not care what kind of ministry they live under? Oh, the curse of God is upon them! We read in Psalm 106:15 that God gave them their requests, and sent leanness into their souls. He gave them their requests, that is, He gave them quails. "They lusted in the wilderness, and tempted God in the desert," and He gave them quails to feed upon, but sent leanness into their souls. We may apply this to those who seek after nothing but "quails," who seek only that which may feed the flesh. Oh, the curse of God is upon their souls! There is leanness there, and they are starved there even unto death; whereas those who know what the sweetness of the Word is to their souls, and have fed upon the Word, would rather feed upon brown bread and water all their days if they may have the Word, rather than have the greatest delicacies in the world without the Word.

I put this to your consciences; answer it as in the presence of God: if this should be put to you, can you say as in God's presence, who sees and searches the hearts of men, that upon the real sweetness and good your souls have found in the Word, that if God should put to your choice either to live with bread and water and have the Word, or to live with all the delicacies in the world without the Word, you would a thousand, thousand times sooner choose to live with the Word with bread and water than without the Word with all delicacies. I remember that Luther had an expression that he would rather be in hell with the Word than in paradise without it.

9. There is another sort who lose their souls by indulging them. Their souls are satiated with the cares and pleasures of this life; they glut their hearts with the delights, pleasures, and cares of this world, until their souls get an excess and die of them. Such give liberty unto their hearts to delight themselves in all outward contentments, especially if they are lawful. Now a man or woman may indulge their souls and undo themselves by lawful things. A man may not only destroy his life by eating poison, but by an excess of good meat; though the meat is good, yet he may over-indulge on it. Though the things of this world, its cares and its pleasures, may be (as some things are) in themselves lawful, yet by an inordinate and immoderate letting out the heart to lawful things, you may over-indulge your soul, and it may die of that indulgence. Many men think themselves out of danger if the things that their hearts are set upon are in themselves lawful. They are not swearers, whoremasters, drunkards, or thieves, as others are, and therefore they think their souls may be saved. I say, you may busy your heart only about that which is in itself lawful, and yet your soul may take an excess and perish eternally.

10. Many lose their souls by forfeiting them, and that by these two ways: first, a man forfeits his soul, as men do their tenured lands, by not tendering that homage to their lord that is due, by which they hold their lands; and so their lands come to be forfeited. And just so do you: God has given you your precious soul, worth more than all the world, and you lease it from God, but so as you must tender up to this Lord that homage that is due to Him; that is, you must worship God. When we

come to worship God, this is that we do: we come to tender up homage that we acknowledge to be due to God for these souls of ours that He has given to us. That is our worship; that is the nature of worship, to tender up something by way of homage, to acknowledge that due respect we owe unto God as that Lord who has the absolute disposal of us. Now by neglect of worshipping God, of tendering up His homage, you forfeit your soul and endanger yourself to perish eternally. And how few people regard any such worship of God! Though they do the things that God requires, such as praying and coming to hear the Word, yet they do not do it in a way of tendering up homage to that God upon whom they alone depend. But this is that which God requires of us, or otherwise our souls are forfeited.

Second, men forfeit their souls by breaking covenant with God. However, there may be some that God will not take the forfeiture of, yet certainly, upon your breach of covenant with God, your soul is forfeited. You engage your soul to God every time you enter into covenant with Him. It may be said of any man or woman who enters into covenant with God that he or she has engaged their soul to God. You engage and bind your soul to God in your covenant and, upon your breach of it, dealing falsely, you forfeit your soul.

By these various ways souls are lost; and, oh, how many thousands of souls perish with such ways and manners as these are! Therefore, seeing that there are such ways to lose a soul, let not people think themselves safe, though they do not go in some ways whereby they may come to lose their souls; for there are very many ways whereby you may lose your soul and miscarry to eternity.

A Sixth Use of the Doctrine

*"For what is a man profited if he shall gain
the whole world and lose his own soul? Or what shall
a man give in exchange for his soul?"*

MATTHEW 16:26

USE 6. If the loss of our souls is so dreadful a thing, and there are so many ways to lose them, then it dearly concerns us to examine whether we are not in such a condition at the present that if our souls should depart out of our bodies, they would certainly be lost. This is a needful scrutiny, and a most necessary inquiry. Many men have these thoughts: "What if I should now die? I have not made my will, and my estate would go such and such ways as I would not have it. It would be squandered away; it would be spent in lawsuits." Aye, but rather let your thoughts run out thus: "What if I should now die? Would not my soul be lost and perish forever?"

Now, though I have said that we cannot set forth such a man or woman, and conclude that their souls shall certainly be lost, because we do not know what God may do hereafter, yet we may say that such a man or woman's soul, in the condition it is, if God does no more for it than He has yet done, then it will certainly be lost. Indeed, a man or woman may come to know and may certainly conclude that they are elect, but none can come to such a conclusion as to know certainly that they are reprobates. The vilest wretch upon the face of the earth does not have sufficient ground to conclude against himself that he is a reprobate, and that his soul shall forever be lost. Therefore, surely, we cannot conclude against another if we cannot conclude against ourselves.

QUESTION. But who are those persons whom, if God should work no otherwise upon them than He has done, that then their souls should be lost?

ANSWER. There are nine such persons:

1. That soul to whom God has not made known, and convinced of the dangerous, natural condition in which it is, if such a soul should depart from the body, it would be lost. Only let me premise these two cautions. I do not speak of infants, but of those who have come to years, and who live under the means of grace. Also I speak of God's ordinary way. I will not limit what God may do in extraordinary ways, but in an ordinary course and way of God's dealings with the children of men, whom He lets live to come to years and be under means, these following rules will discover who they are who at the present are in a lost condition. I say, such to whom God has never revealed and convinced of the evil of their natural condition, in which they were born and in which they are, if God should let them so die, and make known no more to them than He has, such a soul would be lost because without faith it must be lost—and that is acknowledged by all. He who does not believe shall be

damned, and is condemned already. Now, faith in a Savior to save the soul implies that I know what a dangerous condition I am in by sin. For there is even a contradiction implied in my believing in Christ as a Savior if I am not yet convinced of the damnable condition that I am in without this Christ.

2. The soul that has not yet made it to be its great care, above all outward things in this world, to save itself, if it should now depart from the body, would be lost. I say, if God has not first convinced you, and made you sensible of the damnable condition in which you are in yourself; and if he has not taken your heart from the creature, from the things that are here below, and made it to be the great care of your soul to get it to be saved; if He has not made you to be solicitous about the work of saving your soul—such a soul as this is, if it should now depart, would be lost, for God does not save souls but by manifesting Himself to them. He would have all men to work out their salvation with fear and trembling (Philippians 2:12). Certainly, though the principle of our salvation is outside of us, yet the Lord who made us without us will never save us without us. Whosoever God saves, He makes them solicitous and careful about the work of the salvation of their souls. Now, if your conscience tells you that to this day your care has been about many vanities, but as for having your heart taken up with saving your soul, you do not know what belongs to this; if God should work no more in you than He has done, if you should now die, you would be lost.

3. That soul to whom the Lord has not revealed the glory of the mysteries of the gospel, who yet has the gospel kept hidden from it, who does not see into the glorious work of God in the covenant of grace in those great counsels of God, and the great things that God has done for the salvation of mankind in Jesus Christ—that soul would be lost if it should now depart from the body, with no further work of God upon it.

That Scripture that divers times you have heard used is sufficient proof for it: "If our gospel be hidden, it is hidden to those that are lost" (2 Corinthians 4:3). Now certainly, my brethren, if God has revealed to your souls the glorious things of the gospel, they cannot but be taking things to you; they cannot but cause much stirring, much activeness, and many mighty workings in your souls. Once the glorious light of the gospel comes into a soul, it cannot but cause mighty stirrings and workings in such a soul. When I see people sit deadly and dully under the means of grace, under the preaching of the glorious things of the gospel, I cannot but think to myself, "Lord, do these people know who and what Jesus Christ is? Do they understand what the great things are that God has done for the salvation of mankind? Certainly, if they knew the wonderful and strange works of God about the salvation of the souls of the children of men, their hearts could not but stir within them, and work in another manner than yet they have done."

4. The soul that has no other righteousness to tender up unto God but its own, if it should now depart, would be lost eternally. Whatever man or woman it is who has lived most unblameably in his life and conversation, who has been the most righteous, so that no man would be able to blame him for anything, yet if this man or woman has no other righteousness to tender up unto God but his own, certainly this soul would be a lost soul forever. The truth is, even the soul of Abraham, Isaac, and Jacob, the souls of all the patriarchs, prophets, apostles, martyrs, all of them would be lost eternally had they no other righteousness to tender up to God but their own—much more those who have only a civil righteousness, a mere natural righteousness, such righteousness as is attainable by the very light of nature, such a righteousness as Paul speaks of in Philippians 3, that he lived unblameably, how he was a Pharisee, and he

accounted that righteousness of the conversation, to be "gain." Yet afterwards, when Christ was revealed to him, he accounted it "but loss," for he saw that it would endanger the loss of his soul eternally to rest upon that.

QUESTION. Is the soul lost that has no other righteousness but its own to tender to God? Why, what other righteousness is there besides that which is a man's own?

ANSWER. There is a supernatural righteousness, the righteousness of a Mediator, God-man, who has come into the world to stand between lost souls and an infinitely-provoked God; and that righteousness is made over to the soul by faith, and the soul that is saved by the hand of faith offers up the righteousness of that Mediator, God-man, for the satisfaction of infinite, divine justice and the appeasing of infinite wrath. That is the soul that is saved. But the soul that is not acquainted with such a righteousness, that does not have such a righteousness made over to it by faith, the righteousness of the Son of God, the righteousness that is by faith in Christ, that soul, if it should now depart from the body and the Lord work no otherwise upon it than He has yet done, certainly would be a lost soul.

5. The soul that God has not made (in some measure, at least) to feel the weight and burden of sin, to whom He has not discovered sin as a greater burden than all burdens whatsoever, if such a soul should depart, it would prove to be lost, and that upon this reason: because without repentance a soul must be lost. "Except ye repent, ye shall all likewise perish" (Luke 13:3), Christ said. Now repentance cannot stand with feeling sin lightly, much less with joying in sin. Repentance, whether before faith or after, we will not now speak of, whether a legal repentance or an evangelical repentance, yet it must be such a repentance as must be apprehensive and sensible of sin as being

a greater evil than all the evils that the soul is liable to in this world. It must feel sin as it is against God, feel sin as sin, so as to be a burden to it (the measure of it, how far, and how weighty sin should be, we do not now stand upon). The soul must come to realize that sin is a great burden, yea, an intolerable burden, so that were it not for an infinite Mediator, the soul could not stand under the burden. That is necessary in the work of repentance, and so the soul must come to sorrow for sin, as sin. This is the repentance that is unto life, which cannot be unless the soul feels in some measure the weight and burden of sin.

6. Again, that man or woman who walks after the flesh, in a course of sin, to give satisfaction and contentment unto the flesh, who makes it to be its great care and endeavor to satisfy the flesh, such of you whose consciences tell you that the contentment of your hearts is some fleshly thing, and that in the course of your lives you walk after the flesh, certainly if you should now die, your souls would be lost. That is clear out of Romans 8:1: "There is no condemnation to them that are in Christ Jesus, that walk not after the flesh, but after the Spirit." Therefore, those who do not walk after the Spirit, but after the flesh, there is condemnation unto them at the present. Oh, if men had but enlightened and stirring consciences, how easy would it be for men and women to see themselves in a restless condition, and to conclude that if these things are the truths of God, then they are in such a condition. And though they do not know what God may work for a time to come, yet if they should now die, their souls would be lost eternally. Then there is that other place in Romans 8: "They that live after the flesh shall die," that is, perish eternally. If your hearts are after the flesh, after fleshly things, and they are the things that you mind; and if you would speak as in presence of God, you cannot but acknowledge that the things of the flesh are the things that take up your hearts, that are the adequate objects of your spirits, and you think your

great good and contentment lies in them; if you might but live always in this world, and have those contentments to the flesh as you desire, you would care for nothing else, but your hearts would be fully satisfied—this is living after the flesh. Now the Scripture tells us clearly that those who live after the flesh shall die. It is your great care that the flesh be satisfied, and it is God's threat that when you make it your great care to satisfy the flesh, you shall die. So this is a perishing condition unto you.

7. Yea, further, whatever soul is under the dominion of any one lust, that soul, if it should now depart, would certainly be lost. Not only such as live in all kind of sins, so that the constant course of their lives is in every kind of sin, but if there is but any one reigning sin, if there is but any one sinful way that God has convinced your conscience of to be a sin, and yet because of gain, delight, pleasure, honors, or respects you go on in a constant course, way, and practice of that sin; though it is but one sin, so that you are a slave to any one lust—certainly this soul of yours, if God works no otherwise upon it than yet He has done, will certainty be lost. That is clear out of Romans 6:14: "For sin shall not have dominion over you, for you are not under the law, but under grace." I would reason from this Scripture thus: whatever soul is not under grace, under the covenant of grace, and under the mercy that there is in that covenant, that soul, if now it should depart, must perish eternally. But whosoever is under the dominion of any one sin is not under grace; for the Scripture plainly says that sin shall not have dominion over us if we are under grace. If our souls are in such an estate as they be under the grace of the gospel, then there must not be any one sin that has dominion over them. There may be some sin dwelling there, but not reigning there. There is a great deal of difference between sins being in the soul and ruling over the soul.

QUESTION. What is it for sin to have dominion?

ANSWER. Sin has dominion when it sets up a kind of throne in the soul and gives laws like a king, and you obey. It is one thing for an enemy to come with violence and take possession, and hurries one on to do what one would not otherwise do; and it is another thing to be subject, and to yield to the laws and commandments of sin. Sin has dominion when it is as a king upon his throne to whom you yield subjection; and to satisfy your own lusts, you are willing that this sin should rule over you. Now that you may know a little further the meaning of this, sin and Jesus Christ cannot both have dominion together. Thus far we may go safely, that unless Jesus Christ has dominion over you, then sin does.

QUESTION. But how shall I know whether Christ or sin has dominion?

ANSWER. I will appeal to you in this plain and familiar kind of expression of mine: can you say as in the presence of God, who sees and searches your heart, "O Lord, Thou knowest that I have given up my heart to the rule of Jesus Christ"? I would put this to every soul here present, and I beseech you to weigh it; for we are speaking of matters of life and death, of salvation and damnation. Therefore I put this to you. Think of it, can you appeal to God in the sincerity of your heart and say, "Lord, Thou art the Seer and Searcher of all hearts. And Thou knowest that though I have many weaknesses and infirmities, and am often overcome by temptation, yet Thou knowest that I have given up my heart to the obedience of Jesus Christ, and I do yet give it up. And my soul desires above all things that Jesus Christ may rule in it, that Christ may have dominion, that His laws may be set up. And if I knew any more of the mind of Jesus Christ, whatsoever it costs me, Thou who knowest all things, know that I would submit unto it. And if there is anything that is against the mind of Jesus Christ, if it is known to me, Thou knowest that my heart is against it; and I would rather that I were delivered from the power of it than to have all the world"?

Can you speak thus as in the presence of God? Certainly, a Christian, though a weak Christian, can appeal to God in the sincerity of it, and is able to venture itself upon such an appeal to God. And if there is not this dominion of Jesus Christ, then there is the dominion of sin, and then you are not under grace. Therefore, if God does no more in your soul than He has done, you shall perish forever. And that man or woman who can sleep quietly so has a strange pillow to sleep on. It is reported of Augustus Caesar that, hearing of a gentleman who was much in debt, he sent to buy his pillow, saying, "Surely there is a great deal of virtue in that pillow, that such a man could sleep on it who was so much in debt." Truly I may say, it is a strange kind of pillow that men can sleep on who are in such a condition that if God does no more for than He has done will certainly perish.

8. That man or woman who has not yet had such a change wrought by the power of the Spirit of God, as is a new birth, a resurrection from death, a new creation, that soul, if it now departed, would certainly perish. Certainly, every one of you, as you come into the world, as you are by nature, your souls are in a lost estate, and in such a lost estate as unless the Lord makes such a change in your heart as is a new birth, by which you come to be born again; as is a new resurrection, by which you come to be raised from the dead; as is a new creation, by which you come to be a new creature—certainly you must perish. Till this is wrought in your hearts by the power of the Spirit, you are in a perishing condition.

There is nothing more plain than this in Scripture. You know what Christ said to Nicodemus, "Verily, verily, I say unto you, except a man be born again, he cannot see the Kingdom of God" (John 3:3). Therefore, it is not enough that you live somewhat better than heretofore you have done. It may be that when you were a young man you were wanton, unclean, profane, abroad in the fields, and in wicked houses on the Lord's Day. Aye, but now you have more wisdom and understanding, and now you do not do so. This is well and good, and this is to be encouraged, aye, but what is this compared to such a mighty change as to be born again? If your bodies had no other kind of soul than that which is of sense, and afterwards a rational soul should be put into it, what a mighty change would there be in that body? Before they could only see, hear, and feel; but now, having a rational soul, they can understand, understand reason, understand the ways of men. This is a mighty change, and truly there is as mighty a change when God puts a new life into the soul and regenerates it, making it partaker of the divine nature, and even to come to live the life of God, according as the Scripture phrase is. Now this must be in every soul that is saved; and if the time has not yet come that this regeneration is wrought, then certainly your soul is yet in a perishing condition. God alone knows what He intends to do hereafter, but for the present, your soul, I say, is in a perishing condition. The first work that God made (that is, the work of creation) by sin was quite spoiled. Now is the honor and work of Jesus Christ, the Son of God, to rear up a new world, and that is a great deal better world than the former world was; and the special creatures of this world are His saints, and the new creation in their hearts. This is the condition of a converted soul: it is made a new creature. "All old things are done away" (2 Corinthians 5:17). You who live in your old ways and are altogether for your old customs, what will you do contrary to what your forefathers did, and what you yourself have done all your lifetime? Why, you must be a new creature, and all things are to become new in your soul. You must know that the old man is dead in you, and that the new creature is reared up in you, or else you cannot know that if your soul should this night depart but that you would be an undone creature forever.

Yea, I shall yet say further, because it is a point of a wonderful consequence for men and women to put themselves to, I fear that there are many men and women here who yet all their lifetime have not put this question to themselves: "What are the terms between God and me? Why, I hope that God will work grace in me; aye, but what has God done? Is it so wrought at this moment that if I were this moment to die, I would be in a safe condition, and the hazard of my miscarrying to all eternity would be over?" A man may joyfully go through all conditions in this world if he were able to say, "Well, whatever befalls me in this world, yet my condition is such that I know the hazard of my miscarrying forever is over, blessed be God." Oh, that people would but put this question to themselves: "In what estate am I now in if I were to die this instant?"

9. The soul that yet has not gone beyond those whom the Scripture brands and denotes as hypocrites or reprobates, if you have yet no more wrought in you than the Scripture shows that they had, then certainly if you should now die, you must perish. For example, the Scripture holds forth these examples:

Pharaoh confessed his sins. "The Lord is righteous," he said, "and I have sinned."

Saul said, "I have sinned against the Lord."

Ahab humbled himself in sackcloth, and went softly when the prophet threatened God's anger against him.

The Scripture tells you of the "stony ground," which "received the Word with joy."

Scripture tells of Herod, that he heard John the Baptist

gladly, and reformed many things.

It tells of Judas. He came and acknowledged his sin, and brought again the thirty pieces that he had gotten by it, and cast it down. Yet these of whom the Scripture thus speaks, all of their souls were lost forever; and yet I say they went thus far. Now it concerns us very dearly to look to ourselves, and not to think that we are safe upon every slight apprehension. If the Scripture holds forth such examples of those who went thus far and yet were lost, we need to be careful to examine our state. To what end do you think God set down these examples of wicked men whose souls were lost, and showed you how much good they did? Certainly this was God's end, that men and women might not flatter themselves with every little good thing that they do, but that they should be very serious and solicitous in the examination of the estate of their souls, how the terms are between God and them. This was God's end, and this being God's end we are to make the use of it that God aimed at in holding forth these things in His Word unto us. Oh, therefore, do not satisfy yourselves with a little; do not say, "If I should now die this night, and no further work were wrought, yet I hope the work is so far wrought that my soul will not be lost."

SERMON 7

Questions and Objections

*"For what is a man profited if he shall gain
the whole world and lose his own soul? Or what shall
a man give in exchange for his soul?"*

MATTHEW 16:26

QUESTION. You say that we must go further, but how shall a man know that he has gone further than those whose souls are lost?

ANSWER. Can you say with David, "Lord, Thy Word is pure; therefore doth Thy servant love it"? I believe not one of these souls previously mentioned could say, "Lord God, Thy Word is a pure Word. I see a holiness and beauty in Thy Word, and therefore my soul closes with it because it is pure." This is further than any of them went. David could say so, but Saul could not. Ahab could not, nor could Herod. The "stony ground" and Herod rejoiced in it, but it was not from the purity of it that they rejoice; for then they would have rejoiced in all the Word of God, every part of God's Word being pure and holy.

They could not say that they prized Jesus Christ for being a Sanctifier as well as a Savior. None of them looked upon Jesus Christ to deliver their souls from the power of their sin and work righteousness in them, as well as deliver them from the wrath that is to come. Therefore, though some of them would be glad to be saved from hell by Christ, yet to look upon Christ in regard of His purity and holiness as being altogether lovely, this none of them could do.

None of them lifted up God as the highest end of all, and gave themselves and all that they had, were, or could do, being empty of themselves, so as to lift up God as revealed in Christ as the highest end, and Christ to be all in all to their souls. They did not go this far. And therefore do not think that it puts people to great straits to tell them how far many went whose souls were lost, and, if they went no further, their souls would likewise be eternally lost.

Now then, these things being so, what remains but that you should lay them to your hearts? Oh, lay them to your hearts. And perhaps God will be pleased this evening to cause everyone in this congregation to examine themselves, and call their souls into question, to ask, "O my soul, how is it with you? How do things stand between God and you?" Are you in such an estate that if God should call you out of the body this moment you would be saved? Oh, do not be satisfied in anything in the world until you come to a resolution in these things! And if you find that these things speak against you, and your souls are cast down by them for the present, do not slight them; for verily God will make them good upon you. These things shall stand when your soul shall perish.

USE. Wherefore, then, this is the last use about this point of the dreadful loss of the soul. Oh, then, let every man or woman propound this question to themselves: "What shall I then do to be saved?" (Acts 16:30). The world is troubled with a great many questions at this day, questions that have no great necessity in them. But here is the great question, men and brethren, "What shall I do to be saved?" And if people, when they meet together, would be taken up, and would be asking this question of one another, it would prevent a great many wrangling and jangling questions that men spend their time in. Oh, when they are asking you many such vain questions, answer those vain questions this way: "Aye, but do you know what one may do to be saved? Tell me something of the way of God about the salvation of my soul." And this is that at which both ministers and Christians should most aim to help one another in. They should not fill people's heads with curious questions, and specially the heads of young ones; for that is a great deceit of the devil at this day. There was never a time wherein there was a more hopeful harvest of young ones than there was two or three years ago in England, and in this city; and because the devil saw that it was in vain to tempt their hearts to their former profaneness, he labored by all means to cause them to fall into the hands of vain jangling people who would fill their heads with a great many curious questions about controversies, and things that they do not understand, and so take away the very strength and life of the work of the Word upon them. Yet the Scripture tells us plainly that we must not receive the weak in faith unto doubtful disputations (Romans 14:1).

OBJECTION. But we must inquire after all truths!
ANSWER. It is true that we must, but we must do it seasonably, in their due time. It is not for young converts, before they are settled in the main things of religion, to have their heads filled with doubtful disputations. It is the plain Scripture, and it is as

plain, if we would understand it, as "Thou shalt not steal," or "Thou shalt not commit adultery." Oh, this has hindered the salvation of many a soul! Now therefore this is that which I would aim at, to turn the strength of your souls into this great question: What shall we do to be saved? In Ecclesiastes 7:29 the wise man says, "God hath made man upright, but he hath found to himself many inventions." That is how your Bibles have it, but I find it translated in the old Latin this way: "He has mingled himself with many questions." So they turn the phrase. Now may the Lord take your hearts off from those, and give you hearts to attend to this great question: What shall we do to be saved?

This was the question, you know, of the jailor in Acts 16:30. And it concerns those who as yet have no assurance of what condition their souls are in for salvation, to ask this question speedily, and not to put it off till they come to sickness and death, and then send for ministers and godly Christians, and say, "Oh! What shall I do?" How many, upon their sick and death beds, who never thought before to inquire what they should do to be saved, are in dreadful anguish, and then cry out, "Oh, what shall I do? Oh, the distressed condition I am in! I am afraid that my soul is lost forever! What shall I do?" Why do you ask it now? Is this the question to ask now, when your soul is going before the great and dreadful God to have the sentence of its eternal doom to be passed upon it? Oh, it concerns you quickly, you young ones, as soon as ever you come to know that you have souls, to be asking this great question: "What shall I do to be saved?"

We have an example of this in that young man whom Christ looked upon in love because he was inquisitive about the salvation of his soul. The story is in Matthew 19:16: "Behold, one came and said unto Him, 'Good Master, what good thing shall I do that I may inherit eternal life.' " And in verse 20 it appears that this was a young man: "The young man saith unto Him, 'All these things have I done.'" Oh, it would be a comely thing for young men to come to Christ and say, "What shall we do to have eternal life?" It appears that he was a young gentleman, a man of great possessions, and he is called by Luke "a ruler." Some interpreters think that meant only in the family, for the Jews had some chief in the family who ruled and governed there. But this young man came to Christ, and that running, as in Mark 10:17, where you have the story: "And Christ looked upon him, and loved him," as in verse 21. Oh, it is a lovely thing to see young people begin early to inquire what they should do to be saved, and we have had great hopes for young people. But here was the policy of the devil, when the Lord was bringing the greatest harvest of young people within these last three or four years to Himself as ever was, I think, since the beginning of the world. The devil knew that he could not get them to turn to lewdness and profaneness immediately again; therefore he labored to put them to turn all their religion into questions about controversial things that they would not be able to manage and understand, and so put them off the thoughts of that great question what they should do to be saved. Oh, labor to inquire, and to be satisfied and resolved in that question early.

If you ask this question, as you are to do it early, so do it earnestly; do it with a great deal of fervency of spirit, as a matter of infinite concern. Mark 10:17: "When he was forth into the way, there came one running, and kneeled to Him, and asked Him, 'Good Master, what shall I do that I may inherit eternal life?'" He came running with a great deal of fervency and earnestness about the business; and the fervency that youth has should be manifested in being earnest in inquiring after the way of salvation. People who are elderly think that they are well enough, and they have not lived so long, they think, as not to know how to be saved all this while, and therefore will not inquire. Because of this their spirits do not boil with that fervency and heat as young ones do. This man came running to Christ.

If you do inquire, inquire sincerely, with a heart truly willing to do whatsoever God shall make known to you. We are this day about this great question, what a man should do to save his soul. I suppose that many of you would be glad to know what should be done, and I think every one is ready to ask such a question as this. But before we come to answer it, let me speak to you as in the name of God. Do you desire to know it with a heart truly willing to yield to whatsoever should be revealed to you out of God's Word? Put this to your own hearts before we come to give any answer; otherwise, what do you hear this day, if there be not such a heart as this? Can you appeal to God, and profess that whatsoever this day the Lord shall reveal unto you from His Word that you should do to save your soul, that you will do? Can you say, "Here I am, and I profess to yield myself up to the truths of God." If your hearts are so framed, then we may have encouragement to now show you what should be done.

You must inquire constantly too. If you are not satisfied at one time, never be at rest till you are satisfied; do not ask what I should do, and come to hear what you should do, and then pass it over and let every little thing take this out of your minds again. But when you begin to inquire after the way of salvation, resolve that you will never give rest to your souls till you have gotten this question answered. And there is great deal of reason that we should ask this question in such a way. For:

1. Every one of your souls are in a lost condition naturally; therefore, it concerns you to be inquiring after the way of salvation.

2. The salvation of a soul is the most difficult thing in the world; if ever your soul is saved, it must cost more than heaven and earth is worth to save it. It is not, therefore, such a trifling business, the saving of souls. This I dare avouch, as in the name of God, that the soul of the poorest girl or servant who is here, if it is saved, must cost more than heaven and earth is worth to save it. Therefore, there is a difficulty in it.

3. There are but few who shall be saved; nothing is more clear in the Word of God than that there are but few souls that shall be saved. We cannot tell that this or the other soul cannot be saved; we are not to enter into God's counsels concerning particular souls. But this we may say, and have warrant from the Word to say, that there are but few souls that shall be saved. "Strive to enter in at the strait gate, for strait is the gate, and narrow is the way, and few there be that enter" (Matthew 7:13 compared with Luke 13:24). And upon that ground Christ Himself raises that exhortation, "Therefore strive." Therefore inquire after the way of salvation with all your might. If there should come a voice from heaven at this time and say that there are but few in this congregation who shall go out alive, it would make everyone stand still. Everyone would think with himself, "O Lord! Must I die here?" Why, there is this voice from heaven, that there are but few souls in the world but shall perish eternally. Then certainly it is not for us to be quiet; but it concerns us to be restless in our conditions, and for everyone to say, "Is it I? Is it I?"

When Christ said that one of His disciples would betray Him, everyone was inquiring, "Is it I? Is it I?" It is said that the flock of Christ is but a little flock. The words in the original are two diminutives, and may be translated, "a little, little flock." Oh, it concerns you all to look about you.

QUESTION. But now, these things being premised to put you to inquire after salvation with all your might, we come to answer this question: "What we should do that our souls may be saved?"

ANSWER. We must premise further:

There is nothing that any man can do that saves him; there must be something higher than what he can do—and yet God requires that he should do what he can do. Indeed, what any man can do of himself, yea, or by assistance from common grace; yea, I will say further, by assistance from any grace whatsoever, though it may help forward his salvation by an ordinance of God, yet it cannot be the thing that saves him. The thing that saves him is higher than what is done by the creature; it is what is done by Christ, or what is suffered by Christ. It is that which saves the soul, and not what is done or suffered by us.

But we must not make such a vain, foolish, and dangerous inference that therefore nothing is to be done, because the things that we do are not the things that save us. There is a great deal of evil that comes from men and women's presuming to draw consequences; they think that if this is true, the other will follow; and so, through the weakness of their understandings, they come to draw dangerous consequences from true positions. We are dead in sins by nature (Ephesians 2:1), and without Christ we can do nothing (John 15:5). Here is the consequence drawn by many ignorant people who pervert the Word to their own destruction: "If God is not merciful to me, why should I pray, read, hear, or use any means. Let us lay aside all, for we can do nothing; we are dead in sins." Now we are to know that though nothing can be done by us (till God brings us into a state of grace and salvation) that is acceptable, so as certainly to bring us to heaven, yet if it is but that which shall stop us in the contrary way a little, it is worth our labor. If it is but that which in any way may tend to bring us unto any means that may do us good, it is worth our labor, and all our pains.

But let us especially consider that though we are not able to do that which shall save us, yet God is pleased often to convey His strength to those He intends to save through the use of those means, at that time when they improve their natural abilities rather than at that time when they sit idle and do nothing—and therefore you must be up and be doing. We read in the gospels concerning the young man who came to Christ and inquired what he should do for eternal life that Christ professed to him that he was not far from the kingdom of heaven, that is, that he was not so far as others. It is true, if a man abuses his doing, and rests in his doing, that sets him as far from the kingdom of heaven as profane ones; and therefore publicans and harlots may enter into the kingdom of heaven as soon as scribes and Pharisees. But there may be many actions done by a common assistance of God's Spirit that may bring some nearer to the kingdom of heaven than others; and the denial of such a thing as that is would be an extreme boldness in any; for they are the very words of Christ to the young man, that he was not far from the kingdom of heaven. And therefore, notwithstanding your inability, and notwithstanding the things that we do are not the things that save us, yet we have ground enough to put on men and women to do.

Now the meaning of this great question is this: what is the way that God ordinarily takes to bring men and women to salvation? Or how should I follow God in His way? That is a certain truth of the ancients, "Though God made you without you, yet He will not save you without you. God works upon us as upon rational creatures, and therefore it concerns all the children of men who would have their souls saved to observe the work of God, and to stir up what is in them to join with the work of God in the way of salvation. Certainly, whatever conceits there are to the contrary, they are not only foolish, but extremely dangerous; and Satan's policy and cunning is exceedingly much seen in them.

A further thing that I would premise before I come to particulars is this: when I speak of anything that should be done, I prescribe no particular order, knowing that the works of God are various. Sometimes God stirs a soul to do one thing, and sometimes to do another thing; but take them in whatever order you will, yet we must name them for memory's sake in some order. God expects them from you, and you are to join with God in those works if you would have your souls to be saved. And so we come to the great question:

QUESTION. What should we do to be saved?
ANSWER. First, if you would have your souls saved, join with God in what He has revealed to you concerning your lost condition, laboring to understand those truths clearly that are delivered in the Word concerning the lost condition of souls by nature, and work those truths upon your hearts so as to be sensible of them. Those whom God intends to save, He shows them what this salvation is. He shows them from what it is they are to be saved so that they may not run away with the fitting word "salvation" and the saving of souls. Now God reveals this in His Word; and when He intends to save a soul, by His Spirit He stirs it up to join with the Word of God, and work those things upon itself so as to be made sensible of them.

For example, the soul, being solicitous as to how it should come to be saved, searches the Scripture; and there it finds how we are by nature the children of wrath. There it finds that God had made man according to His own image at first, but man has sinned against God and broken the covenant upon which his eternal state depended. In the sin of first man all men have sinned, and are deprived of the glory of God, and now are conceived in sin and brought forth in iniquity; so there is a most dreadful breach between God and the soul, and man by nature has become an enemy to the infinite God. Now he has the seeds of all kinds of sin in him, and all his life, while he continues in his natural estate here, is nothing but fighting against God, flying in the very face of God. He finds that by sin he is brought under a most dreadful curse, the curse of the law, and that he is bound over by the bonds of the law to eternal death as the wages of sin. These things the soul finds in Scripture.

Now if you would be saved, when you find God revealing such things, labor thoroughly to convince your soul of the truth of them. "Are these things so indeed? Is this my condition? Am I thus and thus naturally? Oh, what good then will it do me to have all the world, and be in such a condition as this is? O my soul!"

When were you sensible of this condition? Do you walk as becomes one who is sensible of such a lost estate as this is? Oh, labor to drink in these truths, to work them upon your heart, and cry to God to set them home upon your spirit, to make your soul thoroughly sensible of them, as He uses to make those whom He has a purpose to save.

You must come to a conviction not only of your lost estate, but of your inability to save yourselves, and the inability that there is in all creatures in heaven and earth to save themselves. You must come to a conviction that your fall from God is so dreadful that all the created power in heaven and earth cannot help you, yea, and that you are now unable to help yourself to save your soul. Be convinced thoroughly of this. This was the way that Christ took with the young man: He told him of the law first, and then afterwards, because he was conceited that he had fulfilled the law and done it, Christ put him upon a duty that might convince him to the contrary, which was required in the spiritual meaning of the law that forbade covetousness, and requires that we should be willing to part with all for God when He calls for it. "Go and sell all that thou hast, and follow Me, and take up thy cross, and follow Me," Christ said. Aye, but the young man had great possessions; but because he was not a swearer, nor a stealer, nor a murderer, nor a liar, he thought he had fulfilled the law. But Christ, by saying what He did to him, did as much as say, "Poor young man, you are deceived. You think that you are able to do what God requires in His law; but if you understood the spiritual part of the law, you would see that you are so cast down by it that all you are able to do in your obedience to the law cannot be sufficient (through the sinfulness of your heart and nature), but you must perish if you take such a course as to think to be saved by the law."

Certainly, this it is upon which thousands of souls perish. They think indeed that they are sinners, but hope that they shall do better; and they are able, they think (though not without God, God must help them) to do that which the Word of God requires of them whereby they may come to be saved. Now certainly you do not know your fallen condition, how far off you are from God, and what your sinful estate is naturally, if you have such thoughts as these

Second, if you would have your soul saved, break off the acts of your sin at least.

QUESTION. Why do ministers speak to men to break off the acts of their sin?

ANSWER. Certainly we may well speak, for God gives men much power over outward acts. You cannot do it of yourself, that is true, but there is a common work of God's Spirit that greatly enables men and women regarding outward acts. "Let him that stole steal no more." A man at the day of judgment cannot say, "Lord, I continued in theft because I was not able to stop." Though you cannot change your heart indeed, yet you can forbear the outward act. One who is mute might say, if he could speak, "Lord, I was no swearer because I could not speak." You are ready to say, "I cannot help it," but God will find it otherwise at the great day. Certainly, if you would but use the strength that God gives you, you may as well go to a sermon as to an alehouse. It is a very false reasoning of people that because they do not have true grace, therefore God enables them to do no outward acts. Therefore, do what in you lies to break off the outward acts of your sin.

You who are a company-keeper, a Sabbath-breaker, a swearer, an unclean person, take heed of continuing in the outward way of sinning against God. Resolve this day against those outward acts of sin. Because you think that you can do nothing, profess to God in His presence when you are alone, "Lord, it is true, I can do nothing without Thee, but here I do engage myself to join with whatsoever Thou hast given me or shall give me to abstain from those acts of sin in which I have lived. And this, Lord, I engage myself to do, if ever I expect to be saved in the day of Jesus Christ." Can you not say these words? Express yourself thus to God, and certainly you can say these things, and that is something that you can do. The man and woman who shall willfully go on in those vile, gross acts of sin that are against the very light of nature, and the light of their consciences, for them to come and say, "What shall I do to be saved?" and yet still continue in their sins, it is but trifling with God and taking God's name in vain, unless it is with a resolution to go thus far.

Third, you must labor to take you heart, as much as you

can, from the things of the world, from these outward concerns here, from seeking them as your greatest good. That which was your chief desire heretofore, you must labor to take your heart from, and possess your soul with the "one thing necessary." You must conclude thus with yourself, "It is not necessary that I should be rich, that I should be so honorable, that I should have these and these outward comforts in the world; but it is necessary that I should look to the salvation of my soul." When God has a purpose to save, He takes the heart very much off of creature comforts. Oh, if people's hearts were taken off from the world to seek after salvation in a constant way, as they are in some flashes, when they hear some truths that come near to their hearts, or when they are upon their sickbeds, how far might they have been gone in the way of salvation! But the thoughts of the world have taken their hearts, and all other things have vanished and come to nothing.

Fourth, if you would have your soul saved, your great care and endeavor must be to acquaint yourself with the knowledge of the mysteries of the gospel, of the covenant of grace, of the way that God has chalked out for salvation. Let a man or woman have never so good meanings, never such desires and affections, and live never so fairly and civilly in the world, yet if they are not acquainted with the way that God, in the gospel and in the covenant of grace, has revealed for the salvation of souls, they may perish for all that. God has appointed but one way to save souls, and He is set upon it and determined that whosoever misses that way must perish, whatsoever good thoughts and desires they have otherwise.

What Must We Know to Be Saved?

*"For what is a man profited if he shall gain
the whole world and lose his own soul? Or what shall
a man give in exchange for his soul?"*

MATTHEW 16:26

What must we labor to inform ourselves of in the gospel and in the covenant of grace in order that we may be saved?

I will list thirteen things we must know and do in order to obtain salvation:

1. You must labor to inform yourself of the absolute necessity of satisfaction to divine justice. That is revealed in the gospel, and that you must come to know. "I am a sinful, wretched creature; my soul is in a damnable condition. Now that which must save me must satisfy God's infinite justice. I may not be saved merely by crying to God for mercy. No, if there were nothing

else but my crying to God for mercy, yea, put all my good deeds into the scale, put what I have done, what I can do, what I can be enabled to do, all my prayers, my cries, this will not do."

OBJECTION. It is true, there is not enough in me; but will not God's mercy eke it out?

ANSWER. No, it is neither what you do or can do, or can be enabled to do. But it is a satisfaction to justice, a price paid for the soul. No soul is ever saved unless it is saved in the way of a price that is paid for it. And this you must acquaint your soul with, which thousands of people are ignorant of. Yet they hope to be saved. But how? They will pray to God that they may be saved, and that God would have mercy upon them. But is this all? Certainly, this is not the way of the gospel. But the way of the gospel is that which reveals unto the soul the price that is paid for a soul, even the blood of Christ. The gospel reveals that in Christ, the great Mediator of the second covenant, there is a perfect satisfaction to God's infinite justice. This indeed is a great part of the mystery of the gospel; this is the saving truth of the gospel, and you must acquaint your soul with this truth if you are to be saved.

And when you hear of this truth, perhaps you cannot understand it for the present. Then you need go to God in secret, and be crying to Him that He would reveal this truth unto you.

OBJECTION. But it is not our crying that works anything with God.

ANSWER. It is true, it is not merely our crying; but there is something of God further. Yet God has made many gracious promises of answering our cries, and now, so that He may make good His promises, He will further reveal this mystery of the gospel to you, that there is a necessity of satisfaction to divine justice for your sin that has brought your soul into a lost condition.

2. There is the necessity of a perfect righteousness. I will not speak of anything controversial about it, as to which way it comes to be applied, but all will grant that there is a perfect righteousness that we have need of. The way of salvation is a perfect righteousness. You must have a Surety who has a perfect righteousness for you.

3. The way of salvation reveals an absolute necessity of the application of the satisfaction and righteousness of Jesus Christ. The application of it means that it must be made your own in some way, that you must have your part and share in it by your union unto Christ and by being made one mystically with Him through faith, so that the soul is not merely saved through mercy. Nor is the soul saved thus, in that Christ has come and done such and such things, and therefore God the Father says, "For the sake of Jesus Christ I will save you, for He has satisfied Me by what He has done." No, there is something more.

I confess it is true, in the end we are saved for the sake of Christ, but it is by our union with Christ. We are united to Christ and made one with Him, if what Christ has done for our salvation is tendered up to the Father as ours, we being one with Jesus Christ. So that if you know your miserable estate by nature, and thereupon inquire after salvation, and cry to God that He would be merciful unto you, that is not enough.

The gospel reveals still more. Suppose you come to know more than you can understand by the light of nature; yet the gospel reveals to you that not only must you be saved by Christ, but you must be united to Christ by faith. There must be a spiritual marriage between the Son of God and your soul. You must have Christ to be a head and you a member, He your Husband and you His spouse. You must inquire after this union; and that is the way of believing. This is the substance of the apostle's words to the jailor when he asked what he should do to be saved: "Believe in the Lord Jesus Christ, and thou shalt be saved." It must be through Jesus Christ, the great Mediator of the second covenant, by your believing in Him and being made one with Him that you must come to be saved.

4. The gospel reveals further, as necessary to salvation, a necessity of regeneration, of being "born again," of having the image of God renewed in the soul by the Spirit of Jesus Christ, of being a new creature. If the soul should now depart wanting this, it must certainly perish; but if it comes to be saved, it must have this revealed to it, for in the gospel there is held forth the great work of God in begetting that soul anew to Himself that He intends to save, putting a new life into it, sending the Spirit of Jesus Christ into it whereby it lives, acts, and works—being now carried on not by its own spirit, but by the Spirit of the Son of God. This act of regeneration is necessary to salvation; so Christ tells Nicodemus that he must be "born again." This only the Gospel reveals; and thus our souls should labor to acquaint themselves with the great things of the gospel. And as the wise man says concerning instruction in Proverbs 4:13, "Take fast hold of instruction; let her not go; keep her, for she is thy life," so I say of these instructions that are revealed in the gospel; keep them, for they are your lives. Do not think that God, though He is infinitely merciful, will yet save souls in any other way; for God has set this way. And it is an infinite mercy that we are to admire, adore, and praise His Name for, that there may be salvation in any way at all. And if there may be salvation in any way, you poor, wretched children of men, know that you should be restless till you come to understand further that one way. Oh, that we could make it to be the great business of our lives to search into the gospel and find out these things, for it is through this that we come to have eternal life.

5. If God has put it into your hearts to seek to have them saved, you must walk with fear and trembling before the Lord all the days of your lives. The fear of God must be mighty and strong upon your spirits if you would be saved; and you must labor to keep the fear of the great God upon your spirits. Philippians 2:12 is famous for this: "Work out your own salvation with fear and trembling; for it is God that worketh in you both to will and to do of His own good pleasure." It is as if the Holy Ghost should say, "You need to walk with fear before the Lord for, the truth is, He has you at such an infinite advantage as you are not able to stir one foot to do anything to deliver your souls from eternal wrath without the work of God upon you." You need to take heed what you do so that you do not provoke this infinite God who has you under His feet, so that you are able to do nothing towards your salvation if He withdraws Himself from you.

I appeal to you, suppose that you so depended on any one man in the world that your life lay at his mercy; and if he should but speak a word you were a dead man or woman; would you not, when you come into his presence, come with fear lest you should displease him? Would you say, "What do I care for him? Let him be pleased or not pleased, what is that to me?" You would not dare do it. Now, shall we have less fear because He with whom we have to do is the Lord? If we had as much dependence upon any man in the world as we have upon God, we would fear him. Now, shall God have less fear because He is a God? He should have more fear. "Fear Him," said Christ, "that when He hath killed the body can likewise kill the soul. Yea, I say unto you, fear Him." Christ put an "I say" upon that; and truly, that soul begins to be in a way of salvation that begins to have the fear of the great God to fall upon him.

Most people in the world walk boldly and presumptuously in the presence of God, as if God had nothing to do with them, and as if they had nothing to do with God. Alas! These go on in the ways of death and delusion. But the soul that God has a purpose to save, He begins to reveal His glory to it, and to shine upon it, as He did upon Saul when He shone from heaven in a glorious manner, and stopped him in his way when he was riding unto hell and destruction. He cried to him, "I am He that thou hast sinned against. I am He that thou persecutest." Then Saul fell down trembling and said, "Lord, what wilt Thou have me to do?" It is as if Saul had said, "Lord, I did not know Thee; but I see Thee now to be a great and a dreadful God. I see that I am in Thy hands to save or destroy as Thou pleasest." And therefore Saul came with a trembling heart and cried to God, "Lord, what wilt Thou have me to do?" Aye, he was in a good way of salvation.

And so, when a vile sinner who has gone on without the fear of God upon him shall now come trembling, beholding the dreadfulness of the infinite God, that eternal first Being with whom it has to deal, and shall have His fear struck into it, this soul is in a good way of salvation; it is stopped in the way of destruction, and it is in a good way of salvation. That is very observable further in the text: "Work out your own salvation with fear and trembling, for it is God that worketh in you." This is a place that many people grossly abuse; they think they need do nothing. But mark how boldly these people cross the Spirit of God in the text, for the Spirit of God makes this argument: "Work out your salvation, because God works." And they say, "It must be God who works, and therefore I will do nothing." Oh! If you should willfully go on in ways of provoking God, and upon your sickbed and deathbed cry, "O Lord, now be pleased to work upon my soul, as Thou used to work upon those whom Thou dost intend to save," do not be amazed if God should make this answer, "You are a bold wretch, who has provoked the eyes of My glory all thy days. And do you now cry to Me to do it?"

If any of you think that there will ever be a time when you will stand in need of God's mercy to save your souls, you need to walk with fear and trembling before this God. I put this to the soul of everyone here: do you not think, O you sinful soul, that there will be a time that you shall stand in need of the mercy of God? And what course do you take now beforehand? Is that course that you take beforehand a continual provocation of God? Is it a good preparation for that time?

If there were a man that you lived near—though for the present you did not care for him, but slighted him—yet if you knew that there would be a time that you must stand in need of that man so as if he should forsake you, you would be a lost man, would you dare to provoke that man? We all know what need we shall have of the mercy of God; and therefore we need to walk with fear and trembling before Him.

6. If you would have your soul saved, attend upon those means that God has appointed to save souls; wait at wisdom's post. This one direction, being clearly shown but of Scripture, will be enough to confute all who talk against doing. If God has appointed means to save, then surely He has appointed that we must amend upon those means. In Romans 1:16 the preaching of the gospel there is called "the power of God to salvation." Now if you would be saved, you must bring your souls under that which is the power of God to salvation. Because the Lord in the ministry of the gospel puts forth His almighty power for the saving of souls; therefore it is that the gospel is called the power of God to salvation. You cannot be saved without the almighty power of God, and where is that put forth but in the preaching of the gospel? "To whom is the arm of the Lord revealed?" that is, the arm of God in the preaching of the gospel. You know what the apostle says in Romans 10: "Faith cometh by hearing,

and hearing by the Word of God."

QUESTION. Can we do anything towards our salvation?
ANSWER. Yes, you may hear, it is the duty of us as creatures to come and hear the Word, and faith comes by hearing. So then faith comes by something that we do, but not so that God has tied Himself to give faith to everyone who hears. I would not be understood so. But God has appointed that hearing should be a means for working faith. It is true, it is the blessing of God in hearing, but hearing is the way that God has set. God indeed can convey faith from heaven to any soul immediately. "Aye, but where there is the preaching of the gospel, there I expect that these creatures who intend that I should work faith in them should come and attend upon the preaching of the gospel."

Christ could have opened the blind man's eyes without spitting upon the clay and anointing his face, but He would have that done; and that must be the means by which He will open his eyes. So if God will have hearing the word of the gospel to be the means by which He will work faith in the soul, take heed how this is neglected. Acts 26:18 says that Paul was sent to preach, but to what end? "To open their eyes, and to turn them from darkness to light, and from the power of Satan unto God, that they may receive forgiveness of sins, and inheritance among them that are sanctified by faith that is in Me." That is what the Lord Christ said to Paul. "I will send them to open the eyes of men, and to turn them from darkness unto light, and from the power of Satan unto God, that they may receive forgiveness of sins; and this is the great ordinance that I intend for this end, and that I will accompany to those whom I purpose to save at any time."

Therefore, when you come to hear the Word, you should come to it as the great ordinance that God has appointed to save souls by. Is there any soul that begins in this congregation to be awakened, and to think to itself, "O Lord, what shall I do to be saved?" I tell you that every time you come to hear the Word preached, you should come to it with such thoughts as these: "Now I am going to that great ordinance that the Lord has appointed to convey His power through to the salvation of those souls that are appointed to eternal life. I am going to the 'pool of Bethesda,' as it were, and there I will wait until the Lord shall be pleased to send His angel to stir my heart, and until I have begun to feel some power of Christ already, which encourages me to hope for further power. Many a soul has met with Jesus Christ, and He has brought it from the power of Satan to His own kingdom of light; and why may not my soul meet with the same power of Jesus Christ? However, I am resolved that as long as I live I will wait upon God in the way that He has appointed." Oh, the Word has a great deal of efficacy for the salvation of souls! Therefore, if you would have your soul saved, attend upon it for that end.

I shall apply one Scripture, that may be preparation for what remains. You are inquiring how you should be saved, and I am answering, "Oh, take heed that you are not found in this to be like those wretched Jews (God forbid that there should be anyone in this place found like them) who would fain have the Prophet Jeremiah be inquiring what the mind of God was concerning them, and they professed that whatever the Lord should reveal by him they would do, but when it came, lo they flung all off and it was to no purpose." The Scripture is found in Jeremiah 42:5, where they said to Jeremiah, "The Lord be a true and a faithful witness between us, if we do not even according to all things, for the which the Lord thy God shall send thee to us." In other words, "We desire you to go and know the mind of God, and tell it to us. And here we profess and call God to witness that we will do what lies in us to perform all that the Lord your God shall require." This was a very fair promise, and I hope there are some souls, if not generally all of you, who have such a disposition as to say, "Oh, let His servant search His Word, and find out what should be done; and whatsoever he shall speak according to His Word, that will we do—and God forbid that it should be otherwise. It would be just with God that our souls should perish if we should do otherwise."

But there is a great deal of deceitfulness in the hearts of men. Jeremiah went and did as they desired him, but read chapter 44:16 and you shall see what a different disposition there was in them, compared to what there seemed to be before. First, you shall find in chapter 43 that they began to wrangle at what Jeremiah spoke to them. All the proud men began to wrangle at what Jeremiah spoke. Mark, it is all the proud men; they are proud spirits who contend with God's Word. But mark it, first they wrangled (chapter 43:2), and then they grew resolute and stubborn. Chapter 44:16: "As for the Word that thou hast spoken to us in the name of the Lord, we will not hearken unto thee." What, are these the men who called God to witness that, whatsoever Jeremiah should declare in the name of God, they would do? Yet now, first they wrangled at what he said, and then they resolved that, as for what he had spoken to them in the name of the Lord, they would not hear it. God forbid that ever there should be found among any of you such wrangling spirits with the Word of God. Certainly, God will justify the words of His servants that they speak in His name one day, and will make them good upon you; and they may lie heavy upon the soul that shall neglect them. But where there is first wrangling at the Word of God, there usually grows an impudent, proud, stubborn casting off of the Word of God. "As for the Word that thou hast spoken unto us in the name of the Lord, we will not hearken unto thee. Why should we not do what we have a mind to? Why should we not take our liberty on the Lord's Day if we want, and follow our business if we want? Let ministers say what they will, we will do as we want to do; and we will keep our company if we want to, let them speak till their hearts ache." This was the very guise of this people who made such a profession before the Lord. But the Lord forbid that it should be so with any of you.

7. If you would have your soul saved, you must take heed of resting upon false hopes of your salvation; you must raze down to the very ground all your false hopes of salvation. Nothing in the world hinders the salvation of souls more than false hopes, when men dare build their eternal salvation upon every slight and vain hope that they hold. "The hope of the hypocrite," the Scripture says, "is like the spider's web," spun out of your own conceits; but every little touch is enough to strike it down again. Oh, the poor things that people venture their souls upon! I showed you what caused the loss of souls, that one thing was venturing. People's vain hopes was another, and these must be razed down.

QUESTION. What are those vain hopes that must first be razed down? And what do you mean by razing them down?
ANSWER. First, such hopes as are not Scripture hopes; and if they are not Scripture hopes, they must be razed down. Romans 15:4: "Whatsoever things were written aforetime were written for our learning, that we through patience and comfort of the Scripture might have hope." We have hope through patience and comfort of the Scripture. How do the hopes of those who shall be saved arise? Why, they arise thus, either by reading or hearing something out of the Word of God, and by God darting some light, some truths into their souls through His Word, they come to receive it; and there it lies working in them till at length their souls relish it, and they taste the sweetness of the

Word and come to have comfort in it. And so, through patience and comfort of the Scriptures, their hope comes to be raised.

The Scripture in raising hopes first works patience; it usually beats down the soul first and speaks hard things to it. And the soul that God overpowers to Himself is willing to lie under the power of the Scripture and be patient, notwithstanding that the Scripture reveals such hard things, and puts it upon never such hard duties. The heart, I say, yields to it, and at length the soul comes to find sweetness out of the Scripture, and so hopes come to be raised. That is, the soul sees some eternal truth out of the Word of God, the truth of God Himself that is eternal, a divine truth that it dares venture its eternal estate upon, and upon this it raises its hope; it is able to give an account from some place of the Scripture upon what grounds it hopes. "I hope that God will show mercy to me, and save my soul in the day of Christ," some will say. Aye, but what ground have you for your hopes?

Now, if your hopes are right, then there is something in this Book of God to be shown as the ground of this; and indeed you can have but little comfort of your hopes unless you are able to bring forth some Scripture or other upon which you build your hopes. For when you say that you hope, you may not mean that you think and are persuaded that it is so.

QUESTION. But what Scriptures have any to ground their hopes of salvation upon?

ANSWER. What Scriptures? A great many! I will give you but this one that many have to ground their hopes upon. Romans 8:1: "There is therefore now no condemnation to them which are in Christ Jesus, who walk not after the flesh, but after the Spirit." Upon this a soul that God brings to Himself may say, "What, does God say in His Word (that Word upon which my soul stands, and must be cast one day for eternity) that those who

are in Christ Jesus shall never be condemned? Aye, but who are
they? Such as 'walk not after the flesh, but after the Spirit,' such
as the bent of whose hearts, and the endeavors of whose souls,
are not after fleshly things, the comforts of this world, but after
spiritual things; such whom the Lord has made to be sensible
of spiritual things, and such as the Lord acts upon and guides
by His Holy Spirit in their ways and conversations. God says that
such shall never be condemned. Then upon this I will build my
hopes, for I feel that the Lord has been pleased to work so on
me as to bring me to Jesus Christ, to see Him, to close with Him,
and to rely upon Him. And I feel the fruit of the Spirit of Christ
in me so that, whereas before I walked after the flesh and did
not favor spiritual things, now I find that the lusts of the flesh are
mortified, and I would wrong the grace of God if I should deny
the actings and guidings of the Spirit in my soul. And therefore I
will build my hopes, and rest upon this Scripture."

And the more any soul rests upon any Scripture (if it rests
truly), the more shall it find the power of that Scripture upon
it. Therefore you shall know the difference between a hypocrite's resting upon Scripture and one who rests through the
work of God's grace: a hypocrite rests upon such in Scripture,
and thinks that his heart is according to the Scripture; but
he does not find that the more he rests, the more his heart is
wrought upon by the Scripture, and daily grows to be more and
more like the Scripture, to come nearer and nearer to what is
required in the Scripture. But when a gracious heart rests upon
Scripture, it finds that daily it grows nearer and nearer to the
Scripture, and that works daily more and more upon it. Indeed,
that is the way to grow in sanctification, and to make our hearts
like the Scriptures. Fall upon several places, and let your souls
rest upon them for eternity; and so you will find your hearts to
grow more and more like those Scriptures, and the power of

those Scripture will appear more and more in your hearts and conversations. This is the way of the saints who have hopes of being saved.

Second, those hopes that are to be razed are hopes that are not wrought in the soul by the power of the Holy Ghost. In the forenamed chapter, "The God of hope fill you with all joy and peace in believing, that you may abound in hope through the power of the Holy Ghost." The hope that is right for salvation is such a hope as is wrought through the power of the Holy Ghost. Now, then, the hope that is in men and women, that is born with them, and has lived with them all their days, springs from the root of nature; for so that which is born with us and grows up with us all the days of our lives springs from a root of nature, and so the hopes of most people are none other but such as spring from root of nature. Go from one to another, and ask them, "Do you think to be saved?" And they will say, "Aye, I hope so." If you ask them, "How long have you hoped so?" And they will reply, "Ever since I can remember. I thank God. Aye, I thought so." It is a hope that springs out of the root of nature, and therefore you have had it always, whereas the true hope of the godly for salvation is a hope wrought in their hearts by the almighty power of the Holy Ghost.

I appeal to you now, what almighty power of the Holy Ghost have you felt in your hearts to raise up those hopes that you have in you? For certainly the grace of hope has a difficulty in it, as well as any grace whosoever. Now nearly all people find an easiness in that. But here the Scripture makes it to be the glory of the Holy Ghost to take hopes in any creature; therefore, those hopes that arise from a root of nature, that are not wrought by an almighty power of the Holy Ghost in the heart, must be razed down.

Put this question to your souls: "I have hopes to be saved,

but, Lord, how are they wrought? What power of the Holy Ghost has been in my heart to raise these hopes? Suppose there were no Holy Ghost (as they said in the Acts, that they had not so much as heard whether there was any Holy Ghost or not), yet might not I have such a hope as I have in God's mercy?"

Oh, the hope that will bring you to salvation is such a hope as is raised by power of the Holy Ghost. Now if our hopes are raised by the power of the Holy Ghost, then they will have much of the Holy Ghost in them, and will be suitable to your hopes. So does the Holy Ghost come into your hearts and dwell there; and if He comes and dwells in your hearts, then He enlightens your hearts. He acts and guides you, so that you are led by the Holy Ghost on your way.

Now, can you say that in the course of your lives it is the Holy Ghost who guides you, that you are carried on by the Holy Ghost, and not by your own spirits. It is true, the best of all may be acted and guided by their own spirits in some time of temptation, but for the course of their lives they are acted and guided by the Holy Ghost. Their lives are such that those who live by them may say, "Here is one who is moved and guided by the Holy Ghost." Can you say so? Certainly, if you have true hopes for salvation, they are raised by the Holy Ghost; and if they are raised by the Holy Ghost, He will move your lives in the ways of holiness.

Third, those hopes must be razed down that are not lively and purging hopes, I will put them both together. Hopes that are lively you have spoken of in 1 Peter 1:3: "Blessed be the God and Father of our Lord Jesus Christ, which according to His abundant mercy hath begotten us again unto a lively hope, by the resurrection of Jesus Christ from the dead." There is a great deal in this Scripture: first, that the hopes of the saints are lively hopes, that is, hopes that are mightily working in them. Such hopes will not suffer their hearts to lie dead in any way of wickedness. Indeed, it may be with the hearts of the saints as it is with a fountain of living water that may have some dirt cast into it. Being a living spring, it works out that dirt. So the children of God who have some lively hopes may have some dirt cast in by temptation, some sin, aye, but if their hopes are lively, they will work all out. And mark it, "you are begotten." Therefore you see that the hopes of life and salvation are not bred with us (as I spoke before), but they are that which follow from our new birth. And this is by the resurrection of Jesus Christ from the dead. The power and the virtue of the resurrection of Jesus Christ from the dead being in the soul, and putting a new life into the soul, begets it to this lively hope.

And then it is a purging hope. 1 John 3:3: "And every man that hath this hope purifieth himself, even as He is pure." You think, why do men need be so pure and strict? Are there none of you who ever have scorned at purity, preciseness, and holiness? If you have, consider this text upon which your souls lie. Every man who has this hope, that is, to see Jesus Christ, and to be made like Him, here in this world purifies himself even as Jesus Christ is pure. That is, he makes Jesus Christ to be his pattern in all that he does, and aims at no less purity than the very purity of the Son of God. He aims at it, and makes it his work, though he cannot come fully to it. And that very hope that is in him works him to this. Now what hopes you have had that are not such as these must be razed down to the ground, if ever you would be saved at last.

QUESTION. Razed down to the ground? What is that?
ANSWER. By razing false hopes to the ground I mean this:

First, you should be willing to seek God, and that earnestly, that He would never let you be at quiet in any false hopes. Be earnest with God in prayer. "O Lord, I see that the matter of my salvation is a matter of infinite consequence. If I should mistake, if I should miscarry in it, it would have been better for me never to have been born. O Lord, therefore help me in this thing above all so that I may never rest my salvation upon any false hopes, so that I may not at the last be disappointed of my last hopes."

Be earnest thus with God, and be willing to know the worst of yourselves. "Lord, if Thou seest that the work is not yet done, let me know it; let me know it now before it is too late." It is better to know that the work is yet to begin, while you have time to work, than to know it afterwards, when the time is gone. And then be willing to examine your hopes, to lay them to the rule of the Scripture, and that very narrowly. And if you find that your hopes cannot stand with the Word, then resolve thus with yourselves that the work is yet to be done; the very laying of the foundation of that great work, of the saving of my soul, is to begin.

OBJECTION. But God forbid this. We have not lived all this while to begin to lay the work of saving our souls now; that would be an ill thing indeed. Oh, I would to God it were not so!
ANSWER. But this very thought that some have, that they are not now to begin the laying of the foundation in saving their souls, is that which destroys them; whereas, though a man or woman has lived many years, yea, though they have been professors of religion, yet if upon examination they can find that the saving work of God is not wrought in their hearts, and upon that can conclude, "Lord, it is to begin, for all I know. I must begin the work again, for it is better to begin twice than to be damned once. Therefore, whatever becomes of me, I will begin again." This would be a good sign.

Suppose you should begin again, and it may be you thought too ill of yourselves; for it may be that there was some truth in your hopes or hearts that you could not see. Yet there is no great danger that what was good will not hold, though you do not see it. It is the safest way for men and women, therefore, to be willing to begin often; yea, and sometimes it is the best and the most ready course for people who have lost their evidences for salvation—and who can see no clear evidences out of God's Word to settle their hearts upon, for the great matter of this salvation—to begin again rather than to spend time in looking for their old evidences. A man who has lost his evidences may have them renewed with less charge and cost than he can seek them out; and so sometimes it is with the soul when it has lost its evidences for salvation: it may get new in less time and with less charge than to seek out the old.

It may be that you look to see whether you have not been a hypocrite all this while. Suppose upon examination that you cannot find anything to satisfy your soul but that it has been so; yet now, what hinders you but that you may this instant throw your soul upon Jesus Christ?

OBJECTION. Aye, but I am afraid that when I have come to Christ I have not come rightly.

ANSWER. Aye, but perhaps you may come to Christ in that time so that you may all know whether you have come rightly or not. But the best way for those who are mightily troubled and solicitous about evidences for whether their estate is right or not, I say, let those, rather than spend too much time in discouraging their own hearts, begin the work again. Let such a one present Jesus Christ now as a Savior for lost man, whose grace is infinitely full and infinitely free. And nothing is hindering you from this very instant casting yourself upon Him to be your Savior, to both save you from sin and from condemnation.

QUESTION. Aye, but then I may be presuming, and who has the right to do any such thing?

ANSWER. Nothing can give you a right to Christ but casting your soul upon Him, by believing in Him; the right that we have to Christ is by believing. It is not by any work before believing that gives the right to Jesus Christ. So by this you see what I mean by razing down the old foundation.

8. The next thing you must do is to lay the new foundation of this great work of your salvation, and be sure that you lay it securely.

QUESTION. Lay it securely? What is that?

ANSWER. Christ is the Foundation. No other foundation can be laid but Christ Himself, so lay it there. And then that which is next to Christ the Foundation is the true work of faith, and the true work of repentance. The true work of faith that is next is the foundation of what is wrought in our hearts. Christ is the foundation first, but any work in our hearts is the work of faith. "Believe, and thou shalt be saved."

Now, then, you must rightly know what this work of faith is, the way of thy believing, how you receive Jesus Christ in your believing, the power of how your faith is wrought, and what the work of it is upon your heart. Now, having laid Christ for your foundation, and having understood the mystery of the gospel, then when you come to believe in this great mystery of the gospel, you must consider what it is that you are now to believe. "Why, I am now to believe that the thoughts of God from all eternity were for the good of the children of men; and therefore He has sent the second Person in the Trinity into the world to take man's nature upon Him, to die an accursed death for the sin of man. As for me in particular, the thoughts of God were thus upon me from all eternity, to send His Son into the world to take my nature upon Him, and to be made a curse for my sin, to pay a price for my soul, and through Him (when I believe) I believe all my sin to be pardoned, the infinite, holy, dreadful God to be at peace with me, and my soul to be reconciled. I believe that this wretched, sinful soul of mine will be received into mercy, into the love of God, as the love of a Father, to be made an heir of God and eternal life." When you believe, this is the object of your faith.

Now this is a mighty work; it is a mighty thing to believe such things as these are. Consider, therefore, what you do when you say that you believe in Jesus Christ. Put this to your soul: "Can you, O my soul, close with these things? Can you venture your soul upon such things as these are?"

And when you come to believe, what do you do? It is not that you think that these things are true, but that in your believing you receive Jesus Christ according to the condition of the gospel; that is, your heart opens to receive into it the King of glory. "Oh, it is Christ who is the foundation of the new world that God is to raise up. It is Jesus Christ who brings in all the good, happiness, and glory of God to the children of men. And it is He who my heart opens to receive in, to embrace, to be satisfied with all, as all the good and happiness I expect. It is Christ to whom my heart opens to save me from my sin as well as from punishment, to unite me to God, to bring me to union with Him, so that I may live forever to the praise of the great God. And it is this Christ whom I take into my heart to be King and Governor, and now to rule. Sin, Satan, temptations, and lusts shall not reign as they have done, but Christ shall set up His own government in my soul."

Now, then, upon this must follow wonderful and glorious effects upon the soul. The soul that believes such high things as these are, and opens itself to receive Christ upon such terms, certainly, I say, there must be wonderful effects wrought in that soul. Such things must work the soul up to God, to live for Him in another manner than ever; and that is the reason for that Scripture expression: "Whosoever is in Christ is a new creature; all old things are past away, and all things are become new", (2 Corinthians 5:17). Why? Because the Lord has revealed new, glorious things to such a soul, the Lord therefore now acts and carries on the soul to other manner of objects than ever before it was wont to be busied about. And such a kind of work of faith this is; that is the foundation of the great work of salvation next to Jesus Christ Himself. As the old must be razed down, so a new must be raised up.

Now when you come to think of salvation, that you hope to be saved, you must have recourse to such a kind of work upon you as this: "How have I felt the power of the Holy Ghost razing down old things? And how have I felt the power of God, even that power by which Jesus Christ was raised from the dead, to raise such a foundation as this is?"

And upon this the soul follows the work of humiliation and repentance, that is, godly sorrow, and so mourns as to have the heart to be taken from its former courses and ways, and be set upon the contrary good. Now when the soul finds such workings of God upon it (as certainly these things cannot be, and yet no notice at all taken of them), when the soul takes notice of how God comes in with power upon it, and believes, "surely the Lord intends salvation to me; the Lord has laid such a groundwork upon my soul as I dare venture all upon it. And now I have cause to hope that the hazard of miscarrying to all eternity is over"—this is that which is the "joy of the Holy Ghost, joy unspeakable and glorious," when the soul upon good grounds can have hopes that the hazard of its miscarrying to all eternity is over. Now, "My soul, return unto thy rest" (Psalm 116:7), says such a one. So this is the next thing, the razing down of the old foundation and the raising up of the new one.

9. If you would have your soul saved, you must keep your soul under the authority of the Word, and maintain the authority of the Word, and the authority of conscience over you. This is the way, if you mean to go in God's way for salvation.

As for the Word, the soul that God intends to save, He reveals unto it the dreadful authority there is in this Book of God. "This is that Word," says God to the soul, "wherein I have revealed My mind to the children of men. Those counsels of My will that concern the eternal good of the children of men are in this book, and all your souls are to be cast by this book, by this Word, for eternity." This being revealed to the soul, the soul stands in awe of this Word, and trembles at this Word, fears the authority of it, looks upon every threatening in the Word, every command in the Word, every promise in the Word, as having a divine authority stamped upon it. The soul sees the broad seal of heaven stamped upon everything in this Book, and dares not willfully transgress against any thing in the Word, and so continues keeping itself under the dreadful authority of the Word. And that soul is in a good forwardness to be saved that is kept under the dreadful authority of God's Word in its constant course.

Now I appeal to you, you say that you would fain have your souls saved; but can you say this? "Indeed, I have many sins; yet God knows (who knows all things) that my soul is kept under the dreadful authority of His Word continually, and this I labor to do more and more, and I am willing that it should be so. I am not willing to have the authority of God's Word cast off, but I am glad that ever God revealed to me the dreadful authority there is in His Word."

The next thing is the authority of conscience. If conscience has any enlightening, that will display much of the mind of God to you. Nothing will reveal God's mind more unto the heart of a man or woman than an enlightened conscience; and it will reveal it with power. A minister speaks, and his words many times vanish into the air. But when conscience comes to discover God's mind, it comes with power and speaks particularly to this soul and the other soul. And conscience (when it has light) will be pleading God's cause, and admonishing and plucking the soul out of the ways of death and perdition; and it will not easily be put off. You may easily put off the counsels of such and such friends, but conscience will not easily be put off; it will come with such majesty upon the heart of a sinner that there is no gainsaying of it. Conscience will not regard the vain shifts that people have, but will still come in a commanding power. Oh, keep the authority of conscience! Many men and women, because they cannot go on freely in the ways of sin where conscience and the Word have much authority over them, therefore seek to cast off the authority of the Word and conscience. But know this for a truth, that the soul that has cast off the authority of the Word and conscience is going quickly to hell, is going quickly to destruction. All the while the Word and conscience kept you under, you were in some forwardness towards the way of life. But if you have once cast that off, then, oh, how the soul grows hardened in sin! How easily the truths of God are rejected! And then it goes with greediness to satisfy the lusts of the flesh, and ten thousand to one but such a soul perishes eternally. Oh, if there is ever a soul in this place that had the authority of God's Word and conscience to be over them with power, and now, through the violence of their lusts, have cast it off, let such a one take notice of what is said unto them in the name of God: oh, your soul is going speedily to destruction. But for you who begin to feel any authority of the Word or of conscience upon you, oh, keep it; for this is what will carry and guide you in the way that will bring to life at the last.

10. If you would have your soul to be saved, take heed of sinning against the price of your soul, against the blood of the covenant, and against mercy. Take heed of these three things: take heed of sinning against Jesus Christ who paid the price, against the gospel that revealed the price of your soul; and, oh, above all things, take heed of turning the grace of God into wantonness! Do not let the free grace of God revealed in Jesus Christ be turned to be a means to harden your soul in sin, to think that you may take more liberty to have the satisfaction of the lusts of the flesh just because Jesus Christ came to save sinners. Let me say to you, as Peter said to Simon Magus, "Pray if it be possible that the thoughts of thy heart may be forgiven thee." If you have ever had such reasonings in your heart as these, "Why, Jesus Christ came to save sinners; and the grace of the gospel is free and full enough to save souls, though they are never such great sinners"; and if upon that you have taken more liberty—oh, you need to fall down before the Lord and cry, "If it be possible, let such a thought of my heart be forgiven me." If you look into the Epistle of Jude, you find a dreadful passage against such "as turn the grace of God into wantonness." It is made a sign of a reprobate, and it is as black a brand of a reprobate as any, to turn the grace of God (and especially that grace of God that is in the price that is paid for souls) into wantonness; that is the most dreadful hindrance of saving of a soul that possibly can be. Oh, take heed of sinning against Jesus Christ, the great Savior of souls, but honor Jesus Christ all the

ways you can. Would you fain have your souls saved? Christ is the great Savior of souls, and you need to honor Him. "Kiss the Son, lest He be angry" (Psalm 2:12), and love Him. You need to love His ordinances, all His members, and all His people. You need to give all the respect that may be to Him because He is the only Savior of souls.

As for the blood of the covenant, take heed that you do not sin against that; let it not be accounted as a common thing. Oh, do not prize the satisfying of your own lusts rather than the blood of the covenant, and all the good that was purchased by that blood. When any wretched sinner hears the gospel preached to him, and yet shall prize the living in any base, wicked way of sin, such a one tramples the blood of the everlasting covenant under his feet. And the language of his heart and actions is nothing but this: "Whatsoever is spoken concerning the blood of the everlasting covenant revealed in the gospel, I prize satisfying the lusts of my own heart more than all the good that is in the covenant."

Now, do you think such a soul as this can be saved? Now you sin against the blood of the covenant when you come hand over head to the sacrament, and thereby you come to be guilty of the body and blood of Jesus Christ. People are mighty earnest about coming to sacraments. Do but read 1 Corinthians 11, which is a Scripture I know you who are acquainted with Scripture are not unacquainted with. Verse 27: "Whosoever shall eat this bread, and drink this cup of the Lord unworthily, shall be guilty of the body and blood of the Lord." And what then? Verse 29: "He eateth and drinketh his own damnation." When you would have the sacrament as the seal of the blood of Christ, and yet come in your sin and filthiness, and do not discern the Lord's body, you come to be guilty of the blood of Christ, and so to be guilty of your own damnation. So many think to seal their souls by eating and drinking the damnation of their souls; for there is nothing set out in Scripture that more furthers the damnation of a soul than to sin against the blood of the covenant. I know some make that Scripture their "damnation to themselves," that is, that they are only to be reproved and condemned for doing so; but we are to enlarge Scripture to the uttermost level that may be. And seeing that the Scripture has made the sin against the blood of Christ in other places so dreadful, we may very well understand that place in the most dreadful sense that may be.

Now in case you come unworthily, you hear what the Scripture speaks: it is guiltiness of the blood of Christ, and eating and drinking your own souls' damnation.

Then take heed of sinning against the mercy of God; do not let mercy harden you, but let it soften your hearts. Oh, that soul is in a good forwardness to be saved that every time it thinks of the mercy of God it finds itself to melt before the Lord and mourn bitterly for sin, when as it applies the mercy of God to itself, aye, that is a good evidence.

But when you think or speak of God's mercy, you find your hearts the more hardened in sin, this is dreadful! For how can such a soul be saved that sins against the mercy and love of Jesus Christ? For who shall hear and plead for your soul before God when you are guilty of the blood of Jesus Christ? And what is it that shall be your atonement before the Father? It must be the blood. "Without shedding of blood there is no remission of sin." And what blood must be for the remission of your sin when you trample the blood of the covenant under your feet and when you sin against mercy? What is it that must recover you but the mercy of God, when you come to God in the anguish of your soul? Now if your case is thus, then Jesus Christ shall plead against you and say, "O Father, Father, avenge Thyself upon this wretch, who has not only sinned against Thy work of creation, but against the work of redemption that I went into the world to work. Father, let this soul perish eternally that has rejected Me, and received every base wretched lust before Me."

Now, shall that soul be saved that shall have the blood of the covenant cry against it, and that shall have mercy itself cry to the Lord against it, "Lord, avenge my cause, for I have been most abominably and cursedly abused by this wretch?" When not only the law of God's justice and Satan accuse you, but Christ, His blood, and the very gospel itself, how shall such a soul be saved? Now, then, if you would have your souls saved, take heed of sinning against Jesus Christ, against the gospel, against the blood of God, and against the mercy of God.

11. If you would have your soul saved, take heed of sinning against the Spirit of grace, the good Spirit of God, who must draw you to Christ, and guide you in the way of salvation, if ever you are saved.

Now, take heed of slighting the motions of God's Spirit. Oh, do not slight any motion of the Spirit of God. How do you know but that when there comes any motion of God's Spirit, it comes to save you at this time? You cannot tell but that at any time when God's Spirit assists His Word, your soul may depend upon that time, so as God may say, "Had this soul followed on the work at this time, it might have been saved; but upon its not following on, it shall not be saved." Does God's Spirit begin to move your soul when you are hearing the Word? Oh, do not go into wicked company and so lose all again; but get alone in your closet, fall down upon your face, and cry to God that He would follow on the work of His Spirit that He has begun in you. "O Lord, I lived a long time in a dead-hearted condition, never minding the good of my soul. But Thou hast begun to stir me, and, Lord, I hope it is the beginning of Thy saving work upon my soul. Oh, that Thou would go on with it!"

How many upon their sickbeds and deathbeds would give a thousand worlds (if they had them) to have such stirrings of the Spirit of God as sometimes they have felt? Oh, now, when the Spirit stirs, and temptation stirs, take heed of listening to temptation, and rejecting the motions of God's Spirit. Think of what we read of the people of Israel, when they were going to Canaan: they were very near Canaan, and when they were upon its borders they refused to go into the land when God would have them. And upon that, "The Lord did swear in His wrath, that they should never enter into His rest" (Psalm 95:11). So when the Spirit of God begins to bring you near to salvation, so that it may be said of you as Christ said to the young man, "Thou art not far from the kingdom of heaven," take heed of hearkening to temptation lest the Lord swear that you shall never enter into heaven. The Spirit of God, which is like the dove in the ark, may perhaps come into your heart once, and it may come in again and you send it out again. But take heed of sending it out the third time lest it never comes in to you again, but rather the Lord should say, "Spirit, never strive more (Genesis 6:3) with such a soul." Oh, when God begins to stir, it concerns you to say with Samuel, "Lord, speak, for Thy servant heareth." You who have been forward heretofore, and have lost the work of God's Spirit, need to look about you; for it is a dangerous thing to draw back. "My soul," said God, "shall have no pleasure in these that shall draw back" (Hebrews 10:38). And if the soul of God will have no pleasure in you, how shall your soul be saved?

12. Whosoever would have their souls saved, let them take this course: account the preciousness of the time of your lives to consist in this, that it is a day of salvation. Account it,

therefore, a mercy of God that your lives are continued upon this reason, not because you may get great estates, and live and have your pleasures and delights, but because God has appointed the time of man's life here in this world to be the time to provide for his eternity. Few men and women in the world know how to judge aright of the preciousness of their time, the time of their lives; and that man or woman who comes to know aright how to judge the preciousness of this time of life, and of what depends upon it, such a one is in a good forwardness to salvation.

13. Be sure to go with those who go in the safest and the straightest way. Many of you question many things that others do, whether they need do so or not. "Why," you ask, "can none be saved but those who do so?" But I appeal to your consciences, do you not think the strictest way of goodness is the safest way for salvation? Now, if it is the safest, if you did but understand the infinite consequence of the salvation of your souls, there would need be no other argument to persuade you to any strict way of godliness but this one: "Whatever it is, whether absolutely necessary or not, I am sure it is the safest way." And I am sure that there was never yet anyone upon his sickbed who repented of being too strict and too precise. But I have known many who have repented of being too loose and too careless.

In a matter that is of great consequence, you will be sure to take the safest way. If there are any people in the world who walk so as your consciences tell you they are in a more strict way than others—more holy, more close to God, more self-denying, more faithful—it concerns you to inquire after those, and to walk after those and join them. "Surely those who go on in the safest way for the salvation of their souls, those I will make a pattern for myself. I will not look what the common course of the world, and the generality of the world does. The Scripture tells me that there are but few who shall be saved. And therefore the fewness of men shall never discourage me. Be they never so few, be they never so mean, if I am persuaded in my conscience that this is the safest way, then this is the way that I will walk in."

And surely this is the way for a soul to have comfort at the great day, when it shall appear before the great God and our Savior Jesus Christ. I beseech you to consider this: if you were all now to appear before Jesus Christ to have your eternal estates determined, in what men's conditions would you wish yourselves to be? If it might be in your liberty, and Christ should say, "Now I am to pass the sentence of eternity upon you for your salvation or damnation," what kind of men's estates would you wish yourselves to be in? Who would you rather be like? Who would you venture most upon, to be dealt with according as your consciences think they are most likely to be dealt with? I am persuaded, if this were the case, that most loose, profane, and ungodly men would run and cling to those whom they now scorn and condemn; to those who walk with the most strictness and holiness in their conversations. Certainly, if you would do so then, it is your wisdom to do so now; that which will be true then certainly is true now. And therefore that is a good way to helping to save your souls, to join with those who walk in the strictest and the holiest way, to do that now that, if you were to die, you would wish you had done; and to be with them now who, if you were to have the sentence of eternity past upon you, you would wish you had been with. But this shall suffice for what is to be said concerning that great question about preventing the loss of our souls, and what we should do to be saved.

As for the condition, you have heard divers things already about the way and direction for saving souls. I suppose when first the question was raised that every one of you would be greedy to

hear an answer. There was never anyone in this place but would
fain have his soul saved eternally. So what do you mean to do
now? What are your thoughts? There has been a question, and I
have endeavored in the name of God to answer it.

Now this is that which I desire of you even before you sleep:
Get into the presence of God alone, and give your answer to God
what you mean to do. Are you resolved upon it? Will you engage
your souls now to God this evening that that little time He will
let you live in this world, that your endeavors shall be according to those particulars that have been opened unto you? Oh,
blessed be God if this is in any one soul! But can anyone think
that among such a multitude as this is but that the Lord would be
pleased to dart some thing or other into one or more?

Let me conclude at this time, as the servant of Naaman said
to him when the prophet gave him direction what he should
do to be cleansed, he began to be angry, and was loath to do
what the prophet bid him. "Why," said his servant to him, "My
father, if the prophet had bid thee do some great thing, would
thou not have done it? How much rather then when he saith to
thee, 'wash and be clean'?" So I say to you, considering what the
worth of your souls is and the danger there is of your eternal
miscarrying, if God should have said this, "That your souls may
be saved, I require of every one of you that you should for forty
or fifty years lie as a head block at the fire burning," aye, and
if God should have said unto us from heaven, we all had cause
to have fallen upon our faces and to have blessed God for His
mercy towards us. But God does not require any such thing as
this at your hands. Rather He requires the abandoning of your
lusts, and attending on Him in His ordinances. He requires
the keeping of your souls under His Word and conscience, the
following of the motions of His Spirit, and believing in His
Son. Such things as these the Lord requires, upon which your

souls may eternally be saved. And will you not accept? Well, the soul that God intends to save, He will persuade. And may the Lord persuade your souls in these things, so that you may be saved in the day of our Lord Jesus Christ.

The World Is Not Worth a Single Soul

"For what is a man profited if he shall gain the whole world and lose his own soul? Or what shall a man give in exchange for his soul?"

MATTHEW 16:26

We come to the last thing. As the loss of the soul is great, as in all the respects I have opened, so it is such that were a man to have gained the whole world in a way of the loss of his soul, yet that gain will never recompense it. Job 27:8: "For what is the hope of the hypocrite, though he hath gained, when God takes away his soul?" There are some men who seek the world and yet lose both the world and their souls; they neither gain the world nor their own souls. And there are some who gain the world and their souls both. But there is no necessary connection between either gaining the world or losing one's soul, or losing the world and gaining the soul. One may be severed from the other.

But suppose that God should let a man gain what he will. Many men seek gain by sinful ways, and God crosses them in it. They do not have their gain, and yet they are damned eternally for seeking gain. Suppose a man had gotten all the world, as he would desire, and yet this man is wicked and loses his soul, he is a most miserable man. Now the thing that I have to do is to show unto you what a poor gain a man has who is wicked, though he may get the world, when he has cast up all his reck-onings, it may be said of him, as we usually say of men who have little, they may put all their gain in their eye and never see the worse. So certainly, if you have sought after gain in this world in such a way as you have not provided for your own soul, when you come to sum up all your accounts, you will see that very little has been gotten.

There are many ways whereby a man may come to see all the glory in the world to be but darkness: by seeing the glory of God, the glory of Christ, and the infinite consequence of an eternal estate. Those three things make the spiritual man to look upon all the glittering vanities of this world as mere dark-ness, as nothing. But there are three other things that may help a natural man to see the things of the world to be as nothing, and the gains of it to be very poor gain (I mean one who is not sanctified, who has no grace).

First, if God pleases to wound his conscience and terrify him, he will see all things to be poor things indeed.

A second is when God lays His hand upon him and afflicts him, upon his sickbed or his deathbed. It is reported of Muscù-lus that when he lay upon his deathbed, and his friends came to him, and saw what a poor condition he was in, he who had been an eminent, worthy instrument of God, and an excellent preacher in his time, mourning for the sad condition they saw him to be in said, "Oh, what are we?" As he lay in his bed he overhead them, and said, "Smoke." Many a carnal man, in the time of his sickness and apprehension of death, will say that all this world is as nothing.

A third thing that may make even a carnal heart to see all the things of this world to be as nothing is strength of reason. Though there were not terror of conscience or any afflictions, yet strength of reason may reveal the gain of this world to be as nothing, compared to the soul. And this strength of reason God is pleased sometimes to sanctify by His Spirit, when it is helped by the Word, by the sanctified reason that there is in the Word. I say, when it is helped by that, then God blesses it so as to work the heart from the world to the things that concern the everlasting good of the soul. And it is that which I shall speak to at this time, to convince you what a poor thing the gain of the world is, even by strength of reason, and yet such reason as is founded upon the Scripture.

I have already shown you the things that may make a spiritual heart see a vanity in all things in the world, such as the excellency of God, the excellency of Christ, and the consequences of eternity. The other two, terror of conscience and afflictions, are God's works; and when God is pleased to show the vanity of the world, ordinarily He brings them on the creature, by the sanctified, saving work of His Spirit, the vanity of all things. I shall endeavor to show this you by strength of argument and reason out of the Word.

1. Surely, though you should gain the world, and yet be a man who is likely to perish at last, you have gotten but little, and it appears first in that all those who ever came to have true wisdom, and who are in Scripture commended as men of true wisdom, have looked upon all the things of the world as very poor things. What do you think of him who was the wisest man

upon earth, Solomon? He had the greatest experience that ever man had, of what good the honors, pleasures, or profits of the world could do. And yet, after all his experience, see his testimony of all in Ecclesiastes 1:2: " 'Vanity of vanities,' saith the Preacher, 'vanity of vanities, all is vanity.' "

Observe these things in it:

- The things of this world are not only vain, but vanity in the abstract.
- They are an excessive vanity, "vanity of vanities."
- They are a heap of vanity, "vanity of vanities."
- All is vanity.
- And he adds his name to this: "saith the Preacher."

Now the word that is translated here "preacher," in the Hebrew, as those who know the tongue know, signifies one gathered. And it is in the feminine gender, and so some think it notes the soul of Solomon, who gathered wisdom after he had been gathering vanity so long. And so either he is saying that all things in the world are only vanity, and that vanity of vanities, a heap of vanities. Or else it is a soul gathered to God, after all his departure from Him, says that it is so. Herein Solomon is like a man who has gotten to the top of a high hill; and it is such a hill as there are perhaps hundreds of people of a strong opinion, and upon the top of the hill there are very rich treasures to be had; and they are all scrambling up a hill, treading on one upon another so that they may get up the hill. Now Solomon had gotten to the top of the hill before the rest, and he, seeing men, and seeking to get them out of such a conceit, cries out to them, "Sirs, you are all deceived; you are persuaded that if you could get estates, honors, and promotions, then you would have a great deal of content. Why, I am upon this hill, have a great deal of content. Why, I am upon this hill, and I find there is nothing but dirt here; there is nothing here that will answer all your toil, trouble, and expectation, and you will be utterly deceived." This is the meaning of this Scripture.

And next to Solomon, one of the wisest and holiest men who ever lived upon the earth, was Paul in the New Testament. Mark it, as soon as God worked upon his heart to show him better things, in Philippians 3:8, he professed that he accounted "all things but loss for the excellency of the knowledge of Christ Jesus." Verse 7: "But what things were gain to me, those I counted loss for Christ. Yea, doubtless, and I account all things but loss for the excellency of the knowledge of Christ Jesus my Lord, for whom I have suffered the loss of all things, and do count them but dung," but dog's meat, "that I may win Christ." This was the slight esteem that Paul had of all the things in the world, that men kept such a stir about.

When God began to work upon Zaccheus, when he heard of the salvation of his soul, when Christ told him, "This day is salvation come to thy house," immediately (being a covetous, rich man who had gotten his estate wrongfully) he cried out, "The half of my goods I give to the poor; and if I have wronged any man by forged cavillation, I will restore fourfold."

John was the beloved disciple of Christ, who lay in His bosom, and therefore knew so much of the mind of Christ. You know what he said in his first epistle, 2:15: "Love not the world, neither the things that are in the world; if any man love the world, the love of the Father is not in him. For all that is in the world, the lust of the flesh, the lust of the eyes, and the pride of life, is not of the Father." "The lust of the flesh" is pleasures and sensuality; "the lusts of the eyes" is riches; and "the pride of life" is honors. These are not of the Father, but of the world, John said. You may think they are great matters, they may be world. "And the world passeth away, and the lust thereof; but he that doth the will of God, abideth forever." It would be an infinite task to show you this both in Scripture, and likewise in the whole course of the story of the church, how slightly the martyrs accounted all the things of this world as soon as God gave them any true spiritual heavenly wisdom.

But because that would cost a great deal of time, therefore I proceed to show by strength of reason, further out of the Scripture. Let this convince rational men that that which the wisest men in the world, who have had from God a testimony of great wisdom, have thought to be a little matter, certainly has no greater matter in it. But they have thought the gain of all the world to be as nothing; therefore, certainly, there is no great matter in getting the things of the world, however men esteem them.

2. What if a man gains the world but loses his soul? He is never a whit the better for anything in the world. We say sometimes in our common language that such a man is the best man in the parish, and I have the hands of the best men in the parish. The truth is, we mean the richest men in the parish. But riches and honors make no man one whit better than he was before. "The heart of the wicked is little worth" (Proverbs 10:20). Let a man have never so great an estate, he may have so many houses that are worth so much, but he is worth no more than he was. As a great letter makes a word have no more sense than a little letter does, so great honors and great places make a man no more excellenct than he is without them.

These things in the world have no goodness in them any further than we put goodness upon them. We may indeed make good use of them, and so by our good use we may make ourselves better through God's grace; but possessing them does not make any soul one whit better than it was before. In fact, ourselves better through God's grace; but possessing them does not make any soul one whit better than it was before. In fact, they make many souls worse. Thousands of souls grow worse than they were before by the enjoyment of the world. But where have you one better? None can be better by having the things of the world; no, it must be by some grace of God that a soul grows better, and not by the things of the world.

I will give you this demonstration. You never find in Scripture (that I know of) that ever any child of God was worse for afflictions in the end; but you may find that almost every child of God who was in prosperity was the worse for their prosperity. There are very few exceptions. Daniel and Nehemiah were the only two I know of who were not the worse for their prosperity; but not one was worse for afflictions, from Genesis to the Revelation. Therefore, certainly, there is no such great matter in the things of the world. Daniel 11:21 is a remarkable place: "And in his estate shall stand up a vile person, and he shall obtain the kingdom by flatteries." A vile person, and yet have the honor of the kingdom? How can this stand? Yes, interpreters think it to be Antiochus Epiphanes who was advanced to that mighty height. I remember Josephus saying that the Samaritans in their letter to him give him the title of "the mighty god." He had that title given to him by those who were under him, and also that of Antiochus Epiphanes, which signifies illustrious. He was "illustrious Epiphanes, the mighty god," and yet the Holy Ghost gave him this title: "a vile person." What good do a few herbs that are strewn upon a corpse do? Do they make the dead flesh to be less corrupt and putrefied than it was? Truly, all the finery that wicked men have is at the best but a few herbs and flowers strewn upon a filthy carcass, which makes them no better.

The things of this world, therefore, in Scripture are called the things of "another man's." Luke 16:12: "And if you have the verse before: "If therefore ye have not been faithful in the unrighteous mammon, who will commit to your trust the true riches?" The riches of this world are called unrighteous mammon; now these are opposite to the true riches, as if there were no true riches. Then in verse 12, if you have not been faithful in that which is another man's, that is, in these riches of the world, who shall give you that which is your own? So that nothing is a man's own, to make him better, but grace. The things of the soul are a man's own, but the other things are the world's things; they are not a man's own. Therefore, what does it profit a man that he has gained the world, for he is never a whit the better man?

3. All these things are things beneath the soul, things of an inferior nature. What good is it for a man who has gotten never so much food laid up for his horses and dogs, but he has nothing for his children or for himself? So if a man has gotten the world, he has gotten something for his body, his inferior part, aye, but he has gotten nothing for his soul, which is more important than his body. These are things beneath and under the soul. What good would it be for a soldier to have a gilded scabbard, if he has a broken, rusty sword within, or but a wooden sword within? Therefore I find in Scripture that the bodies of men and women are called the sheath of their souls. Daniel 7:15: "I, Daniel, was grieved in my spirit, in the midst of my body." So it is translated in your books; but those who understand the original text know it is a word that signifies a sheath. So Arius Montanus translates it, and likewise in your margins, "in the midst of his sheath." And by comparing this Scripture with 1 Chronicles 21:27, it is plain that that is the propriety of the word. 1 Chronicles 21:27 says, "The Lord commanded the angel, and he put up his sword again into the sheath thereof." Now the word that is here translated "sheath,"

I find by comparing them together, is the very same word in the original that Daniel translates body; for the body is but as the sheath unto the soul—and what will it gain a soldier to have a brave sheath, and in the mean time have nothing within it, or that which is of no use at all?

Thus it is with many: they seek great things for their bodies, but their souls are left in the meantime without any succor or help, and in a most miserable condition. All things that are in the world should be servants to your soul if they are all inferior to it. We account it a great dishonor to a man to marry his servant. If we heard that a man of estate in this world married his servant, who was very low, we would account it a dishonor. Now for your heart to mingle itself with the things of this world as its chief good, what is that but to marry your soul to that which should be your servant? For all these things are but as servants to the soul; and for the heart of a man to be set upon the things of this world is to have the curse of Ham to be upon him: "A servant of servants shalt thou be." For the things of the world should be your servants; yet you are their servant, and so are a servant of servants. The curse of Ham is upon you when you are a slave to your estate, your honors, or to your brutish lusts. You are a servant of servants.

4. They are such things as God in His ordinary administration of providence has denied to His choicest servants, especially in the times of the gospel. Many of His choicest servants in former times were in very low and mean conditions. But as for the times of the gospel, how Christ Himself, who was the Son of God, lived? He did not have a hole to hide His head in. The fowls of the air had nests, and the foxes had holes, but the Son of man had nowhere to lay His head. Jesus Christ, who was infinitely beloved of the Father; and all the apostles, were in a poor, mean condition. Every one of them died a violent

death but John. We have records of their several sorts of death. Some were crucified, some were stoned, and some other kinds of death; but all were put to death save John. Read in the latter end of Hebrews 11 about those whom the world was not worthy of, how they wandered up and down in sheepskins, in goatskins, in dens, and in caves of the earth. This was a little before Christ's time, and he is speaking of those in the time of the Maccabees.

Now certainly, if God had so ordered things in His general administrations towards such as are most dear in His eyes, as to deny them these things, so that they shall have but little of them, there is no great matter in them; surely if there were any great matter in them, God would not deny them to His servants. When a wicked, rich man shall look upon a poor man who walks humbly before God, and would not commit the least sin willingly for all the world, I think such a man should think thus: "O Lord! What a difference there is between such a poor man and I; and yet my conscience tells me that God has more honor from him in one day than He has from me in all my life." Surely there is no such great matter in the things of the world if God has denied them to him. If there were any great matter in them, certainly such as walk most humbly with God, and most closely with God, would have them, if they were absolutely good. And indeed, this is one great reason that God's own dear servants have so little of the world and others so much. It is that He might hold this forth to all the world, that the things of this world have but little in them.

5. All the things of this world—the pleasures, profits, and honors of this world—surely have no great matter in them; for they are no more than may stand with God's eternal hatred of His creature. Now certainly, those things that have no higher excellency in them than may stand with the eternal hatred of

the infinite God have no great excellency in them. Those things that reprobates may have surely have no great matters in them. That which you give to your swine, you make no great matter of it. So take all the things of the world, and they are no more than God gives to swine, than God gives to reprobates, than God gives to such as He eternally hates.

I remember that Luther had such an expression as this of the Turkish empire: "It is but a crumb that the great master of the family casts to his dog." Now if all the Turkish empire is no more than a bit of bread that you would cast to your dog, what is your estate? The Lord who is so infinitely rich in mercy can afford such bones for dogs as these are, surely there are no great matters in these things that reprobates may have as well as children. Therefore, you poor people (and yet godly) who lack these things, quiet your hearts. What if you do not have such an estate as others? Oh, do not murmur! Why, it is no great matter you lack; you only lack that which God gives to reprobates. Suppose a man gains the world; if he loses his soul, what does he get? He gets a bone that dogs have in exchange for the loss of his soul.

6. The things of this world have no reality in them at all, no real good in them. According to the language of Scripture, what are the things of the world divided into? Take the division that you had before from John: "The lust of the flesh, the lust of the eyes, and the pride of life." Take pleasures, riches, and honors, and see what the Scripture says of them all.

As for sensual pleasures, you think that they have a great deal of reality in them. Why, in the Scripture phrase "they are nothing." In Amos 6, compare the former part of the chapter with verses 4-6: "That lie upon beds of ivory, and stretch themselves upon their couches, and eat the lambs out of the flock, and the calves out of the midst of the stall, that chant to the sound of the viol, and invent to themselves instruments like David, that drink wine in bowls, and anoint themselves with the chief ointments, but they are not grieved for the afflictions of Joseph." Here the pleasures that these men lived in are described; but mark what he says in verse 13: "Ye which rejoice in a thing of naught." You rejoice in that which is nothing. All these pleasures, these fine merriments, when you get into a tavern there you drink, boast, and have pleasure and music— and what a brave life this is! Aye, but you rejoice, says the Holy Ghost, in "a thing of naught." It may be a great matter in your eyes, aye, but the truth is that it is nothing.

As for riches, see the testimony of the Holy Ghost concerning them in Proverbs 23:5: "Wilt thou set thine eyes upon that which is not?" They are that which has no being at all; no, only grace and godliness have a being. Proverbs 8:21: "That I may cause those that love Me to inherit substance." Junius translates it, "to inherit that which is." You think that the things of grace are but imaginations; and only worldly things are real. No, the things of the world are but fancies, and the things of grace are real.

As for honors, you have Acts 25:23: "And on the morrow when Agrippa was come and Bernice with great pomp," literally, with much fancy; it was but all a fancy. And the truth is, the excellency that these things of the world have is an excellency that our fancy puts upon them. A piece of gold that heretofore was worth twenty shillings may be raised up to two and twenty shillings, aye, but though men may raise it up in their fancies to be worth more, the amount of gold is the same. So we may raise up the things of this world very high by our fancies, but there is no more real good in them than there was before. They are but shadows, and though a man's shadow is longer or shorter, yet a man does not grow longer or shorter with his shadow; for though a man's estate is more or less, yet his happiness does not grow more or less according to his estate. Therefore, what does it profit a man if he gains the world? Why, he gains a shadow; he gains that which has nothing in it; he gains a fancy, a dream, and he loses his soul for all this.

7. Suppose there were some reality in these things, yet there is nothing that can satisfy the heart. Isaiah 55: "Why do you lay out your money for that that is not bread and for that which satisfies not?" Only grace is that which satisfies the soul; these things have so much mud at the bottom that you cannot have a full draft of them. And besides, there is a curse of God upon them, that they should not satisfy. Yea, God has so fashioned the hearts of the children of men that they shall never be satisfied with these things. And the eager desire after these things comes from a great distemper. Maids and young women sometime have chlorosis, and it makes them long for coals, it may be, dirt, and green fruit; but though they long for it, yet this cannot satisfy them because it is but trash. So the heart of a man or woman who longs for the things of this world is in a distemper, just as one who longs to feed upon dirt may do so, but he can never be satisfied with it.

8. How can the gain of the world make up for the loss of any spiritual good? One who goes on in ways of looseness, that soul, whatever he gets in the world, has it without God. God in His ordinary providence may cast it in, but he has it without the blessing of God with it. What if a man had never such fine flowers in a garden, if the sun should never shine upon them? Truly, so it is with many wicked men: they have brave and fine offices, but they never have the sunshine of the blessing of God upon anything they have. Yea, that which they have in a way of sin, they have it with the curse of God along with it. That which wicked men feed upon is but swill; it is like hog's meat that is

wrapped up in the dirt. Their meat is filthy and stinking by itself, but when it is wrapped up in dirt, then it is worse. And so are their estates: the Scripture calls all in the world but as dog's meat, and it is wrapped up in their sin, and the curse of God is upon it.

Suppose that what you feed upon had no curse of God upon it, yet it is but as a piece of carrion; but now it is wrapped up in your sin, and so long as you go on in your sin the curse of God is upon it. But the good of all the things in the world consists in this, the communication of God's goodness towards me in them, and Christ's blessing of them to draw my heart nearer to God, and to be instrumental for me to serve God all the better. But how few men know wherein the true chief good of these things consists. "I have more of the things of the world than others have, aye, but wherein am I more happy? Wherein? Oh! I see God letting Himself out to me in the way of His goodness, and He gives me this to do Him more service than others who are poor." Oh, if you could say this, it would be a sign of a gracious heart indeed! A man who loses his soul and gets the world gets dog's meat wrapped up in dirt and filth. Oh, what a poor price for an immortal soul!

9. I must also tell you something about the uncertainty of all these things. "Charge those that are rich in the world that they trust not in uncertain riches" (1 Timothy 6:17). The whole world is, as it were, upon a wheel. The Scripture says that the tongue sets on fire the whole course of nature; it is in the original the "wheel of nature." All these things are turning up and down, as it were, on a wheel.

You have heard of the wheel of him who was a great king. Having overcome four other kings, he made them draw his chariot. But as they drew his chariot, he took notice of how they continually looked back to the wheel and asked them what the reason was. "Why," said they, "by this we see the turning of the things of this world. The nail that is now on the top will by and by be on the bottom. We were high enough for a while, but now are low enough." And the consideration of this abated the pride of that great prince who made these four kings draw his chariots.

So this world is but a wheel of nature. And will you venture your soul for these things that have no certainty in them? I remember Philip de Colisine's report of a Duke of Exeter, who married one of the sisters of the King of England. And yet he says that he was seen in the low countries begging for bread barefoot. Oh, therefore would a man venture the loss of his soul to gain these things that are so fading and passing away! All flesh is grass, and as the flower of the field, it passes away, and comes to nothing; yea, at those times when we have most use of the things of the world, then they are gone from us. When Absalom was caught by the tree, and had the most use of his mule, then his mule left him hanging by the hair of the head. So worldly things are most out of the way when you have the most need of them. And will a man venture the loss of his soul to gain these things that will leave you when you have the most need of them? When you lie upon your sickbed or deathbed, what good will it do you to think that you wore fine clothes, and had so much riches coming in yearly? "Riches avail not in the day of wrath; but righteousness, that delivers from death." All theses things are but fading, and will fail a man when he has the most need of them.

I remember our *Chronicles* [*Chronicles of the Kings of England,* by William of Malesbury] telling a strange story of Richard, the third king of England. And you who have them, they are worth your reading. I do not know that I ever read of a more magnificent coronation for a king than his, set out in abundance of glory. He had one earl who bore before him his crown, and four earls carrying four swords before him, one a sword of state, and another without a point to be a token of mercy; then two glittering swords, one in respect of the secular, and the other in respect of the clergy; four barons bearing a canopy over his head, and himself in a long purple velvet robe, and his queen in all her pomp and state. He had a duke to bear up his train, and his queen had a countess to bear up hers.

Divers other particulars might be shown to set out the greatest pomp and glory almost that could be conceived for a man to be in; but behold the revolution of things, for within little more than two years after this, this glorious prince was slain, and his body, lying naked to the view of all, was carried on a horse with his hands and head hanging down on the one side and his heels on the other, as butchers carry swine or calves. He was carried to Leicester, and there lay several days above ground naked and contemptible, and the very stone in which his body was laid was afterwards made use of to be a trough for horses to drink from at a common inn. Such hatred did they show to him who a while before was in such a glorious condition.

Thus we see that these things that are here will not hold long; and for one to seek to make his life rest in these things is as if a bird should build her nest in a little bush that is floating up and down in the sea. These things will carry you a little way, but nor far. We all have to provide for eternity. If a man had a voyage to the Indies, and he would purchase a little boat that would carry him from Westminster to the London Bridge, it would be a poor provision. So when we provide for outward comforts and no more, we think little of the great voyage that we have to go. All of us have to sail to eternity, and what is a boat of these outward comforts to carry us that long voyage? The things of this world may well be compared to a tree in the time of a storm. When you are traveling on the way it begins to rain, and you ride under an oak or an elm tree. Now if there falls but a little rain, it may keep you dry; but if it rains much, the longer you stand under the tree, the worse you will be. So the things of this world may comfort and quiet us against a little trouble, but riches, as I said, "avail not in the day of wrath." They will not keep off the dreadful storm of God's wrath. All these things are uncertain, and will disappoint us.

Now these, and divers other considerations that might be added, are the strength of reason grounded upon the Scripture, to convince a man of the vanity of all the things of the world. Now put all these considerations together, and well may we say, as it was said of the price that was given for Christ, of which Zechariah prophesied, "those thirty pieces, a goodly [considerable] price" that was given for Him. You hear sometimes of Judas's sin, that he betrayed Christ for thirty pieces, a goodly price. I may well apply this to your souls, you who venture the loss of your souls for getting the world. Though you could possibly get all the world, considering what has been said, it is a considerable price. Do you not see what a considerable price is given for your soul? If these things have been made real to you, it would be of marvelous use to help against any temptation to anything of this world.

Now that you have seen what darkness is upon all things, how they are all but glittering vanities, and not worth the venturing of the soul for, take heed of hazarding your souls upon any of these things. You will curse yourselves hereafter when it is too late: "O cursed wretch that I was, that I should yet venture upon sinful ways that I was told would endanger the eternal destruction of my soul! And notwithstanding I heard what a vanity was in all these things, yea, for such a vanity I was drawn aside to lose my own soul." Well, you see the upshot of all, that to venture your souls for the gain of the world is to venture the loss of pearls for pebble stones, to venture gold for dirt, yea, for dirt that has a great deal of poison in it, for so it has. All these things in the world, being separated from God, are not only dirt, but there is poison in them.

Now, then, these things being laid together, you see the point cleared. And all that remains is but to bind up this in several uses and applications. If all these things are so poor and mean, what use are we to make of all these meditations and considerations?

APPLICATION

1. If these things are so, we learn not to envy the prosperity of ungodly men, whatever it is. Let them ruffle it out for a while here in this world, and carry all before them; let man have his day here in this world, there is no great cause to envy him if he is going on in such a way as he is likely to lose his soul. Poor, miserable, wretched creature that he is, better ten thousand times that he had never been born. Poor people who are wicked (as many are) have the curse of God mingled in water; and rich men who are wicked have the curse of God like poison in their wine. Now we know that, of the two, the poison will work more strongly in wine than in water. And so certainly ungodly rich men, who have most of the world, are the most miserable creatures; for they have more to answer for than others have, and their estates are usually fuel for their lusts, and so their condition is worse than the condition of any beggar who begs his bread from door to door. And certainly there is no wicked, rich man upon the earth but if he dies so, will hereaf-

ter curse the time that ever he had an estate. He will wish that he had been a beggar, and had gone begging up and down in his rags, for then he would not have had so much to answer for before God. Oh, he is not a man to be envied! What man is there who would envy a malefactor condemned to die, though he had on fine clothes? Would not any one of you rather save your woolen plain suit, or a leather suit, than a suit of velvet, and go to be executed in it?

I read of Chrysostom who, being invited to a feast, as he was going, met with one going to be executed. And it fell out that the way to the execution was a very fair way, but the way that led him to his friend's house was a dirty lane. So he made this meditation of it: "Oh, how much better is it to go in this dirty lane, to go and rejoice with my friend, than in a fair plain way, and go as the other does to his execution!" He was not willing to go that way, though it was a fair and plain way, but rather to go his own, though foul and dirty; he considered that the end of the way was different.

So do not look much upon men and women, what their present condition is, but look at what their end is likely to be, and do not envy them. I suppose you cannot but have heard the story of a poor soldier who, having a command from his general not to touch anything upon pain of death, came by a vine and took a bunch of grapes. The general, being very strict, condemned him to die because of his disobedience, and as he was going to his execution he went eating the bunch of grapes. His fellow soldier rebuked him, but he gave him this answer: "I pray you, do not envy my grapes to me, for they cost me dearly."

So truly we have little cause to envy the men of the world their grapes, that they have their mirth, their merry meetings, whatever they have; for it is likely to cost them dearly; it is likely to cost them their souls. They endanger their eternal perishing; and therefore there is no cause at all to envy such. David indeed was troubled a while when he saw the prosperity of the ungodly; but when he went into the sanctuary, there he understood their end (Psalm 73). O my brethren, you are come into the sanctuary; you are come now in the exercise of the Word thus to hear what is likely to become of ungodly men who enjoy all the world for their portion. Their end is likely to be the loss of their souls eternally. Do not envy them. You envy them, but suppose that God should say to you, "Well, it shall be with you as with them; that is, you shall have as much as they, and there is all the good you are likely ever to have from Me." Would you not see cause to give a dreadful shriek, if such a message should come from heaven to you? What a foolish thing it would be for a child who had a loving father, and who expected a great inheritance from him, because he sees a stranger who comes and sits at the table, and has better provision than he has, to grumble and murmur because he does not have such provision made for him every day? Oh, he has no cause to do so, for the inheritance is reserved for him!

God is a rich householder, and He can give such things as these are to His enemies, as we speak of, but the inheritance is reserved for you. Do not envy the ungodly in the enjoyment of the world, for the truth is that their portion is but very little; it is but a poor pittance for an immortal soul to have, though he should have all the world. It is true, we should be sensible of our unworthiness of the least crumb of any good thing; yet though we should be sensible of our unworthiness, yet we should not be satisfied with having all the world for our portion. It was a most admirable speech of Luther, when divers of the princes of Germany made much of him, he began to be afraid lest he should have his portion in these outward things, and here should be all. He broke forth in this expression, fear-

ing lest God should give him his portion here: "I protested to
God with all my power and strength that He should not put me
off so with these things." He would not be content with them.

There is little cause to envy the men of the world; for, the
truth is, it is but a poor pittance they have, and they have made
a most miserable bargain. If you saw someone who professed
himself to be a merchant, and he ventured many thousands of
pounds, but brought home nothing but a fair, painted bauble
for children to play with, would you envy it to him? Just so it is
with the men of the world: they flatter and please themselves
with baubles, but their souls are gone in the meantime.

2. Let all those seek to get the world in those ways wherein they
are likely to lose their souls lay this Scripture to heart. And, oh,
that God would settle it upon their spirits, so that, when you
awake in the night, you might think of it. When you walk up and
down, when you are in your shops or in your business, think of
this text. I told you in the beginning of one who counseled one
of the kings of Portugal to think of this text for a quarter of an
hour every day. Oh, that you, every time you awake, especially
you who have been seeking after much of the world, would
think seriously of this Scripture. "Am not I the man or woman
who has hazarded my soul by seeking after something of the
world?" Have you never sought to gain anything of the world in
a way of sin? And has your heart been thoroughly humbled for
it and repented? It may be that to this day you have not made
restitution. Has not the eager pursuit after the things of this
world taken your heart up so much that you have not favored the
things of God and eternal life? You look upon the things of the
world as if they were the only realities, but on spiritual things
as imaginations. Have not the things of this world so taken up
your spirit as made you to have slight thoughts of spiritual and

heavenly things? Have you not blessed yourself in the enjoyment of these things, though in the meantime God has not made known to you the riches of His kingdom? Yet you have thought yourself to have enough in the enjoyment of what you have.

Have you not often, when you have been hearing the Word, had your thoughts and spirits about the things of the world as things suitable to you, but the things of the Word you have not relished? Yea, and anything in the Word that has come close to that covetous corruption of yours, your heart has secretly derided. There are no men in the world who more secretly condemn and deride the things of God, spiritual things, than worldly-minded men. In Luke 16:13, we read that Christ preached to the Pharisees against their covetousness, and told them that "no man could serve two masters, but either he will hate the one, and love the other, or else he will hold to the one, and despise the other; ye cannot serve God and mammon." You cannot think to have your hearts set upon the world and your gain, and yet serve the Lord; but if your hearts are set so upon your estates, you will be presumptuous with God; you will venture upon the ways of sin to gain the things of this world.

But the Pharisees, who were covetous, also heard all these things and derided Him. The word in the Greek is, "they blew their noses at Him." When a man scorns and derides another, he will show it by his nose; so they did in a jeering, scorning way; they derided Jesus Christ, who talked after this fashion: "A man cannot serve God and mammon too; a man cannot look after the things of the world and the things of God too." Carnal hearts hear things in religion as unsavory things, because those hearts are after the things of the world.

This is not only true of riches, but also of your reputation. Have you not often ventured to lie, to save your credit in something? And have you been more troubled when you have been discovered in anything that goes against your credit and esteem than in the sin that you have committed against God? Now by such kind of evidences it is clear that men enjoy the world in such a way as they are likely to lose their souls for all eternity. Oh, look upon your estates that you have, and think what they cost you and what little comfort you will have in them! It is observed of David, when he longed for the waters of the well of Bethlehem, and there were men who ventured their lives to get him the water, when it came to him he would not drink it. "Oh," he said, "it is the price of blood!"

So when you look upon your estate, when you sit at your table and see that you have more there than another man, when you look into your chest and see there that you have plenty of garments, and that your children are fine and brave, and the like—these are pretty things for a while to please the fancy with, aye, but what do they cost? A man who would reckon his clothes that the dyeing and the spinning cost him so much, aye, but what did the wool cost? Why, that was his own, and he thought nothing of that.

Such and such things that you have, what do they cost? They cost this much and this much, aye, but has your soul not been lost in the bargain? And can you have pleasure in it, when it cost you as dearly as it has? In Psalm 31:6, the spirit of holy David rose up in indignation against such men as these are: "I have hated them that regard lying vanities," that is, "my spirit cannot but with indignation and abomination rise up against them. What? That men should follow after vanity when there are such glorious things to be followed after, when there is the blessed God, and the glorious riches of grace and salvation that are revealed in His Word that may make the hearts of the children of men, and yet they follow after vain things? For men who have immortal souls, capable of eternal communion with the Lord in the highest heavens, to follow after vanity and satisfy themselves in such things, I hate them."

Certainly, it is the curse of God that is upon the hearts of men that allows them to follow after such things, and especially in the times of the gospel, when such glorious things are revealed to their souls, I say the curse of God is upon them. Isaiah 44:20: "He feedeth on ashes; a deceived heart hath turned him side, that he cannot deliver his soul, nor say, 'Is there not a lie in my right hand.' " He feeds off ashes. A deceived heart has turned him aside so that he cannot deliver his soul. Therein lies the sore evil of it: he has a deceived heart. He does not need to cast it upon the devil, but it is his own bare, filthy, corrupt heart that dares not trust God for his soul for eternity. He will have present things, come of it what will come; he knows what the meaning of present things are, but what those are that are to come, he does not know. A deceived heart has seduced him, and he cannot deliver his soul, nor can he say, "Is there not a lie in my right hand?" That is, "Is not the strength of my endeavor set upon falsehoods? The chief of my strength and endeavors, is it not set upon a lie?"

Chrysostom said that if he were to preach to all the world, he would choose this text as soon as any: "O ye children of men, why do ye love vanity and follow after leasing?" And it would be a happy thing if it were always sounding in the ears of every one whose hearts are after present things, so that such a one may hear a voice behind him, saying, "This is not the way; but this is the way, walk in it. You have deceived your soul all this while and wearied yourself, and that through the curse of God upon your heart. Habakkuk 2:13: "Behold, is it not of the Lord of hosts that the people shall labor in the very fire, and the people shall weary themselves for every vanity?" Is not this of the Lord of hosts?

So we see men and women who have understanding in the things of the world, yet for the matter of God, they have none at all. They are very industrious and laborious to get outward things, the outward comforts of this world; they tire themselves; they can sit up late and rise early. Oh, is it not of the Lord of hosts that people should thus weary and tire themselves?

By way of similitude, we may apply it to the spirits of men who are wearying and tiring themselves after vanities. It is the Lord's curse that is upon their hearts. It is said of Dionysius that when he was upon his sickbed he heard Thales, the philosopher, discoursing excellently about divers excellent moralities; and he cursed those pleasures and delights that had taken his heart from attending to such things. When you come upon your sickbed, what will comfort you then? It cannot be your silver or gold. Oh, that the Lord would make you for the present to see your vanity and folly before it is too late, and you curse yourself and there be no hope for you!

But if this point shows the folly and madness of those who seek after never such great things in the world with the hazard of their souls, but then, what shall we say to those who will hazard their souls for every trifle? We spoke of that in the aggravation of the dreadfulness of the loss of the soul, and I will only speak a word or two more of it here. In Amos 2:6, God complained that the righteous were sold for silver, and the poor for a pair of shoes. They put such a poor price upon righteous men and poor men. It as if God should say, "Know that I put a greater price upon My righteous servants than all the silver in the world." Oh, now, the complaint may be against many people who sell their souls for silver, yea, even for a pair of shoes, for a trifle, for a toy, for nothing—not for all the world, but for every little pittance. What is that which you have, or are likely to have? Why, they are very poor things in comparison of the world. It is reported of Alcibiades, a young gallant, that Socrates came jeering unto him for his pride, and brought him a map of the world and said to him, "Show me, I pray, where your land can be found here."

Now, if I were to speak to princes and emperors, this text would speak dreadfully to them, that they should venture their souls for kingdoms and empires. But for you who are never likely to have any such things, for you to set your hearts upon such trifles, and so to damn your souls, what can you get? Look upon a map and see what all England is. Europe is but a fourth of the known world, aye, but then what is England to Europe, and then to all the world? And then what is one county in England, and one city, or one house? "I have a great many tenements in a parish," says one. But what is all this to the world, and all this world unto heaven, and heaven and the world unto God? But to think that you are blessed because you have but a few rotten tenements, oh, what a seduced heart has deceived you, that you can be satisfied with such things as these are? This one meditation I think might sink into the hearts of those who will venture their souls for every trifle.

If ever your soul is saved, God must set such a price upon it that He must give more than a thousand worlds are worth to save it. He must give no less than the blood of His Son. And can you think that the infinite God should prize your soul at such a high rate, when you yourself prize it at such a low rate? If a man had lost anything of his estate, and it could not be redeemed without some great sum of money, if his friends came to know that he did not prize what he had lost, will any friend be so mad as to lay down five hundred pounds to redeem that for his friend which he knows aforehand that man does not prize at even twelve pence? So, can you think that that soul of yours that you prize as nothing, that the infinite God should lay down such a price to redeem it?

3. From the consideration of the comparison of the gain of the world to the loss of the soul, here is a use of exhortation to teach us to answer all temptations, or to work upon our hearts to answer all temptations to any way of sin with this: "You offer me too little. Whatever you can offer me to draw me to think well of sin, certainly it is too little; for it endangers my soul. The thorough understanding of this point, and the working of it upon the heart, is a very great help against whatsoever temptation should come to draw you to sin.

Surely, if these things are so, then this can be no argument for me to neglect any duty that God calls for at my hands, or to venture upon any way that my conscience tells me is sin. A man should think with himself, "Oh, if I do this, it will endanger my estate." But instead he is likely to think, "If I do such a thing, I shall get so much by it." Certainly there can be no strength in this, if what has been spoken out of this text is true. But when there comes a temptation and it prevails over you, you deny this Scripture to be the Word of God, and you set your judgment against the truth of God. But consider with yourself which is likely to stand. Know that God will make His Word stand. He will make it good, when you and a thousand, thousand such as you are shall perish forever. You who are merchants, when men offer you less than your wars are worth, you scorn and condemn them; and so you should do when temptation offers you less than your soul is worth.

We read that when Saul saw the people following David, he said, "What can the son of Jesse do for you? Can he give you olive yards and vineyards," and the like? So when temptation to sin comes, ask it, "What can you do for me? Can you save my soul in the time of distress? You would draw me to such and such courses, such and such companions would draw me to such and such ways." Aye, but you may put them off with this, "Is this the way to save my soul? If it is, then I will do it; but if it will not do that, God forbid that I should meddle."

Oh, therefore, remember "that the fashion of this world passeth away" (1 Corinthians 7:30–31). The apostle would take the hearts of men from the things of this world, and so he brings this argument: "The fashion of this world passes away. Therefore use the world, as not abusing it." The phrase that you have in your English Bible is "passes away." Two very learned writers translate it by a word that signifies to deceive. The fashion of the world will deceive you at last. Another translation uses a word that signifies "to go quite cross." The fashion of the world either deceives, or it goes on quite cross. The outward show of the world deceives thousands and thousands of souls to their eternal perdition. And then it goes quite cross; it seems to promise you this and this much, but it will go quite cross in the conclusion, and will be your undoing if you do not take heed. Therefore, do not let anything in the world tempt you to commit the least sin that possibly may be.

Augustine, in his book about an officious lie, had this passage: "A man must not tell an officious lie (that is, a lie without an intention to do anybody hurt) for the gaining of the world, nay, for the gaining of all the souls in the world. The least sin is a greater evil than the gain of all the world is good, because it is dangerous to the soul upon that very ground." And therefore it is said of Basil, when the persecutors terrified him with the loss of all that he had, but that did not prevail, then they made him fair offers of great advantages that he should have. But Basil laughed at them, and bade them go and offer such things to children.

So the book of the martyrs tells us of Austinius, that godly man, who had been a means to demolish a place for idol worship. The idolaters afterwards came upon him and put him to extreme torments; they set children upon him to take his flesh with their knives. But at length they said that they would be content if he would but give never so little for the building up of the idol temple again, to let him go free, "No," said he, "not one halfpenny." Certainly this point will be enough to justify any who shall lose estate to endure anything in the world rather than do anything that may in the least degree hazard their souls. Martyress Juletta, when one accused her and said that she was a Christian, then the judge said, "You will not have liberty of the law," "No?" said she, "Then farewell riches, life, and all." She would be sure to keep her soul safe, whatever became of all other things.

4. The last use is a use of encouragement to those who will rather venture all in the ways of God than to hazard their souls. You are the wise merchant, who is willing to sell all for the pearl. And bless yourself in God that ever He has put into your heart to look to that which is the main chance, as we used to say. If God had left you to yourself, you might have gone on in such ways as others do. But can you say, "The Lord has caused the fear of Himself, and the fear of eternity, to fall upon my soul; and I can appeal to Him that whatsoever comes of me in regard of outward matters, I think that I can be satisfied if all things are well with my soul."

I say, bless yourself in God. A man is not to praise himself, but in God. When you consider that God has drawn your heart to Him, and given you your interest in God, you may bless yourself in God, in the grace of God, who has given you a heart that has been taken off from creature comforts, disengaged from them, and is set upon the things that concern the eternal salvation of your soul. Bless yourself in God, and do not be troubled though you are cut short in the things of this world. One would think that what has been said about the vanity of the things of this world would make people who are crossed in them (if they are godly) to be satisfied. What if you are plundered of all, and have little provision for your family, bread for just one day, and do not know where to get bread for the next? Aye, but is your soul safe?

We read in Genesis of the king of Sodom, who said to Abraham, "Give me the souls, and take the goods to yourself." Though he was but a heathen king, he spoke of their natural lives. So you whose hearts God has inclined to soul-saving ways, say to the men of the world, "Take the riches, but let me have the safety and welfare of my soul."

Oh, if God has assured you upon good grounds that your soul is safe and your sin pardoned, what great mercy this is though you do not have some of the lumber of this world! If a malefactor who was in danger of dying should go to seek a pardon for his life, and, when he had gotten it, and was coming from the presence of the king, perhaps he lost his glove or handkerchief upon the stairs, would it not be an unseemly thing for such a man to fall crying and wringing his hands because he had lost his glove? Just thus, for all the world, is the madness and folly of people who say that they have some comfortable hope that God will have mercy upon their souls, and will save them forever, yet when they are crossed and wronged, they cry out that they are undone.

Man and woman, you are not undone, for your soul is safe. "Lord, strike, strike," said Luther, "only pardon my sin." And, my brethren, well may you be encouraged to undergo any difficulties, and to bear the loss of the comforts of this world, to save your souls; for indeed the Lord has granted to us the way of salvation of souls at an easier rate than our forefathers had.

If I should tell you the way that many of our forefathers had for the saving of their souls, and many of the saints of God in former times, you would have said then that it was a difficult way to save souls and go to heaven.

I will give you an instance of one man and one woman, how hardly they came to salvation. That blessed martyr Bersesius, see what a way he had to heaven for professing the Christian religion. The persecutors came to him, and because he would not deny the truth they struck all his body members out of joint; and when they had done that, they made wounds in all parts of his body. Then they brought iron combs that had been sharpened, and so raked them upon his body that had been thus wounded; and when they had done that, they laid him upon an iron grate, and with instruments of iron opened those wounds. After that they melted hot burning salt, and strewed it upon those wounds, and then they came with hot irons and seared him with those. After that they dragged him by the heels into a dungeon where they had prepared sharp shells, and there he lay and perished. "Here is one who went to heaven upon hard terms," you will say. But God does not call you to do so, but merely to deny yourselves in some base lust, in some sinful and ungodly way, in something that you may spare as easily as you would the water out of your shoes, as we used to say.

Then there was a woman who was of noble birth. She was brought before the magistrate for her religion and, answering boldly and resolutely, she would not yield. So, after many temptations and fair speeches, they dragged her by the hair of her head from the seat of judicature and pulled one joint from another; having done that, they took the teeth and claws of wild beasts and raked her flesh from the bones. Then they came with hot irons, torches, and burning flames, and scorched and burned her to death, and yet she went on constantly. If she might save her soul, she was willing to endure all this misery.

I do not know what God may call you to before you die; many of our brethren have suffered very hard things, and God may call you to hard things. Oh, that this text might prepare you!

And now, my brethren, as it has been a means to carry others through temptations and many difficulties in this world, so lay these truths to your hearts. And if you cannot think of every particular passage, yet think of this text. Take this one note, that whereas God calls others to spend their strength in suffering such great evils to save their souls, be willing to spend the strength that God gives you in doing and in serving. Spend your strength in active obedience so much the more, by how much the less you are called to spend it in the way of passive obedience, so that you may have cause to bless God forever in heaven, when you shall come to see soul and body to be blessed and saved eternally. You may bless God forever in heaven for revealing such a truth, and setting home such a text: "What shall it profit a man, though he gain the whole world, and lose his soul? Or what shall a man give in exchange for his soul?"

Finis

THE LIFE OF

Jeremiah Burroughs

(1599-1646)

This very amiable divine was born in the year 1599. He was forced to leave the university, and afterwards the kingdom, on account of his nonconformity. After he later finished his studies at the university, he entered the ministerial work and was chosen colleague to Edmund Calamy at Bury St. Edmunds. In 1631 he became rector of Tivetshal in the county of Norfolk, but upon the publication of Bishop Wren's articles and injunctions, in 1636 he was suspended and deprived of his living. He sheltered himself for some time under the hospitable roof of the Earl of Warwick, but, on account of the intolerant and oppressive proceedings of the ecclesiastical rulers, the noble Earl, at length, found it was impossible to protect him any longer. Shortly after, to escape the fire and persecution, he fled to Holland and settled at Rotterdam, where he was chosen teacher to the congregational church of which Mr. William Bridge was the pastor.

Upon his arrival, he was cordially received by the church, and continued to be a zealous and faithful laborer for several years, gaining a very high reputation among the people. After the commencement of the civil war, when the power of the bishops was set aside, he returned to England, says Granger's *Biographical History*, "not to preach sedition, but peace, for which he earnestly prayed and labored."

Mr. Burroughs was a highly honored and esteemed person, and he soon became a most popular and admired preacher.

After his return, his popular talents and great worth presently excited public attention, and he was chosen preacher to the congregations of Stepney and Cripplegate, London, then accounted two of the largest congregations in England. Mr. Burroughs preached at Stepney at seven o'clock in the morning, and William Greenhill at three in the afternoon. These two persons, stigmatized by the historian Anthony Wood as notorious schismatics and independents, were called by Mr. Hugh Peters, one "the morning star," the other "the evening star of Stepney."

Mr. Burroughs was chosen to be one of the Westminster Assembly of Divines, and was one of the dissenting brethren, but a divine of great wisdom and moderation. He united with his brethren, Messrs. Thomas Goodwin, Philip Nye, William Bridge, and Sydrach Sympson, in publishing their own "Apologetical Narration" in defense of their own distinguishing sentiments. The authors of this work, who had been exiles for religion, to speak in their own language, "... consulted the Scriptures without any prejudice. They considered the Word of God as impartially as men of flesh and blood are likely to do, in any juncture of time; the place they went to, the condition they were in, and the company they were with, affording no temptation to any bias."

They asserted that every church or congregation has sufficient power within itself for the regulation of religious government, and is subject to no external authority whatever. The principles upon which they founded their church government were to confine themselves in everything to what the Scriptures prescribed, without paying any attention to the opinions or practices of men; nor to tie themselves down too strictly to their present resolutions, so as to leave no room for alterations upon a further acquaintance with divine truth. They steered a middle course between Presbyterianism and Brownism: the former they accounted too arbitrary, the latter too rigid, deviating from the spirit and simplicity of the gospel.

These are the great principles of the Independents of the present day.

Richard Baxter, who knew his great worth, said, "If all the Episcopalians had been like Archbishop Usher, all the Presbyterians like Stephen Marshall, and all the Independents like Jeremiah Burroughs, the breaches of the church would soon have been healed." The last subject on which Burroughs preached was his *Irenicum,* an attempt to heal the divisions among Christians. This title has been published by Soli Deo Gloria Publications. His incessant labors, and his grief for the distractions of the times, are said to have hastened his end. He died of tuberculosis on November 14, 1646, at the age of 47. The historian Granger says, "he was a man of learning, candor, and modesty, and of an exemplary and irreproachable life." Thomas Fuller has classed him among the learned writers of Emmanuel College, Cambridge. Williams' *Christian Preacher* says that his *Exposition of Hosea* is a pleasing specimen, to show how the popular preachers of his time applied the Scriptures in their expository discourses to the various cases of their hearers. He published several of his writings while he lived, and his friends sent forth many others after his death, most of which were highly esteemed by all pious Christians.

A *Summary* of *The Gospel*

by Jeremiah Burroughs

From Gospel Conversation (1657)
and reprinted by Soli Deo Gloria Publications

The gospel of Christ in general is this: It is the good tidings that God has revealed concerning Christ. More largely it is this: As all mankind was lost in Adam and became the children of wrath, put under the sentence of death, God, though He left His fallen angels and has reserved them in the chains of eternal darkness, yet He has thought upon the children of men and has provided a way of atonement to reconcile them to Himself again.

Namely, the second Person in the Trinity takes man's nature upon Himself, and becomes the Head of a second covenant, standing charged with sin. He answers for it by suffering what the law and divine justice required, and by making satisfaction for keeping the law perfectly, which satisfaction and righteousness He tenders up to the Father as a sweet savor of rest for the souls that are given to Him.

And now this mediation of Christ is, by the appointment of the Father, preached to the children of men, of whatever nation or rank, freely offering this atonement unto sinners for atonement, requiring them to believe in Him and, upon believing, promising not only a discharge of all their former sins, but that they shall not enter into condemnation, that none of their sins or unworthiness shall ever hinder the peace of God with them, but that they shall through Him be received into the number of those who shall have the image of God again to be renewed unto them, and that they shall be kept by the power of God through faith unto salvation.